The Economic Renewal Guide

*A Collaborative Process
for Sustainable
Community Development*

Michael J. Kinsley

Rocky Mountain Institute

1739 Snowmass Creek Road

Snowmass, CO 81654-9199

(970) 927-3851

Rocky Mountain Institute is an independent, nonprofit research and educational foundation whose mission is to foster the efficient and sustainable use of resources as a path to global security.

We undertake to use professional care in our research and publications and to verify our information from sources believed to be reliable. Please contact Rocky Mountain Institute with any corrections or comments for future editions.

We do not imply endorsement of any product, service, or company mentioned in this publication. The information and statements contained herein do not necessarily represent those of funders or reviewers of this publication.

Permission is granted for unlimited photocopying of pages of this book for use in local Economic Renewal efforts only.

This book is dedicated to that small, determined group of people who are committed to preserving and enhancing their communities.

Editor: Dave Reed
Desktop Publisher: Kate Mink
Cover Illustration: Curt Carpenter
Illustrations: Bruce Towl

ISBN 1-881071-06-5

Acknowledgments

To write this book, I collected wisdom from hundreds of people—from the citizens of Pitkin County, Colorado, who taught me how to be a county commissioner in a volatile, creative community, to such rare elders as Dan Kemmis, the Mayor of Missoula, Montana, whose life and work in communities is an inspiration; and David Brower, the visionary who carries on the tradition of John Muir.

Among colleagues who strongly influenced this guide are Hunter Lovins, President of Rocky Mountain Institute; George Gault of Cheyenne, Wyoming; John Eldert of Wallingford, Connecticut; Jerry Wade of Columbia, Missouri; Don Harker, Liz Natter, and Carol Lamm of Berea, Kentucky; Brad Ack of Flagstaff, Arizona; Mark Gimby of Saskatoon, Saskatchewan; Lenise Henderson of Haines, Alaska; and Bob Dettman of Lakewood, Colorado. Additionally, Rick Carlson of Aspen, Colorado; Barbara Cole of Denver, Colorado; Alice Hubbard of Basalt, Colorado; and Marilyn Mehlman of Stockholm, Sweden aided in the development of the Economic Renewal process as it evolved over the last ten years.

In more whimsical moments, I imagine myself an oral historian, staff in hand, treading a dusty road from village to village reciting news and stories heard on my travels. Though travel usually finds me crammed in an airliner, the principle of my occupation is the same. In every community I've worked in—in 33 states and four countries—I've learned something new to add to Economic Renewal. Someone has a story, an idea, or a new twist that I can talk about in the next community. I've learned from such committed people as Akira Kawanabe of Alamosa, Colorado; Cindy Adams of Fairbanks, Alaska; Jeff Boyer of Boone, North Carolina; Debra Becker of Orange, Massachusetts; Maria Varela of Tierra Amarilla, New Mexico; Stella Marshall of Union County, Kentucky; Helen Shortell of Melbourne, Australia; Greg Sweval of Bayfield, Wisconsin; Sioux Plummer of Skagway, Alaska; Roy W. Hunt of Snowflake, Arizona; and a group of lobstermen on the dock in Stonington, Maine.

Several colleagues provided essential help in the creation of this third edition of the guide. Dave Reed of Rocky Mountain Institute served ably as editor, and Kate Mink patiently handled the layout. Robert Alcock helped with proofreading. JoAnn Glassier provided clerical assistance.

Chapter 14 required help from Shanna Ratner of Yellowood Associates, St. Albans, Vermont, and Bob Barton of Catalyst Financial Services, Denver. It also reflects ideas found in *Take Charge: Economic Development in Small Communities,* by the North Central Regional Center for Rural Development, Ames, Iowa. Most importantly, Randy Russell, a consultant from Denver, Colorado, guided and contributed significantly to the chapter's development.

The Economic Renewal program would not have been possible without the help of several foundations and federal agencies: the Allen-Heath Memorial Foundation, the Merck Family Fund, the Benedum Foundation, the Golden Rule Foundation, the Tides Foundation, the G.A.G. Charitable Corporation, the Small Business Administration, the U.S. Forest Service, the Environmental Protection Agency, and the Department of Energy.

The Economic Renewal Guide

Leaders are best when people scarcely know they exist,
not so good when people obey and acclaim them.

Leaders who fail to honor people are not honored by them.

But of good leaders who talk little,
when their work is done, their task fulfilled,
the people will say, we did this ourselves.

—Lao Tzu, sixth century BC, China

So You Want a Successful Community

"The greatest sin is to do nothing because you can only do a little."
—Edmund Burke (1729–97)

You've heard those community success stories—maybe in Reader's Digest or around the big table at your local cafe. They tell of great things done by average folks—people who said: "We're not going to take it anymore. We're not going to get pushed around by a contrary world economy or wait for the government to come save us; we're going to stand up and do it ourselves."

Now it's your turn to create a successful community. The first step is personal commitment. Once you've made that commitment, everything changes: instead of wondering if you might be able to do something to help your town or neighborhood, you're focused on how to make it happen.

This manual is a practical tool to help you achieve success. You've joined with thousands of people who have something important in common: volunteers working in many different ways to help their communities. Though they may not be getting all the support and help they need, and few are completely satisfied with the results, they're making genuine progress. Their communities are stronger as a result of their efforts.

You deserve thanks for the commitment you've made to help your town or neighborhood. It's people like you who make communities great places to live, work, and raise families.

How to Use This Guide

This book is for anyone who wants their community to discover a brighter future. It's especially useful for people seeking a more sustainable local economy or more effective and collaborative ways to solve local problems. Above all, it's for people who want to make things happen instead of just talking about them.

The guide describes a process for organizing and conducting a series of town meetings that can lead to your community's success story. Though it focuses on a particular approach developed by Rocky Mountain Institute called Economic Renewal (ER), it can serve as a useful resource in any community development effort. Field-tested in dozens of towns since 1986, ER is a practical means by which communities can improve themselves sustainably. It's a way to approach development that integrates economic, community, and environmental concerns. Development projects are chosen by community residents and leaders through a thoughtful process that minimizes controversy and maximizes creativity. Economic Renewal is planning, yes, but not planning for its own sake; quite the contrary, it's planning for action.

If you were to compare Economic Renewal to a class, then you as "teacher" would use this book as if it were a teacher's guide. Community participants use worksheets and other pages copied from this book as if they were class materials. They may also use other ER books (see appendix) to support their efforts.

Because the information in this book is generalized for use in any community, don't regard any portion of it as obligatory. It's a guide, not a rulebook. One of your responsibilities is to adapt this material to work in your community as you see fit—if, for example, your town has already done one of the steps in the ER process, feel free to skip it and move on to the next. However, if you change or discard a particular component of this manual, do so with caution. Each is based on practical experience in communities. Agricultural technician Mark Gimby, who uses this guide to support his work in Saskatchewan, advises: "You must be flexible. I depend on the basic tenets of the ER process and I change the details when needed."

Neither should you feel that you must read the book from beginning to end. Look over the table of contents so you know what's where and can refer to chapters as you need them. Although the ER process is described in chronological order, you'll find that much of the advice given for some steps pertains to other steps as well.

If the material in this book isn't enough to get you going, Rocky Mountain Institute also offers training seminars that teach active citizens, leaders, and professionals how to conduct the Economic Renewal town meeting process. You'll find more information about these in the appendix.

What, Me a Leader?

You may not think of yourself as a leader. That's OK, it doesn't matter if you've never been a leader before. To get your community moving, you need not be an elected official or an economic development professional. In fact, it's probably better if you're not. ER requires only commitment, patience, and a willingness to stick your neck out a little.

You'll be most effective if you're respected, respectful, persuasive, a good organizer, and a confident speaker. But if you're a mere mortal with just a few of these qualities, then it'll help if you can find allies and supporters whose qualities complement your own. For instance, you may be good behind the scenes, organizing and coordinating, while someone else is comfortable speaking in front of groups.

Many people who have become leaders never wanted to lead anyone anywhere. They just wanted to get things moving. They couldn't just passively watch and hope things would get better. They couldn't sit back while others were confounded by vexing problems.

Maybe it started for you the way it started for others. To learn more about what was going on, you attended a few meetings of a citizen's group.

Then, once, when nobody else had time, you represented the group at a public meeting. As time passed, you became more familiar with the issues and more comfortable with speaking out. You began to offer your own ideas, some of which may have been off the mark and others of which were right on. These efforts didn't require a rocket scientist, just someone willing to go out and do it as well as they knew how.

It often takes a while to realize that you've become a leader. But there you are, leading—not because you sought power or notoriety, but because you wanted to help bring positive change to your community.

You probably wouldn't be taking the time to read this manual unless you were a leader. But you're not the old TV-western kind of leader—the big guy with the big hat who tells everyone what to do and makes them like it. You're a different kind of leader—someone who doesn't seek power, but rather new and better answers in a world that is very different from just a few years ago. You're not the kind of leader who manipulates or pushes people around. You understand Frances Moore Lappé, co-founder of the Center for Living Democracy, when she says, "Power is derived from relationships among people, not simply authority over them." You know that you've got to work with people and respect them to find the solutions that will work in your town.

It's said that great leaders inspire hope, build morale, bring adversaries together, and make the impossible achievable. They help others transcend obstacles and realize breakthroughs. When you hear a description like that, it's reasonable to think: "Hey, I'm no Gandhi. I'm just a regular person. I can't do all that, so I guess I must not be a leader." The truth is that there was only one Gandhi, one Washington, and one Martin Luther King. Only one person in a billion can consistently deliver those kinds of goods.

But average people can make a difference—not by touching others with a magic wand, but by example. Leaders like you inspire hope by being hopeful. You bring adversaries together by being respectful toward those with whom you disagree and by being willing to talk with them. You make difficult goals appear achievable by proceeding as if they are achievable. Normal, fallible people can make excellent leaders precisely because they're normal and fallible. Other normal people see that they can do the same.

Your leadership begins with trust. When you commit to serve the people of your community by helping with something like Economic Renewal, when your statements and actions serve the needs and priorities of others, they'll begin to trust you. Successful community organizers know that the way to build support is not to attempt to persuade others that your way is correct. The most effective path is to ask others what they need and want, determine how your needs fit with theirs, and then invite them to join you in developing and achieving mutually advantageous goals. They'll support your efforts when they see you support theirs. They'll join you when you join them.

Normal, fallible people can make excellent leaders precisely because they're normal and fallible.

As you assume a leadership role, for your own sake remember that you're not taking on the burden of the community's problems. Your purpose isn't to solve problems so much as to help the community develop its own solutions. Nor is your purpose to become personally influential—on the contrary, you're helping others become influential. In doing so, you will become influential. In other words, the more power and influence you give away, the more you get. Instead of feeling you've got to do everything yourself, make yourself dispensable by encouraging and helping others take the reins of leadership.

Many people learn about leadership through trial and error—a painful and inefficient process. Though foul-ups are a natural part of any creative process, there's no point in repeating the errors of others. This guide was written so you don't have to. You can learn from both the successes and mistakes of others.

Typically, these mistakes have less to do with what was done than how it was done. In working on economic development, community leaders often get caught up in the rightness of a particular solution and forget to deal respectfully with those who have different ideas. They think, "I'm doing this for the good of the community, so everyone should agree with me." It can take a long time to realize that economic development efforts can't be successful unless they're created by the whole community. When everyone who wishes to be involved is involved, then each person feels some ownership of the results. Each is part of the solution.

Sustainable Development: Prosperity Without Growth

The assumption that economic prosperity requires growth seems so reasonable that most of us don't think much about it. After all, it's what we've always been told; politicians, business boosters, economists, and the media all seem to take it for granted. The assumption is so pervasive that virtually every American community is looking for ways to grow out of its economic problems, even when those problems are themselves the result of growth.

The trouble is, the word "growth" has two fundamentally different meanings: "expansion" and "development." Expansion means getting bigger; development means getting better, which may or may not involve expansion. This is no mere semantic distinction. Many communities have wasted a lot of time and energy pursuing expansion because that's what they thought they needed, when what they really needed was development. To avoid confusion, let's define growth here only as getting bigger—expansion—and development as getting better.

Though a sound economy requires development, including vigorous business activity, it doesn't necessarily require expansion of community size. An analogy can be made with the human body. Human growth after maturity is cancer. When a town continues to expand after maturity, its cancer becomes manifest in many ways: spiteful controversy, higher taxes, traffic, sprawl, lost sense of community. Sound familiar?

But after reaching physical maturity, humans continue to develop in many beneficial and interesting ways: learning new skills, gaining deeper wisdom, cultivating new relationships, and so on. Similarly, a community can develop itself without necessarily expanding. It can create affordable housing, protect public safety, and improve employment, health, cultural, and educational opportunities. In fact, a good definition of development is the creation of jobs, income, savings, and a stronger community.

This is not to say that all expansion is bad, but it's essential to distinguish it from development in order to make choices that truly benefit the community.

Looking for Growth in All the Wrong Places

Chances are your town's current economic strategy is based on the expansion sort of growth. If your town is booming, the strategy probably involves riding the growth for all it's worth. If it's declining economically, the solution typically proposed will be some sort of business recruitment to stimulate growth. In either case, local boosters may use the words "growth" or "development," but what they really mean is "expansion": more people, more businesses, more commercial and retail space. The emphasis is on getting more, instead of on doing better with what the town has already got.

Sometimes, at least in the short term, doing better requires getting more. But a community that limits its development efforts to finding new business is missing opportunities and squandering local potential.

Declining communities and expanding communities face different sets of challenges, but one thing they often have in common is an overreliance on expansion. Let's look at this in more detail.

Declining Communities

Business failures, loss of jobs and population, lack of opportunities for young people, deteriorating infrastructure, loss of hope…these are some of the daunting problems of a declining community. The local economy is probably based on one or two salable resources such as timber, coal, wheat, or a manufactured product. Such communities may seem prosperous until the international economy makes a slight "adjustment" and their products are no longer worth more than the cost of production.

When a community's basic industry is threatened, the usual response is to call for economic development—any economic development. Local government officials come under intense pressure to do *something*. Residents want to see action. Traditionally this translates into a single, cure-all strategy: business recruitment, which, when pursued indiscriminately, can be termed smokestack-chasing. Chambers of commerce and development groups across the country commonly fall victim to the siren song of business recruitment.

If communities knew the odds they were facing, they would broaden their approach. Each year some 25,000 economic development committees from large and small cities bid for about 500 major plant sitings—a 50-to-1 ratio. To stay in the running, they must give away land, infrastructure, and tax breaks, or offer special exemptions from regulations. It's not uncommon for a competing government to offer an incentive package worth millions of dollars and still lose the bid. To land a new Mercedes assembly plant in 1993, the state of Alabama offered a record $200,000 worth of incentives *per job created*. Though lesser amounts are offered to smaller firms, very few towns or neighborhoods can play in this high-stakes league.

If a community does manage to bring in a major new business, the reality rarely matches the expectations. Often, promised jobs simply don't materialize. If jobs are created, they may last only a few years until the industry is offered an even bigger giveaway somewhere else, leaving behind unemployed workers and a precarious tax base. Meanwhile, incentives become a community tar baby as existing local businesses begin to demand similar breaks to remain in the community. Eventually, the hidden costs of incentive packages come home to roost, forcing officials to choose between higher taxes and reduced public services.

Gambling and "big-box" retail, the latest business-recruitment fads, present their own pitfalls. Casinos generate encouraging sales tax revenues but also huge demands on local infrastructure and services—especially police services. Big-box retailers typically locate just outside town boundaries to avoid municipal taxes. Local businesses are quickly squeezed out by the superstore. Downtown windows are boarded up and trash piles up in doorways where, broom in hand, shopkeepers once greeted long-time customers with a friendly smile.

Whether it chases smokestacks or superstores, a community pays another price that is impossible to measure: lost opportunities. By the time residents realize they've squandered precious time and money on inappropriate recruitment efforts, years may have been lost—years when the community could have been pursuing more practical and sustainable development options.

Instead of doing the wrong thing, some declining towns, paralyzed by a community-wide bad attitude, do nothing at all to strengthen their economies. One town may be in denial about a plant closure: "They'll change their minds," residents say, or, "The economy is sure to turn around." Another may have realized there's a problem, but is focusing all its energy on blaming those who it believes caused the problem: the government, the company, environmentalists. Both these towns will continue to decline until they realize that revitalization can begin only when inhabitants decide to take positive action—the kinds of actions described in this book.

Rapidly Expanding Communities

A rush of new economic activity can be as harmful as a decline. Some towns near a valuable natural resource suddenly become boomtowns through no effort of their own. This can seem like a good thing, but all too often booms are followed by busts: a raw material or product may be in demand one year but out of favor the next. Worse, demand for the resource, and the profits to be made from its extraction, may encourage those in the industry to exploit it for short-term gain. Many logging and farming communities have learned to their detriment that even "renewable" resources like trees and soil can be depleted more rapidly than they're being renewed, undermining their long-term basis for prosperity.

In other communities, quality of life fuels the expansion. They have clean air and water, little traffic, and low crime. They feel a lot more like home than many cities. These "high-amenity" places may be resort towns or communities that are attractive to retirees and second-home buyers. They may be desirable suburbs within commuting distance of a city, or more isolated communities that attract the new wave of information busi-

The vicious circle of expansion hits business owners, too.

nesses and individuals who do their work by telephone, fax, and modem, and therefore can live and work wherever they like.

Freed by new technologies, the number of Americans seeking a safer, less complex existence is on the rise. According to Joel Kotkin of the Pacific Research Institute, "After losing population for decades, rural areas are now adding people at three times their 1980s growth rate. Between 1990 and 1994, more than 1.1 million net migrants moved into rural areas." Kotkin calls this the "Valhalla syndrome" because migrants are "yearning for a heavenly retreat."

Whatever the cause of the influx, rapid expansion—more than about a 2-percent annual increase in population—generally brings more harm than good. Communities can't seem to keep ahead of problems created by expansion in excess of this rate. Before one problem can be defined and solved, another arises, then another. They pile up and complicate one another. Local leaders are overwhelmed.

Virtually every fast-expanding town plays out an unpleasant scenario. Townspeople accept almost any new proposal for expansion because they think it will maintain a healthy economy. More people move into the area and things look pretty good. But then the side effects begin to hit home. Newcomers often take the newly created jobs and bring increasing crime, social stress, and higher housing costs. Clean air turns gray, traffic slows and snarls, parking becomes impossible, doors must be locked. Intolerance increases and respect for traditional leadership declines. In the case of high-amenity communities, traditional income sources—tourists, second-home owners, retirees who cherished the small-town character and clean environment—begin to look for the next unspoiled paradise.

As with any inflationary economy, rapid expansion results in a few winners and many losers. Many real estate professionals, big builders, heavy-equipment owners, retail property owners, and large landowners do very well; most others are caught in a spiral of inflation. But expansion is seductive. The winners are very good at convincing the losers that they just need more expansion to be winners, and reassuring them that new taxes from expansion will pay for the solutions to expansion's problems. And indeed, no matter how serious the problems, each increment of expansion has attractive aspects that obscure the long-term downside.

But almost invariably, the problems only worsen while taxes increase to pay for the solutions (more schools, police, fire protection, roads, human services, sewers, etc.). New revenues seldom cover the true costs of expansion (which include such things as the replacement or expansion of capital facilities). Since the excess costs are spread among all taxpayers, existing taxpayers unwittingly subsidize the expansion—in effect, the losers subsidize the winners. Worse, in many communities that are experiencing sudden second-home expansion, existing taxpayers are subsidizing the well-to-do.

Having bought into the growth premise, local government, businesses, and individuals all find themselves locked into a vicious circle. Local government is forced to finance past expansion by authorizing still more expansion, which will in turn also fail to pay for itself, but on an even larger scale. If officials instead raise taxes, more residents are likely to join the chorus for growth, believing that it will relieve their tax burden. By this point the expansion has acquired its own momentum, because even a slight slowdown can cause serious fiscal crisis.

Business owners, for their part, naturally see community growth as a fast track to higher profits. It may work out that way for some, but for others—particularly retailers—expansion attracts not only more customers but also more competitors and an upward spiral of costs: higher rents, taxes, and wages. Cash flows faster out of business people's hands. Formerly relaxed and friendly businesses become tense and frenzied. "Gone fishin'" signs fade into memory.

Similarly, many individuals support expansion, assuming it will result in more and better jobs. More, yes; better, maybe; but it will also attract more

Rapid expansion results in a few winners and many losers.

workers, which will maintain competition for jobs. Wages may increase, but probably not as fast as the cost of housing and other essentials. Residents may well find they have to work even harder just to make ends meet. Yet even though many business owners and workers are worse off than before the town expanded, they don't understand why and they call for more expansion to solve their problems.

Comfortable towns seldom turn into teeming cities overnight. Rapid expansion occurs in small increments, each seemingly benign, many arguably beneficial. Cumulatively, however, the vast majority of citizens don't benefit from rapid expansion. Many communities are beginning to examine more carefully each new expansion-generating proposal to determine if benefits outweigh side effects. But most just keep stumbling down the path of rapid expansion without looking where they're going.

Slowly Expanding Communities

Given the problems of declining and rapidly expanding communities, you might conclude that the best strategy is to chart a course somewhere between these two extremes. But while slow expansion does offer a happy medium in many respects, it is no silver bullet. A community will face most of the same problems whether it expands rapidly or slowly—the key difference being that with slow expansion, the community will have more time to address them.

However, no matter how gradually it proceeds, expansion cannot continue indefinitely. By definition, a constant rate of expansion is exponential: a mere 2-percent annual expansion rate results in a quadrupling of size in just 70 years. Sooner or later—usually sooner than we think—an expanding town, country, or species will reach the limits of its space and resources. Island residents tend to be acutely aware of these limits, but the basic principle is the same for people living on the mainland, too: the number of people, buildings, roads, etc. cannot continue increasing forever.

As it approaches its physical limits, even a slowly expanding community will experience the problems of rapidly expanding communities. When there's no more room to build residences inexpensively, for example, housing prices will quickly increase; when conventional means of acquiring water have been exhausted, expensive means will have to be employed.

And though slow expansion theoretically allows a community more time to understand and cope with problems before they become acute, as a practical matter, most communities don't begin to confront problems until they become crises. However, when a community has learned to work together using a process such as the one described in this book, it will be better able to anticipate, confront, and manage expansion problems.

Expansion

cannot

continue

indefinitely.

EXPONENTIAL GROWTH

We've accommodated our increasing human population by using more resources and producing more wastes, counting on the planet to provide whatever we want and absorb whatever we discard. Each of these factors—population, resource use, and pollution—has been growing exponentially. The annual rates at which these factors are growing might sound trifling, yet the nature of exponential growth is that it compounds, like interest. Each year, the number increases by a greater amount than the year before.

When problems grow exponentially, you don't get much reaction time; they sneak up on you. Imagine a pond with a few water lilies on its surface that are doubling in number every day. Suppose it takes 30 days for the water lilies to cover the pond. On which day will they cover half the pond? Answer: the 29th day—on the 30th day they'll double again and cover the entire pond. In other words, exponential growth may not seem like a problem for a long time, then suddenly it's a major problem.

In much the same way, our global resource use is growing at about 5.5 percent each year—which means it's doubling every 13 years. If that trend continues, in 2022 the human race will be consuming four times the resources it consumed in 1996.

What's your community's annual growth rate? How long will it take to double? How long will it be before it's four times as big?

Adapted from the newsletter of the Northwest Area Foundation (January 1996).

The Viable Alternative: Sustainable Development

A growing number of communities are discovering that there's an alternative to economic "development" strategies based on expansion. They're embracing sustainable development, a more balanced approach that weighs social and environmental considerations alongside conventional economic ones. Expanding towns need not give up prosperity as they slow their expansion. Communities with little prospect for expansion need not give up their dreams. There are plenty of development options that don't require expansion.

The term "sustainable development" would be doomed to the scrap heap of short-lived and overused buzzwords were it not rooted in a traditional value, stewardship—the careful, economical, long-term management of land, community, and resources. It's a value that some towns have recently let fall by the wayside. But it's alive and well in many others, even if they don't notice it. People who care deeply about their community and who think conscientiously about the long-term implications of their actions are working for sustainability and stewardship, whether or not they use those words.

When placed in front of the word "development," the word "sustainable" offers both opportunities and constraints. It offers opportunities because its new perspective reveals development options that previously weren't obvious. Many such opportunities are described in the next chapter. It offers constraints because, when proposals are considered in light of their long-term effects, some options that might otherwise appear attractive are seen to be unworkable, or not worth their negative effects.

Taking a long-term perspective isn't easy. For instance, it takes guts to turn down a big-box retailer, knowing that you're also saying "no" to lower prices for some products. But a few communities have done just that—because they understood that, in the long run, the local retailers would be better able to survive, keep their profits in the community, and keep their employees working. These towns have said "yes" to the long-term viability of the overall community.

They chose one form of sustainability. Your choices may be quite different. There's no standard way to achieve sustainable development. Every community's situation is unique. Perhaps more important is that there is no point at which a community arrives at sustainability—it's a goal, a moving target that requires a community to continually learn about itself, its external influences, and emerging opportunities.

The following interrelated guidelines will help any community move affirmatively toward sustainability. Not every guideline will be applicable everywhere.

When natural resources are spent like income, the economy operates like a business in liquidation.

Use Renewable Resources No Faster Than They Can Be Renewed

A timber town will be able to log indefinitely if it cuts timber no faster than the forest can regenerate. A farm town can remain viable only if farmers add nutrients to replace those removed by wind, water, and harvest (and only if the nutrients don't irreversibly pollute area water supplies).

Renewable natural resources—timber, soil, quality of life, etc.—are the chief capital assets of many communities. Unsustainable communities spend these capital assets as if they were income. That's how a retail business is liquidated: tables, counters, and cash registers are sold to pay the bills. When natural resources are spent like income, the economy operates like a business in liquidation, leaving nothing for future generations.

In the business world, there are often economic incentives to operate this way. For example, if the CEO of a large timber corporation is forced to choose between clearcutting a forest to make a 15-percent profit or harvesting it sustainably to make only 9 percent, he's likely to choose the short-term profit from clearcutting and then move the corporation on to another forest, or even another business. Oil, mineral, grain, and other large resource-extraction industries are similarly driven by the quest for short-term return. A community whose economy is based on natural resources may find it extremely difficult to resist these corporate pressures to spend down its precious capital. Yet in the long term it can't afford not to: the corporation can always move on to the next forest, but the community can't.

Use Non-Renewable Resources Understanding that Someday a Renewable Substitute Will Be Required

Activities such as mining and oil drilling aren't necessarily wrong or harmful, but the fact is that they deplete finite resources. Someday the silver, oil, and coal will run out (if the market doesn't make them uneconomic first).

All towns based on the extraction of non-renewable resources must eventually find another basis for their economy. Many have transformed themselves into tourist towns. Others have attracted software designers, stock traders, and other entrepreneurs of the information age. Still others have evolved local economies based on arts and crafts. In general, the smart ones anticipate the shift and ensure a hospitable environment for other, more renewable economic activities well before the change takes place.

Seek Ways to Strengthen the Economy Without Increasing 'Throughput'

Any material process has its inputs and outputs. The sum of the materials that are processed, used, and turned into waste can be termed "throughput."

Many communities think that the way to improve themselves is to increase throughput, to do more of what they're already doing—harvest more corn or trees, make more widgets, attract more tourists. Sometimes this works in the short run, but over the longer term the full social and environmental costs of these enterprises—often hidden—may outweigh their benefits. If so, increasing throughput will only dig the community deeper into the hole.

Innovative communities and businesses create more jobs by further refining their products before exporting them out of the community. Instead of harvesting more, they "add value" to what they've already harvested; instead of making more widgets, they make better widgets; instead of wooing more tourists, they create more interesting experiences that encourage tourists to stay longer.

Throughput can be likened to cashflow in a business. Increasing throughput, like increasing cashflow, doesn't necessarily solve problems, and it may even make them worse—we've all heard the one about the guy who was losing money on every unit he sold, but he was "making it up in volume."

Here's another anecdote that neatly illustrates the problem of throughput:

An enthusiastic middle manager, having been laid off from his job, buys a truck and a load of wholesale fruit and vegetables to sell out on the highway. Business is good. By the end of the day, he's sold nearly all his produce.

When he gets home, he tells his wife about his successful day. When he's finished, she asks him how much he paid for the produce.

Two thousand dollars, he says.

And how much did he earn selling it?

I don't know, he says, I haven't counted it yet. So he goes and counts the money. He comes back and announces he earned $1,800.

Hmm, his wife says, there seems to be a problem.

Yeah, the man says, I need a bigger truck.

Focus More on Getting Better, Less on Getting Bigger

As mentioned earlier, a smart community looks for ways to develop itself without necessarily expanding. It understands that communities have more options than just accepting another subdivision, a big-box retailer, a casino, or another industry. The next chapter highlights a number of creative alternatives to the standard bigger-is-better approach.

Seek Development that Increases Diversity and Self-Reliance

It's well known that a town with several kinds of export businesses is stronger and more resilient than another with only one. With more diversity, fewer jobs are likely to be jeopardized at one time by fluctuations in the national or international economy.

Diversity tends to come not only from big, attention-grabbing plant openings, but also from "micro-enterprises" starting up in garages, living rooms, and barns. Other things being equal, twenty new businesses with two employees each are far preferable to one new business with forty employees.

Some businesses increase local self-reliance by supplying goods and services that had previously been imported into the community. Businesses that serve the local market are less vulnerable to the uncertainties of the international economy. Diversity and self-reliance are also strengthened when businesses and families save money through resource efficiency, as the next chapter will show.

Put Waste to Work

We've grown used to throwing our waste away because "away" was always free. But in the process, we've polluted the land, water, and air that were so conveniently "away." In recent years the public has demanded more stringent health and environmental protections, and governments now require expensive waste-disposal facilities. Meanwhile, land for disposal has become increasingly valuable, making "away" even more expensive.

But waste is simply a misplaced resource. Innovative business people and communities are finding less expensive—even profitable—ways to reuse, recycle, or biodegrade discarded materials, and they're putting people to work doing it. The motto these days is "waste equals food": the byproduct from one business or process may be useful as the raw material for another. Market forces are gradually bending the old linear path of extraction (or harvest)–production–consumption–disposal into a closed circuit, where the last step loops around to connect with the first. Many materials that once came from virgin sources are now recycled from waste, and people are now finding jobs, for example, processing discarded plastic and wood into composite building materials.

Waste is simply a misplaced resource.

Regard Quality of Life as an Essential Asset

High quality of life is usually good for business. Most companies looking for a place to start or move seek not only a positive business environment but a community with good schools, clean air and water, and safe and quiet streets. Many communities that have allowed their quality of life to be degraded have found it much harder to attract and retain good employers.

Wise community leaders are realizing that quality of life and a strong sense of place aren't intangible options, they're vital assets that nurture residents and support the local economy. In addition, an increasing number of community residents are willing to say out loud that development means more than business, it means preserving and enhancing a great place to live. They're saying that they want their towns to continue to be places they and their children can call home. They won't sacrifice their home for short-term gain.

Consider the Effects of Today's Decisions on Future Generations

In 1987, the United Nations Commission of Environment and Development declared that sustainable development "meets the needs of the present without compromising the ability of future generations to meet their own needs."

If a community economy is based on the stewardship of such important local assets as trees or the nutrients in the soil, then future generations will be able to make a living in the same way. In contrast, economic activity that depletes resources creates a daunting future for a community's children. This concept is also sometimes referred to as "generational equity."

Consider the Off-Site Effects of Decisions

Many development proposals look good when analyzed only for their direct costs and benefits. Unfortunately, most communities fail to consider all the off-site and indirect impacts. For example, the drawings for a proposed motel in a tourist town may look terrific. Maybe the owner is proposing to plant lots of trees on a formerly degraded industrial site. But a broader look at the proposal might disclose dramatic increases in traffic past a school or through a quiet residential area. Off-site concerns may lead the community to turn down the proposal, or they might lead to creating a better one with more appropriate access that hurts no one.

Consider the Cumulative Effects of a Series of Decisions

A decision may appear sound when judged in isolation, but how does it hold up when placed in the context of other decisions that are being made or have been made?

Here's a real-life example. A small town in Colorado had a state highway running along its outskirts, with the local school occupying land on the near side of the highway. The owner of an undeveloped tract opposite the school proposed building a modest shopping center. On its own, the proposal sounded good: the stores would generate tax revenue and they'd be easy to access. The town council approved it. Later, because so many kids were dodging traffic to purchase treats at the new shopping center, the highway department decided to build a bypass a half-mile further from town. The town council then figured it would be OK to approve more commercial and residential development along the old highway, but that in turn overcrowded the school to point that the school board had to build a new one. But because expansion had helped escalate land prices, the new school had to be built on cheaper land on the far side of the bypass. As a result, students now must cross the new highway to get to it.

By failing to consider the cumulative effects of decisions, local leaders only worsened the problems they were trying to solve. They didn't ask themselves what unintended consequences might result from each "solution" they chose.

Measure Whether Actions Actually Do What They're Intended to Do

Sustainable development views the economy, community, and environment holistically; it looks at the big picture, paying careful attention to underlying causes and effects. Communities and businesses working toward sustainability therefore need to listen closely to feedback—not just the verbal kind, but all the various indicators of community health, trends, and cause-and-effect relationships. When weighing an idea or strategy, they should examine its direct and indirect effects, look for unintended negative consequences, and discontinue or modify it if it doesn't appear to be working. When conditions change, they should alter their strategy or actions in order to achieve the same goals. This approach is often referred to as "adaptive management." It may sound obvious, but communities, like individuals, tend to get stuck in certain patterns of thinking and don't always notice that their views are based on obsolete information.

Consider a community that's experiencing rapid increases in housing prices. Officials conclude that the problem is insufficient supply for the demand, so they start encouraging more housing construction. This strategy has the desired effect in the short term, but after a couple of years, expansion-fueled speculation and an influx of buyers from more expensive housing markets start driving prices up again. Delayed reactions such as this are common in complex systems like communities; it can take years or even decades to receive feedback on certain decisions. While it's better not to create a housing boom in the first place, the community may not have been able to foresee it. The important thing is to be sensitive to the first signs that the policy might not be working, and be prepared to alter it accordingly.

Where Do We Go From Here?

While expansion was once seen as the only track to prosperity, the good news for both declining and expanding communities is that there is an alternative. Prosperity doesn't necessarily require expansion, it requires development that is sustainable.

Though this chapter challenges common assumptions about growth, it's only a brief exploration of these ideas. The questions it raises are sufficiently complex to justify entire books. Those working to put sustainable development into practice soon learn that the concept can be ambiguous and even elusive. For example, if a corporation proposes a facility that hires most of its workers from outside, imposes a tax burden on community inhabitants, or endangers the quality of the ground water, most people will recognize that it's a bad idea because it can't be sustained over time to benefit the community. But most proposals aren't so easily judged. Often, the best a community can do is determine whether a particular proposal will move the community toward or away from sustainability.

Though the answers may not be easy or clearly defined, the above guidelines provide a general framework for approaching sustainability. The rest of this guide sets out a more specific process for incorporating sustainability into community decision-making.

The controversy, uncomfortable changes, and side effects of expansion aren't confined to a few places. They're being played out in communities across the planet as the global economy touches each individual's life, as the population swells, as resources become scarcer, and as humankind's wastes (from greenhouse gases to pesticide residues to nuclear waste) exceed the planet's capacity to absorb them. It's becoming clear that if our development strategies aren't sustainable, they will be terminal.

But within this crisis are substantial opportunities and solid reasons for hope. Increasing numbers of citizens in overgrown communities are unwilling to drown passively in someone else's prosperity. Those in declining communities are organizing to ensure a better future. Committed people are speaking out and acting for humane and sustainable development to create the kind of economy in which future generations can thrive. Increasingly, they find that others are listening.

Opportunities and reasons for hope are found in the next chapter, which explores Economic Renewal as a practical way to move communities in the direction of a more sustainable future.

If our development strategies aren't sustainable, they will be terminal.

VITAL SIGNS OF SUSTAINABILITY

Once a community has decided to become more sustainable, how does it know if its efforts are working? A growing number of communities—including Seattle, Portland (Oregon), and Jacksonville (Florida)—have devised "indicators of sustainability" to gauge their progress, raise awareness, and develop tools for decision-makers. Though different for each community, these indicators often include such vital signs as daily traffic volume, employment, air quality, housing, literacy, biodiversity, energy use, voter turnout, land use, and recycling.

Indicators aren't new—sales tax, housing starts, and per-capita income have long been used to measure what we've always called progress. But the new emphasis on sustainability recognizes that the old indicators offered, at best, a partial picture of a community's health. The booklet *Monitoring Sustainability in Your Community* (see page 221) gives tips on choosing indicators to create a more complete picture of your community's progress.

An Introduction to Economic Renewal

As discussed in Chapter 1, sustainable development stands in sharp contrast to conventional, business-at-any-cost economic development strategies. It:

➤ Redefines prosperity, weighing quality of life, community character, and the environment alongside economic considerations.

➤ Seeks true development, in the sense of getting better, instead of expansion, which is merely getting bigger.

➤ Advocates the long-term stewardship of community resources, ensuring that present actions don't erode the basis for future prosperity.

➤ Pursues self-reliance and a more democratic approach to decision-making, representing community-wide interests over those of an elite few.

➤ Stresses diversity, resilience, and a conviction that many small efforts work better than a single one-size-fits-all solution.

You may be saying to yourself, "Sure, sustainable development sounds like a fine idea, but how do I translate it into something useful for my own community?" This chapter answers that question. It introduces a practical way to achieve sustainability, called Economic Renewal, which has been successfully implemented in dozens of communities throughout North America.

Although Economic Renewal refers to a particular process for bringing about sustainable development at the community level, it's based on set of guiding principles and tools that many communities are already using, even if they don't use the term Economic Renewal. The principles, described in the first section of this chapter, will help guide you in identifying specific projects to strengthen your community and its economy. The tools, explored in the second section, can be applied in every stage and aspect of your economic development effort. Together, they offer new perspectives on old problems, revealing opportunities that might otherwise be overlooked.

The final section of the chapter gives an overview of the eight-step Economic Renewal (ER) process, which is designed to get practical results in communities experiencing real-life problems. Based on the concept of collaborative decision-making (discussed in Chapter 3), the process is an approach to community problem-solving that meaningfully involves all different kinds of people, many of whom seldom talk to one another. With ER, they're no longer passive observers who can only briefly comment at some long, dreary public meeting. Instead, they become active participants who may even lead fun and creative problem-solving sessions.

To heighten your creativity, as you read about the following principles and tools, think about how to apply each to your local situation. This moment is the beginning of your journey to a more sustainable community.

Four Principles of Economic Renewal

Think, for a moment, about the economy of your community. What makes it work? In many ways a local economy is like a bucket that the community would like to keep full. However, economic buckets invariably have holes in them. Every time someone buys something from outside the community, dollars leak out.

To balance the dollar drain, money must flow in from outside the local economy. Money comes in when people in other places buy products or services created by local people. Extracted raw materials, harvested crops, or manufactured goods are "exported"; many communities also earn income from tourists and other visitors. However they do it, communities must bring in at least as much money as they spend or they will wither and die. When income falls short of outgoings, communities typically react by trying to recruit outside businesses—a risky and expensive strategy whose pitfalls were discussed in Chapter 1. Even if its accounts balance, a local economy that's heavily reliant on only one or two industries may be vulnerable to swings in the national or global economy. To achieve greater diversity, the usual response, again, is business recruitment.

Recruitment is an attempt to find new ways to pour more money into the community's economic bucket. Though it can be useful in many circumstances, this strategy rests on the often unquestioned assumption that new business from outside the community offers the best—or the only—solution to local economic problems.

Economic Renewal focuses on easier, cheaper, and less risky means to achieve the same end. And while this approach may lack the fanfare and ribbon-cuttings of a business-recruitment campaign, it typically fosters a deeper kind of community spirit and self-reliance that comes from solving problems locally instead of waiting for salvation to come from outside.

The Economic Renewal path to sustainable development is based on four principles. Although they're described separately here for clarity, in practice they're interrelated and often overlap. For instance, many things done in a community to pursue the first principle (plug the leaks) will assist in the second (support existing business). A smart community integrates all four, but it takes them in order, since the earlier strategies, as a rule, give more bang for the buck than the later ones. Going for the surer bets first gives a community momentum and puts it in a stronger position to reap the benefits of the subsequent strategies.

Plug the Leaks

The lively interchange of commerce is an important part of community vitality. Your days may begin with coffee grown in Africa, Latin America, or Hawaii. You may drive to work in a car bought from Detroit, Japan, or Europe, made from metals mined in dozens of countries. Television brings you news, culture, and sports events from different continents. Almost no part of your life stands alone without commerce from outside your community.

These products of international trade enrich our lives. However, many other imports—notably such necessities as energy, food, water, health care, and housing—can often be supplied locally at no extra cost, and sometimes at a saving. In our analogy of the community bucket, these expenditures are leaks; before trying to pour more money into a leaky bucket, a town should simply plug some of its leaks. Economists call this strategy "import substitution," but it's little more than practicing the old adage, "a penny saved is a penny earned," at the community level.

Leak-plugging is an important, but all too often overlooked, economic opportunity. When a community plugs an unnecessary leak, it puts money back into the local economy just as surely as if it had earned it through new industry. Likewise, as individual residents spend and respend the money they've saved, the local economic benefit multiplies in the same way it does with new income: more money in circulation creates more value, pays more wages, finances more investments, and ultimately creates more jobs. Unlike income, however, savings are inflation-proof—once you've cut out an expense, you no longer need to worry about its price going up. Further, money spent on local goods and services often goes to small businesses, the backbone of most local economies.

In every community, many goods and services that are purchased from out of town are, or could be, produced or marketed locally. Food, for instance. A study by students and faculty of Hendrix College in Fox, Arkansas revealed that the college was buying most of its food from distant suppliers, even though the majority of those food items were, or could be, produced locally. In 1987 the college changed its purchasing policy and is now committed to buying locally, and area farmers have learned how to produce for the college's specific food needs.

A community's economy is like a leaky bucket—instead of pouring more water in, it's easier to plug some of the leaks.

Leak-plugging can turn a town's whole attitude around. For instance, in the early '90s the future looked bleak to many residents of Tropic, Utah. The timber mill had closed and ranching was part-time for most. But some made a living serving tourists visiting nearby Bryce Canyon National Park, and high school students in an entrepreneurship class noticed that tourists were buying a lot of bottled water. In 1995, with the help of their teacher, Kaylyn Neilson, they started producing and selling Bryce Canyon Mist, local spring water bottled with an attractive label depicting the national park's red and yellow cliffs rising out of the morning fog. The new product hasn't single-handedly saved the town, but it has demonstrated to residents that they can improve their local economy by replacing imports with local products. By late 1995, there was talk of Bryce Canyon beef jerky (using local beef), lollipops, and crafts.

Even when a commodity can't be produced locally, it can often be used more efficiently to achieve the same net result. Indeed, this is probably the most reliable economic development strategy of all. Energy is a case in point. According to energy analyst Amory Lovins, a typical community spends more than 20 percent of its gross income on energy—and 80 percent of those dollars immediately leave the local area. Plugging this leak through efficiency is typically much easier (and cheaper, as it turns out) than trying to produce more energy locally. For example, the University of Northern Iowa spent $7,000 once in 1994 to install efficient showerheads, and is now saving $67,000 each year on water heating. Osage, Iowa (population 3,800) plowed $7.8 million back into its local economy between 1974 and 1991, thanks to a series of weatherization and energy-efficiency projects that continue today through the efforts of the local utility and service groups. As a result of efficiency, 1995 electric rates were 50 percent lower than the state average. Much of the saved money is respent locally.

The untapped economic potential of energy efficiency is enormous. It has been calculated that the United States could save $200 billion worth of energy annually—and create millions of jobs in the process—simply by being as efficient as Western Europe or Japan. Since those countries aren't as energy-efficient as they could be either, the savings potential is probably much greater still. It's as if every town in America had an invisible, clean-burning, maintenance-free power plant just waiting to be hooked up to the grid.

To promote a spirit of leak-plugging, some communities have encouraged residents to buy locally by creating their own currency. "Ithaca Hours" are a currency that "entitles bearer to receive one hour labor or its negotiated value in goods or services." In Ithaca, New York, that's equivalent to about $10 an hour, the average local wage. Twelve hundred local individuals and businesses of all kinds accept Ithaca Hours, approximately 4,600 of which are in circulation.

Of course it doesn't necessarily take an official program to plug a leak. Most towns have some sort of barter, or "informal," economy (see page 145) that enables local goods and services to replace imports. While the informal economy is virtually ignored by economic-development experts, its importance was quantified by Shanna Ratner of Yellowood Associates in Vermont, who estimated its economic value in Crown Point, New York to be equal to approximately 100 jobs. In a town of less than 2,000, that's a lot of jobs.

Leak-plugging—through import substitution, resource efficiency, buy-local programs, and a stronger informal economy—is an important step toward greater self-reliance, and a crucial aspect of any community's development strategy in an increasingly globalized and unpredictable economy. The more efficiently resources can be used, and the more local purchases (especially necessities) can be produced locally at reasonable prices, the more resilient the local economy will be, and the more able it will be to withstand externally created shocks and changes.

Support Existing Businesses

The economic heart of a community is its small businesses. Many development experts are convinced that the fastest way to increase jobs and strengthen a community's economy is to encourage existing businesses to become more efficient and successful. A 1991 report by the National Conference of State Legislatures notes that smaller businesses—those that are most likely to start up in your community—"while not providing the windfall of jobs promised by a Saturn plant…are the largest source of new job creation and tend to be less mobile and more committed and loyal to the…community over time and more willing to endure economic hard times." Yet, caught up in the dream of high-tech industrial recruitment, many communities overlook local opportunities.

The Ithaca and Osage examples demonstrate that one way to support existing businesses is to plug the leaks. Ithaca Hours are a substantial incentive to patronize local small businesses. And, though Osage residents started their energy-saving effort to save money, they also found that lower electric rates strengthened local businesses. Fox River Mills, a major employer in Osage, was able to cut its production costs by 29 percent thanks to lower electric rates and more efficient electric motors, making possible a plant expansion that nearly tripled jobs.

Though these and other innovative ideas can be powerful ways to support local business, any community's development effort must deal with the two most important causes of failure: inexperienced management and inadequate financing. Federally supported small business development centers (SBDCs, see page 218) are often a big help, offering classes in such basic business skills as management and accounting. Central to many communi-

Caught up in the dream of industrial recruitment, communities overlook local opportunities.

ties' development efforts, SBDCs are easily accessed in colleges throughout the United States.

Community development corporations (CDCs, see page 206), which lend to businesses, develop commercial and industrial space, and create housing, are also crucial to many towns. Nationally, there are more than 2,000 of these community-owned corporations, usually targeting services to lower-income people. An excellent example is the Mountain Association for Community Economic Development: operating statewide from Berea, Kentucky, it works on issues of forest products, micro-enterprise, displaced workers, affordable housing, water quality, and access to local government.

A CDC in Eugene, Oregon was the birthplace for a simple but extraordinary idea in the early '80s. One of its board members, Alana Probst, asked ten local businesses each to list forty items purchased out of state. She then called other local businesses that might be interested in bidding on items from the list of 400. In its first year, "Oregon Marketplace" created 100 new jobs and $2.5 million in new contracts. In 1987, this simple program blossomed into a statewide computer-based service that now matches all interested purchasers with Oregon suppliers. The concept works both at the local and state levels.

Oregon Marketplace not only boosted local businesses, in some cases it even created whole new markets. For example, an airline meal company had imported processed chickens all the way from Arkansas, despite a host of chicken growers just outside its home base in Eugene. Oregon Marketplace secured a commitment from the airline meal company so that a local bank would lend the growers enough money to build a processing facility. Some might suggest that Oregon Marketplace is an attempt to isolate the area from the national economy; on the contrary, equipment for the facility, unavailable in Oregon, came from a Chicago firm that in turn bought its steel from an Indiana company. Therefore, buying locally made Eugene a stronger trading partner in the national economy, supporting jobs in Eugene, Chicago, and Indiana.

Other successful efforts to strengthen local enterprises have focused on business networks. A bright light in the troubled wood-products industry of Washington state is WoodNet, a loose-knit network of small- to medium-sized wood-products manufacturers that helps members help each other. It finds markets, connects suppliers with buyers, encourages the use of waste products, pursues joint manufacturing and purchasing opportunities, creates forums for sharing business ideas, and seeks to stretch the region's dwindling wood supply. In an otherwise fiercely competitive industry, WoodNet members routinely communicate with each other, tour each other's shops, and enter into flexible business relationships. Acting together, members reduce costs for materials, professional services, and marketing. They gain access to larger markets by jointly manufacturing products no small firm could supply alone.

The business relationships nurtured by Oregon Marketplace and WoodNet can evolve into practical "flexible manufacturing networks." In Eugene, a group of cottage manufacturers joined together to secure a contract to make band uniforms for a local school. Similarly, small businesses within WoodNet partner to bid on wood products contracts.

Farms are businesses, too. A way to support farms that's spreading rapidly throughout the country is community-supported agriculture (CSA), which generates up-front capital for farmers and secures markets for their products. Farmers sell "shares" of their crops in the fall and winter, when farm income is typically lowest. For their investment, customers are assured a supply of fresh fruits and vegetables. Everyone benefits: the farmers get winter cash, consumers get summer discounts, and the community strengthens its local food supply and agricultural economy. In addition, members share in the satisfaction, as well as the risks, of agriculture. Rural Action, an Ohio-based nonprofit organization, found that ranchers participating in this approach to agriculture made at least $1,000 more per animal by processing and selling their livestock themselves.

Another source of support for family farming is community land trusts. Communities use CLTs to preserve the availability and affordability of land to low-income residents, farmers, and others to whom rising property values can mean dislocation or bankruptcy. One example is the Wisconsin Farmland Trust, which helps farmers withstand development pressures, encourages stewardship of the land, invigorates local agriculture activity, and stimulates farmer-to-farmer cooperation.

City-dwellers are also taking action to support existing business. According to the publication *ZPG Reporter*, residents of Washington, DC's Marshall Heights neighborhood decided in the early 1980s to do something to stem the exodus of neighborhood businesses. They conducted a study that showed retailers how much pent-up purchasing power existed in the area, then persuaded the DC government to pave their unpaved and gravel streets. They established the Marshall Heights Community Development Organization, which now provides a 90,000-square-foot space for start-up businesses and co-manages a shopping center that it bought and renovated. Which brings us to the third principle of Economic Renewal…

Encourage New Local Enterprise

In any dynamic economy, businesses are constantly folding and being created. In most communities this process goes largely unnoticed unless business failures outnumber start-ups. However, your community can do a

Farms are businesses, too.

lot to tip the balance toward success by encouraging new local enterprise. Pursuing the previous two steps will lay a firm foundation for this effort. They create an exciting business climate: a town that's plugging leaks and supporting existing businesses is a great place to start a new one. And plugging leaks will often lead automatically to opportunities for creating new businesses—such as the water-bottling plant in Tropic, Utah, mentioned earlier.

Many communities whose industries are based on limited resources can create new businesses and jobs by adding more value to the products they export. A classic example is the logging town with its own timber mill: by shipping milled lumber instead of raw logs, the town creates more jobs per trees cut down than a town without a mill. Some troubled logging communities are taking this concept a step further by processing milled lumber further into furniture or other finished goods, thus supporting even more jobs with a limited resource base.

Whether the resource is timber, grain, cattle, or coal, adding value is a powerful strategy for stimulating a local economy. A group of organic farmers in Saskatchewan has harnessed this principle both to support their own businesses and create a new one. In 1995, in a project that grew out of their participation in Economic Renewal, they built a facility to process their grain products instead of shipping them unprocessed. Similarly, corn farmers in Marshall, Minnesota, formed a co-op in the 1980s that built a plant to process local grain into syrups, oils, and meal.

Another well-tested method for encouraging new local enterprise is the business incubator. Developed by private businesses, local governments, and colleges and universities, these facilities vary widely from place to place, but generally provide affordable (sometimes subsidized) space, business services, and consulting under one roof. A typical incubator is a cluster of small offices or shops around central secretarial and computer services. Businesses are often required to move on to other conventional space after a specified period of time.

Encouraging new business activity often requires creative financing. For example, many local start-ups are so small or risky that conventional banks won't lend to them. Based on the overwhelming success of "micro-enterprise" loan funds in developing countries, the Good Faith Community Loan Fund of Pine Bluff, Arkansas, was created by a public-spirited foundation to provide financing to very small local businesses. Because the mostly low-income borrowers stand little chance of getting conventional bank loans for their fledgling businesses, the nonprofit fund is putting needed money behind self-employment and new economic activity in depressed regions of rural Arkansas.

Some communities are developing their own creative ways to finance local enterprise. Residents of Oberlin, Kansas gathered risk capital from current and past residents at no more than $1,000 per person—very patient capital that no one expected to get back—and invested in a feedlot, which later went private. Ivanhoe, Virginia sells deeds to square feet of land in a town park to raise money for sustainable development projects. They have land owners from all over the world! The project creates community pride, develops community capacity, and raises money.

After establishing Oregon Marketplace (see page 21), Alana Probst moved on to yet another groundbreaking idea, helping found the ShoreTrust Trading Group in 1995. The nonprofit organization offers business support, marketing assistance, and high-risk, non-bank credit to businesses in the lower Columbia River region that reduce waste, save energy, limit chemicals use, add value locally, or improve fishing, farming, and forestry practices.

A more exhaustive discussion of community development financing mechanisms is given on page 205.

Recruit Compatible New Business

Having pursued the first three steps, your town will be in a much better position to recruit new business. A community that's plugging leaks, supporting existing business, and encouraging new local enterprises won't be desperate for any economic activity, regardless of the harm it may cause. Businesses looking to relocate will be more attracted to a community with vibrant local enterprise and a high quality of life. Government agencies and foundations will also be more likely to direct their resources toward a community that's working hard to improve itself.

Business recruitment can bring significant rewards, especially if undertaken in a sophisticated way. It can attract new enterprises to develop underutilized resources and meet needs unfulfilled by existing businesses. Incoming companies can bring fresh capital, new jobs, economies of scale, technical expertise, and participation in national or international networks. If these characteristics complement local resources, the new company can bring renewed vigor to your community.

However, as explained in Chapter 1, business recruitment pursued without regard for community and environmental values can also create serious problems that outweigh benefits. Many communities have sought new industry at any cost, believing that any economic expansion is better than none. However, a community should add up whether a proposed new business will bring a *net* benefit. Will the advantages outweigh the costs? Will it be compatible with the community's goals? Residents of sleepy Cripple Creek, Colorado, assumed nothing but benefits would accrue from the gambling casinos that moved into town in 1993. Many spent a lot of personal time and money to ensure success of a state ballot question to allow gambling in their town. Within two years, demands for new public services

Having pursued the first two steps, you'll be in a better position to recruit new business.

to the new industry had resulted in a 350-percent increase in property taxes, forcing many residents to leave their own community.

If you decide to offer incentives to entice a new business to relocate to your town, understand that they usually don't work and often backfire (see page 2). Incentives should play only a limited role within a larger development effort. They should be used very cautiously, only with strict safeguards in place, and only when there are solid guarantees of net new jobs.

A cautious approach is the most cost-effective way to attract new business. By choosing the most promising and compatible development for your community, you'll be able to take your best shot at a range of possibilities, and make the best use of limited resources and time. Where industrial recruitment seems appropriate, make it work on your terms. A responsible company will be confident moving to a place where community values and goals are clearly stated, and local government and businesses collaborate to achieve those goals. It won't mind firm local rules if they're clearly stated and fairly enforced.

Taken together, these four principles offer an important message to every community: do better with what you have, instead of seeking "saviors" from outside the community such as footloose companies and government programs. It's not unlike the advice you might offer a good friend who's having problems at work or home. You might say, "Don't expect them to change—work on yourself." Similarly, a community that attempts to strengthen itself by knocking on government and corporate-boardroom doors would be well advised to acknowledge its weaknesses, work to change them, and build on its strengths. Whatever direction your community chooses, taking care of what you already have will give your economy the strength to multiply the benefits of any later economic development.

Nine Tools of Economic Renewal

The preceding four principles are the foundation of a smart community's development efforts—they offer a framework for thinking about how to approach development sustainably. But case studies of successful community development efforts compiled by Rocky Mountain Institute reveal a number of other specific tools you can employ as your community considers ways to strengthen itself.

Ask Why

In any community development effort, one of your most important tools is the question "why." Asking why helps strip away unfounded assumptions and establish what's really needed. It shifts the focus from particular proposals, which may divide the community by appealing to entrenched positions, to the underlying goals that unite the community. Having asked why, you can then choose the best way to achieve those goals rather than narrowly focusing on one-size-fits-all solutions.

This simple technique helps identify the most creative, sensible solutions to community problems. It can be applied to virtually any issue. For instance, during one community's meeting on development, one participant repeatedly insisted that the community needed a big arch over Main Street. Though most participants rolled their eyes or ignored his idea, someone finally asked why he wanted the arch. "We have no pride," he said. "We need something to make people feel good about this community." Another participant said, "I agree, we need to build our sense of community. So let's say *that's* what we need to do. Maybe then we can find additional ways to build pride, including the arch."

The second participant illustrated the point: when discussing a possible solution, ask why it's being considered. Maybe it's only one of several possibilities. Others may be more attractive, less controversial, and less expensive. One may appeal to the whole community, including the guy who wanted the arch.

Asking why can help reveal alternative paths through many thorny dilemmas. Struggling with economic problems, many earnest town leaders assume that a new industry is the solution. If they discover later that their chosen new industry will cause big problems, they may forge ahead anyway, blinded by their original assumption. But when an assumption leads to a painful conclusion, the sensible response is to question it: Why new industry? The answer may be increased income, more jobs, or more savings. New industry is only one of many ways to fulfill these needs.

Assumptions about how to achieve the community's goals are very different from the values that underlie those goals. Therefore, challenging the assumptions doesn't threaten community values. On the contrary, it's the most effective way to achieve the goals that support the community's values.

Old assumptions blind communities to new opportunities. As your community's development effort proceeds, notice and respectfully question the assumptions—your own as well as others'—that underlie particular ideas. Are they limiting the community's possibilities? Are they leading the community down an unwise path? Continually asking why will expose limiting or damaging assumptions and clear the way for more productive problem-solving.

Manage Demand

The conventional response to running out of something is to look for more of it. For instance, facing burgeoning demand in the 1980s, many electric utilities invested in new power plants. They assumed that con-

Old

assumptions

blind

communities

to new

opportunities.

sumers would pay for this new supply, whatever it cost. But the new power plants were so expensive that electric rates soared. In response, consumers reduced their demand, eventually bankrupting several major utilities.

Such "supply-side" solutions often overlook the true nature of demand. It isn't electricity that people want, it's the services that electricity makes possible: refrigeration, lighting, hot water, home heating. But it's typically cheaper to find more efficient ways to provide these services than simply to increase the supply of electricity. That's why utilities like the one in Osage, Iowa (see page 19) have learned that they can often meet customer demand more effectively by investing in weatherization and appliance-rebate programs rather than in new power plants. It sounds counterintuitive, but the utility can actually make more profit by paying its customers to use less of its product. The customers, for their part, still have hot showers, cold beer, and so on—and they have more money left over, which filters back into the local economy.

The solutions to many problems are often far less expensive when they address demand rather than simply adding new supply. "Demand management," as this approach is called, starts by asking what job the user wants done, and then determining the most efficient way to do it. It usually turns out that no kind of new supply can compete with the more efficient use of what you've already got.

Some community organizations have found they can play a vital—and lucrative—role in managing demand. In Southern California, for example, a group called the Mothers of East Los Angeles teamed up with water utilities to implement a toilet rebate program. The utilities were willing to pay customers $100 to trade in their old toilets for new, water-saving models, but the program was failing in low-income neighborhoods because many residents simply couldn't afford to shell out $100 and wait weeks to be reimbursed. The "Mothers," backed by a private consulting firm, bought the new toilets up-front, hired local people to install them, recouped their expenses with the utility rebate, and had money left over to fund a child-care program. The utilities saved money on distribution costs in the long run, and residents who took advantage of the offer benefited from lower water bills.

Demand-management solutions are not only better for the economy, they're better for the environment. For example, some cities are realizing that widening roads and highways doesn't solve traffic problems. "Traffic demand management" programs, such as ride-sharing, can accomplish the same objective much more cheaply. Lester Prairie, Minnesota reduces demand on roadways while supporting local businesses with "Rideshare Bucks," which commuters earn by giving rides to fellow residents. Funded by a state energy grant, the bucks can be redeemed at local retail outlets. In the program's first two years, Lester Prairie commuters saved $600,000 in travel and fuel costs (and in the process prevented 100 tons of carbon dioxide from polluting the atmosphere).

Pursue Development, Not Necessarily Expansion

As discussed in Chapter 1, growth and development aren't the same. Growth, in the sense of expansion, is an increase in *quantity*; while development is an increase in *quality*. This distinction is particularly important to the many communities that are learning the hard way that growth is not the solution to their economic woes. While they enjoy the benefits of growth, they're also vexed by the problems it causes: higher taxes, traffic congestion, crime, long commutes, air pollution, increasing intolerance, disrespect for traditional leadership, increasingly cutthroat business competition, higher rents, housing shortages, spiraling costs, and demands for higher wages to meet the higher cost of living.

Fortunately, communities have many opportunities to develop that don't require them to get bigger. They can create jobs, increase income, improve conditions, save money, and provide opportunities for subsistence (non-cash) activities—all of which strengthen the local economy without necessarily requiring its expansion. It's true that expansion creates jobs in a community; but sustainable development puts people to work, too, without the problems often associated with physical expansion.

Successful communities confronting important decisions about proposed development should ask hard questions: Is this particular kind of development sustainable? Is it something that will support or detract from the ability of our grandchildren to make a living? Will it create problems that the community cannot adequately deal with? Is it compatible with the traditional values of the community? Sustainability can be difficult to determine. Some development ideas are clearly unsustainable; others are less clear. However, it's worth asking questions early to save yourself the grief of unintended consequences.

Seek Small Solutions

Communities with big problems often seek big solutions. But the bigger the solution, the harder it is to pull off, and the greater the risks. When a community puts all its eggs in one basket and someone drops the basket, the community's development effort cracks.

Consider the community that puts its hopes in attracting a particular industry. It usually takes a couple of years before the new company makes the final decision to move in. As time passes, unhappy news may come to light. Local leaders hear that the new company will buy (in some cases, take) water from local farmers. "That's unfortunate, but we need new industry," say the overburdened leaders. Then they discover that the industry can't afford to avoid dumping chemical effluents that may seep into the

Small solutions are more flexible, less expensive, and more manageable.

ground water. Leaders, who have already committed themselves beyond the point of no return, say, "There's no proof that it'll end up in the ground water and, anyway, we need the jobs." Later, distressing news: the company will import most of its workers. "Well," say local leaders, "that's too bad, but we're committed now."

In contrast, small solutions are usually more flexible, less expensive, and more manageable than large ones. When a community embarks on a diverse effort that includes many small projects, each of which can produce results, then the potential for success is high. If a few projects turn out to be duds, no problem. Others will succeed, making the overall effort a success— the kind of success that builds toward a better future.

In 1995–96, Snowflake, Arizona used the Economic Renewal process to select several projects intended to strengthen the community: historic tours for tourists, business education and mentoring, and niche marketing and cooperation among local farmers. Even if one of these projects doesn't succeed, others will thrive and provide a big win for Snowflake. Better, each of Snowflake's three projects is diverse by itself. Some parts can fail while others flourish. If Snowflake instead had sought one big solution, it could have netted one big failure. By pursuing many solutions, its strategy was resilient and durable.

This is not so say that your community shouldn't attempt a large project—just don't *rely* on that big project as the sole basis for your community's success.

Find Problem-Solvers Who Care

Many communities pursuing development seek saviors—a big corporation, government, or maybe a foundation—someone from outside the community who'll wave a magic money wand and save the community from disaster.

It may happen. But the success of this approach depends entirely on an important decision made by people with no direct stake in the community. They may be terrific people who love their children, but their personal goals probably don't include ensuring the success of your community. They've got other responsibilities, other needs, other demands on them. Entrusting your community's future to such disinterested outsiders is likely to lead to delay, disappointment, and an unacceptable loss of control over the outcome.

This not to say that a community shouldn't fully use outside resources; on the contrary, an effective development strategy taps outside resources. But don't rely on them for your sole support. Depending on outsiders is worse than putting all your eggs in one basket—it's handing the basket to someone who doesn't care if the eggs break.

The people who found and provided the fledgling solutions in Tropic, Utah (see page 19) lived there and by all accounts cared about the community. All understood that a stronger local economy was in their interest—they didn't need to be altruistic to understand that the community's success would make them more successful.

When looking for problem-solvers, don't overlook local business people. They, as much as anybody, have an interest in seeing your community thrive. Many care so much about the community that they started a business to remain in it. They're in it for the long haul. In contrast, outside businesses might be induced to move in, but they'll move out just as easily if they're offered a better deal elsewhere. Locals don't move to Asia to save labor costs.

Increase the 'Multiplier Effect'

When a dollar enters a community and is then spent outside the community, its benefit is felt only once. If that same dollar is respent within the community, its benefit is multiplied: it adds more value, pays more wages, finances more investments, and ultimately creates more jobs. Thanks to this "multiplier effect," each additional transaction in which the dollar is involved creates just as much wealth as a new dollar from the outside, but relies on local decisions made by people who care about the community.

Let's say you sell your particular product outside the community (or you provide a service to a visitor from outside the community) and receive new dollars for it. After you pay your business's operating costs, you spend some of your new dollars to buy a jacket from a catalog. A tiny fraction of your expenditure returns to the community to pay the driver or postal worker who delivers the jacket. If you buy the jacket from a local factory outlet or superstore, more of your dollars return to pay salaries of the store's staff. But if you buy the jacket from a locally owned dry goods store, even more of your dollars stay in the community. Its owners spend some of their profits and a much larger share of their operating costs locally. They may even buy one of your products. It's unlikely the superstore owners or the catalog company would do the same. The greatest multiplier effect, and thus the greatest benefit to the community, is achieved when you buy the jacket from a locally owned business that made the jacket itself.

Your community can increase its multiplier effect by plugging leaks, supporting existing businesses, and creating new local businesses—especially if those new businesses supply locals with things that had previously been imported.

Find Hidden Local Skills and Assets

Colquitt, Georgia was a community that appeared to have nothing much to work with. In fact, it had an asset whose importance had, for a long time, gone unrecognized. The mayhaw berry had grown around Colquitt since before the town was settled, but no one thought of it as having any "economic development" value. They thought of the berry simply as something that families canned for their own use.

But one autumn, a small group of creative women canned more mayhaw jelly than their families could eat. They made labels and tried selling small jars of the jelly to specialty stores. The stores thought the product was great and wanted more. The women created a business that went on to employ 50 people who prepared mayhaw jelly and a dozen other products for sale in 36 states.

The women of Colquitt put to work an asset that was literally growing on trees. Though the mayhaw business has since been purchased and moved to another town, it demonstrated that virtually every community has some unique asset or skill that can be put to work creating wealth. It could be a raw material, a recreational opportunity, perhaps a traditional craft or a historical affinity for a certain industry. Hidden opportunities can even be found in waste: in Rifle, Colorado and Hazleton, Pennsylvania, huge greenhouses are kept warm with the waste heat from local power plants. The trick is to examine your community with a fresh eye.

What asset or skill is hidden in your community? As you consider this question, think beyond those that are literally hidden. Opportunities may be right there for everyone to see but waiting for someone like you to recognize and put to work. After all, some of the best ideas are those that, once you hear them, seem obvious.

Build Social Capital

A community's most important strength is the capacity of its people to work together for the common good. This capacity is often referred to as "social capital." Like more conventional forms of capital, it's essential to successful development. Unlike other forms of capital, the more you give away, the more you get back.

According to Harvard political scientist Robert Putnam, social capital is indicated by such things as voter turnout, newspaper readership, participation in community decision-making, and membership in arts, sports, and service organizations. Many people regard these things as not very important, just something you do because it's fun or necessary. But Putnam's twenty-odd years of research indicates that each of these activities is an important thread in the fabric of a community. The stronger the fabric, the better residents feel about living there, and the better a place it is in which to do business. In other words, a community's economic success is based on its social capital rather than the other way around.

Towns succeed because they're communities, not just collections of buildings and people. This is not to say that residents all agree with one another. On the contrary, they have important disagreements, but they deal with those disagreements in a civil way. They solve problems instead of

A community's most important strength is the capacity of its people to work together.

attacking one another. They know that they can't just sit back and wait for prosperity; they must work together to seize it.

Successful communities have committed volunteers who serve in many ways, some organized, some quietly individualistic. They have lots of organizations, meetings, events, festivals, and parties. There's not a night in the week that something isn't going on. Though one of these activities alone may seem insignificant, together they create the foundation for a community and its economy.

Successful development can result from one person's great idea, but a community that sits back and waits for that person to come forward is likely to drift in complacency, hoping things will get better. In contrast, a proactive community sails to success by gathering residents to examine where the community wants to go and how best to get there. That gathering is the place where many ideas, including that one person's great idea, can be offered, considered, and improved upon.

This guide will help you involve your community's inhabitants in a development effort. Chapter 3 in particular offers more ideas about how to develop social capital. At each step in the Economic Renewal process, you'll add another building block of social capital to serve as the foundation upon which your community will succeed.

Organize Regionally

Though prosperity for your own community must be the ultimate aim of your development effort, your community is not an island. Taken too far, community-centeredness can crush creativity ("We're gonna do it this way because we've always done it this way"), provoke petty rivalries with neighboring towns or neighborhoods, or, worse, cause residents to retreat into narrow-minded hostility toward anyone from the outside.

Just as your family needs the community, the community needs its connections to neighboring towns, the region, the nation, and the world. The human scale of a community—which is its strength on a social level—can make for limited economic options and few opportunities to make business connections. A smart development effort looks for ways to tie in more fully to the regional economy.

Regional cooperation may take many forms. Perhaps the most common is the regional development organization, formed by neighboring rural towns to provide staff support and assistance for members. These partnerships may be public (local governments), private (for example, chambers of commerce), or both. Leaders from twenty isolated and fiercely independent towns in the far-flung Alexander Archipelago of Alaska created the Southeast Conference in 1956 to start a ferry system that today is essential to the region's commerce. In other cases, businesses may lead the way by initiating cooperative marketing to regional urban centers. Organic farmers in Saskatchewan (see page 23) reached beyond their individual communities to other farmers over a wide region to build a cooperative processing facility for their products. In 1993, the Arkansas Rural Enterprise Center created WoodWorks, Inc., which markets Arkansas wood products to support businesses, create jobs, and promote sustainable forestry practices. The center helps wood-products businesses of all sizes work together and make sales regardless of what town they're in. The result is stronger, more diversified towns.

WHEN TO DO ER

The timing of your Economic Renewal effort is crucial to its success. Choosing the right time to start requires intuition and a knowledge of the inner workings of the community. In general, though, a community is probably ready to work toward bettering itself when one or more of the following conditions exist:

➤ Residents recognize that something must be done and no one else is doing it.

➤ A crisis (e.g., a natural disaster, closure of a major business) brings the community together.

➤ A few people have begun talking seriously about organizing some effort to seek a better future. Where a few are acting, many others are thinking.

➤ One or more people are committed to take action.

It will be more difficult to conduct ER when there is:

➤ Overwhelming apathy or lack of recognition that something should be done.

➤ A belief that something is coming that will save the town: "We don't need to do anything, we'll just wait till…"

➤ A crisis so deeply divides the community that people on opposing sides of the issue can't be in the same room together.

Though these are useful thoughts about timing, don't regard them as rules. Many communities have achieved success despite apparently bad timing. Some have accomplished results even in the face of rampant controversy. Others that appeared to be drifting aimlessly have taken dramatic action to improve themselves. Even a relatively apathetic community can be galvanized to action by a few credible and assertive people. However, your effort will have the best potential for getting off to a good start when at least one influential resident is actively enthusiastic about the idea.

Eight Steps to Economic Renewal

Economic Renewal is a process by which community residents from all walks of life work together to find and develop projects to strengthen their community and its economy. With the exception of the first preparatory step, it's a series of town meetings, each designed to build on the results of the previous session. At first, this community-based approach may appear long and cumbersome, but because it develops sound decisions, builds trust, and diminishes opposition, it saves time in the long run.

The Economic Renewal process is carried out by a small team of residents with the help of larger group of volunteers and sometimes a professional facilitator. While many factors can affect the length of time required to organize and conduct the eight-step process, most communities find it takes two to six months. The process culminates with the development of project action plans; actually carrying out the chosen projects, which is beyond the scope of this book, can take as little as a few weeks or as long as several years, depending on their size and complexity. The number of participants in the process varies widely from town to town, from as few as 25 to more than 200.

Each of the eight steps summarized below is the subject of a complete chapter later in this guide.

Step 1: Mobilize the Community

The first step in the ER process is to mobilize a broad cross-section of community residents to participate in the rest of the process. This preliminary step is arguably the most important of all because, unless it's done well, the rest of the process may not be worth doing. If an important decision that will shape a community's future is made by an elite group of insiders or by outside experts, community residents who are left out may not stand for it. The result can be delay, distrust, controversy, litigation, or inaction. In contrast, when decisions are developed by all different kinds of people in the community, they're likely to enjoy broad support.

Mobilization usually starts with a small group of people who, having decided that ER sounds appropriate and worth pursuing, schedule the first town meeting (Step 2) and try to generate as much interest in it as possible. This is done in a systematic manner, initially by personally contacting representatives of every organization and interest group in the community, whether official or not. Every possible viewpoint should be represented, including those that are typically ignored in local public processes. Having enlisted the support of key representatives, organizers publicize the process and the upcoming meeting through media announcements and, optionally, special presentations.

Step 2: Envision the Community's Future

This is the first town meeting of the Economic Renewal process. It assembles residents who use worksheets to identify their values, goals, and perceptions, and from them project the community's "preferred future." The effect of this exercise is to itemize what the community wants to preserve and what it wants to create anew. Unlike many economic development efforts that begin with a narrow focus on jobs and business, this meeting gives participants the opportunity to say what's important to them. They're assured that these things, in addition to business and jobs, will be the basis for the community's development effort.

In the course of discussing what they care about, participants often are amazed that others—even people they regard as adversaries—value most of the same things. This realization begins to build the trust that's crucial to the success of the program. The information generated by this session is useful later on when, in Step 6, participants refer back to the preferred future to ensure that prospective projects are compatible with it.

Because many people who attend this first meeting haven't been thoroughly briefed on the ideas of Economic Renewal, the session usually includes an introduction to sustainable development, the ER process, and the people who are conducting it.

Step 3: Identify What You Have to Work With

The serious work begins with this meeting, in which participants inventory the community and its economy. This provides a sound and factual basis for the community's subsequent development effort. Without it, many opportunities would be lost.

Participants break up into smaller groups to discuss seven important aspects, or factors, of the local economy: business environment, access to capital, infrastructure, quality of life, the informal economy, natural resources, and human resources. Each group then itemizes community problems, needs, and assets specific to its factor. The product of the session—worksheets listing problems, needs, and assets—becomes the raw data for the next step. If available, other economic and demographic data can be offered at this point in the process.

Step 4: Discover New Opportunities

Now the community's inventory from Step 3 is displayed so that everyone can see it as a whole and find opportunities that might otherwise be obscure or hidden among innumerable everyday details. Prior to the meeting, the Step 3 worksheets are transcribed onto large sheets of paper and attached to the walls of a large meeting space such as a high-school gym. The visual effect is a huge map of community conditions. The task is to make connections—literally—between community problems, needs, and assets.

In addition to being challenging and creative, this exercise is also fun: lots of people milling around in front of the lists, pointing at items, comparing notes, and making connections. In the course of the evening, participants list dozens or even hundreds of actions that might be pursued to strengthen the community.

Step 5: Generate Project Ideas

Freewheeling and creative, this step concentrates on identifying more projects the community might pursue to strengthen itself. Participants brainstorm project ideas based on what they learned in Step 4 and on ideas gleaned from case studies of other towns.

Some communities find they've already generated so many project ideas that they need very little time to complete this step, and are able to combine it in the same meeting with Step 6.

Step 6: Evaluate Project Ideas

Steps 4 and 5 generate more project ideas than any community can deal with. Many will be impractical, incompatible with the community, or too difficult or risky. The worksheets employed in this step provide a framework for evaluating how well project ideas fit the community's needs.

Participants form committees to evaluate project ideas. Each committee starts by clarifying and adding details to the idea, which may originally have been stated in general or vague terms, then evaluates the idea for its practicality, sustainability, compatibility with the community's preferred future, and other appropriate criteria. Projects that aren't chosen for evaluation are set aside for future consideration.

Step 7: Select Project Ideas

Though Step 6 reduces the number of prospective projects, there usually remain too many ideas for the community to implement at once. In this step, participants compare project ideas to one another to select the few that are most promising for the community at this time. Depending on the number of project ideas, this step may require more than one meeting.

Committees present the results of their project evaluations, which, tempered by comments from all participants, are summarized on a wall-sized "project menu." When the presentations have all been made and the project menu filled in, participants discuss the comparative merits of each project and agree by consensus which projects should proceed.

Finally, participants form project development committees and a committee to create a permanent organization to carry on the Economic Renewal work after Step 8.

Step 8: Develop Project Action Plans

This final step is a bridge from the Economic Renewal process to specific project implementation. It begins with a public meeting, which ensures that the committees get off on the right foot, but after that they work independently.

The committees' task is to create a written action plan for each project. In the process of developing their plans, they'll refine project concepts, recruit technical assistance, analyze alternatives, identify barriers to implementation, create budgets, secure financial support, and deal with resistance.

THE MEASURE OF ER'S SUCCESS

The outcome of the Economic Renewal process will be a few realistic projects chosen by participants—projects that will build toward a more sustainable future. Because many residents will have participated in selecting the projects, or at least followed and understood the process, they'll feel some ownership in and commitment to them. To enhance community support and enthusiasm, participants will choose at least one project that can be implemented quickly and easily to achieve a short-term, measurable success.

Many community residents and leaders, especially those who participated, will better understand the community economy; they'll be more comfortable with economic development. Participants will have experienced a genuinely collaborative process, which, if your community is like most, will be much more creative and less contentious than the usual ways of getting things done. They'll better understand each other and be more willing to work together. This experience may lead to more effective decisions in the future.

Each community that has used Economic Renewal has created and chosen development ideas compatible with its particular circumstances. A few examples:

➤ **Alamosa, Colorado.** Residents dramatically revitalized their downtown, launched alternative crop and fish-farming initiatives, started a community recreation program, conducted a business-needs analysis, planned a community/conference center, and instituted a flood-control program that saves $115,000 in insurance each year. Moreover, Economic Renewal "helped bring the town together" and "fired up the people," according to town manager Mike Hackett.

➤ **Kentucky.** The Mountain Association for Community Economic Development used Economic Renewal in three economically distressed counties. Participants selected a variety of development projects including a farmer's market, a co-op art gallery, a tourism committee, a small-business assistance effort, a value-added wood products business, and downtown improvements.

➤ **Plateau Valley, Colorado.** Residents of this rural area started a local newspaper, upgraded their fairground, and inventoried historic structures, and are now investigating alternative local crops.

➤ **Snowflake, Arizona.** Economic Renewal participants decided to support local business with a mentoring program, improve tourism by training local tour guides, and support local farmers with a co-op for specialty produce.

➤ **Saskatchewan, Canada.** Farmers built a value-added processing facility and started a marketing campaign for their organic products.

Some people may shrug off these successes as flukes, or assume that they resulted from some lucky break. However, though each received some help from the outside, these communities didn't score any big government grants or industrial sitings, nor were they particularly lucky. They created their successes largely on their own.

Like you, the residents of these successful communities were trying to make a living and didn't have a lot of time for meetings. But they balanced their commitment to their community with their family obligations, juggled their schedules, goaded their neighbors. After false starts and a few dead ends, they pulled it off.

These are ordinary folks who chose an extraordinary path, the steady and deliberate course to a sustainable future. It's a path that's yours for the taking. It relies on your understanding that a prosperous future for you, your children, and your grandchildren is based on stewardship of your community, its environment, and its economy. It starts with your commitment to act.

Collaborative Community Decision-Making

Community is the thread that binds towns and urban neighborhoods together. It's the human support system that helps people survive during hard times. It's the joy of a barn dance and the tittering over the gossip column, the powerful continuity of a forty-year friendship, lively conversations picked up mid-sentence at the post office, doing whatever it takes to get someone's car out of a snowy ditch on a frigid January night. It cannot be bought or constructed. The fabric of community is woven over time from the networks of caring people that make a place feel like home. It permeates the soil, the streets, the homes, schools, and businesses of your town.

We have strong emotional ties to our communities. In his book *Community and the Politics of Place*, Dan Kemmis observes, "We mostly live in these places because that is where we want to be." We've made a conscious and often difficult choice to come to, or stay in, our communities. Kemmis, who is the mayor of Missoula, Montana, also writes, "I think we are, in some fundamental way, not only chosen, but shaped by the places we inhabit. Different kinds of places claim different kinds of people."

The notion of community can be romantic—people working together for the common good. But it's also practical. You don't have to feel warm and fuzzy about everyone in your community to understand that you have a common future, and that sometimes differences must be set aside to get a job done. Such an attitude is just as important today as it was in the old days when, more out of hard-headed necessity than any sense of romance, neighbors worked with neighbors to raise a barn. They knew they'd need that neighbor's help the next time there was a big project on their land. A successful local economy in today's volatile world requires at least as much attention to neighborliness. Community inhabitants must work with one another whether or not they like or agree with one another.

Community is the foundation for prosperity. Economic development efforts are most successful in towns where residents work together for the common good, and where controversy isn't avoided but accommodated and channeled constructively. A community where locals have met, argued, agreed, and organized to revitalize their economy is far more attractive to someone looking for a place to locate their business than a town desperately grasping for any business to which it can sell itself.

Economic development professionals tell stories of towns that have steadily declined despite having all the conventionally correct ingredients: a railhead, a nearby interstate highway, a resource to extract, etc. Consistently, these are towns where residents and leaders never seem to talk about—much less agree on—important decisions. Yet development profes-

Community is the foundation for prosperity.

sionals also tell of those few exceptional communities that have thrived with few physical advantages. Despite apparent shortcomings, they achieved success because residents were willing to work through their differences, develop a vision for the future, and put that vision to work.

The primary barrier to successful economic development, therefore, is not the economy. It's not the price of wheat or coal, nor is it the number of tourists that come through. Rather, it's the capacity of community residents to work together.

Collaborative decision-making is the basis for rebuilding trust and respect that may have been marred by years of wear and tear; it's a way to replace boring or painful meetings with fun and creative ones; it's the vehicle by which people who have been ignored can finally fully participate. Collaboration makes it possible to discuss such innovative ideas as sustainable development in a town that might otherwise be closed to all but conventional wisdom. It's a way to incorporate community values into decisions that might otherwise be dominated by a small elite.

The fabric of any community is strengthened by improving and more tightly weaving each thread. The better the weave, the less stress and wear is felt by each individual thread. A strong community fabric will support your effort to bring success to your town. Genuinely collaborative decision-making will tighten the weave and increase your potential for success.

A HEALTHY COMMUNITY

Community may have a far more profound influence than previously understood. Health researchers began studying Roseto, Pennsylvania in the early 1960s because its inhabitants were among the healthiest people in the United States. They were surprised to find that Rosetans smoked as much, exercised as little, and faced the same stressful situations as other Americans, but somehow they experienced far lower rates of heart disease, ulcers and senility.

But the close-knit Italian-American town possessed one unusual characteristic: a strong sense of community. In *The Healing Brain*, researchers Robert Ornstein and David Sobel concluded: "People need people, not only for practical benefits which derive from group life, but for our very health and survival. Somehow interaction with the larger social world of others draws our attention outside of ourselves, enlarges our focus, enhances our ability to cope, and seems to make us less vulnerable to disease."

Community is a Whole New Ballgame

Communities face an increasing number of tough decisions and divisive forces at a time when community spirit and traditional forms of participation are declining. Several major barriers to community decision-making have emerged in the past generation:

➤ **Decisions are tougher.** Not long ago, local leaders focused most of their attention on which road to pave next, when to replace the old water line, or who would fix the church roof. Today, they may have to decide if a rich wetlands is more important than a housing project for local families. They could be asked if a proposed rural subdivision will provide a net gain to local tax coffers. They're supposed to know if heavy metals left on an old industrial site will contaminate the wells of nearby homes.

An increasing number of decisions demand a breadth of technical expertise that only a genius could hope to possess. Local leaders seldom have the knowledge required to answer many technical questions or the money to hire adequate technical advice. The normal response is to avoid the decision, deny the problem, or blame someone else (the government is at the top of the current blame list). Of one thing local leaders can be certain: whatever they do, someone will blame them.

➤ **Decisions are coming faster.** Rapid expansion increases the rate at which difficult decisions confront a community. Local officials feel increasingly like the ball in a pinball machine careening out of control from one tough choice to the next. Planning-commission agendas are backed up six months or more. Almost as soon as one tough decision is made, it's negated by something unanticipated. Even communities that aren't expanding are profoundly influenced by the fast-changing world around them. The normal response, again: avoid, deny, and blame.

➤ **Participation is down.** Nationwide, participation in traditional community organizations is declining measurably. Harvard political scientist Robert Putnam notes that membership in such old standbys as churches and bowling leagues has declined 25 percent in the past 25 years. Regardless of age, income, or race, we're not working together and talking with one another the way we used to. After church or while our teammates were bowling, we used to talk about the school bond issue or the city council's current quandary. Through these informal contacts we informed ourselves, formulated decisions, and came up with solutions to community problems. Despite a recent upsurge in new kinds of community-building efforts such as those described in this book, too many of us, tired from working too many hours, tend to stay home and watch TV instead of communicating with our fellow citizens.

➤ **Partisanship is up.** During the same quarter-century there has been a marked increase in partisanship, factionalism, and special-interest rhetoric. Where once people wrangled over tough issues, then walked outside still good friends, now they leave angry and deeply divided. In many cases, single-issue groups are a reasonable reaction to poor treatment. People get fed up after years of being shut out of decision-making, and it should come as no surprise if they react tactlessly or show up with lawyers and demand that their position prevail. But when combined with the above trends, the result can be deep discord. Increasingly, community politics is "us" versus "them"—and if you're not with us, you must be one of them. Factionalism leads naturally to alienation, adding frustration and anger to the mix.

Community Decisions—Top Down or Bottom Up?

Faced with these challenges, community leaders attempt to make constructive decisions. Whether they're business people, religious leaders, elected officials, community organizers, labor leaders, human-service workers, or active citizens, they work long and hard to find solutions to community problems. But to their surprise and frustration, when they try to implement their solutions in a highly charged atmosphere, sparks fly. They run smack into resentment and resistance from the rest of the community—citizens who didn't have the opportunity, or didn't take the time, to participate in the long process of finding the solution.

Many frustrated leaders, sincere in the belief that they're acting in the public interest, react to criticism with anger. They may throw up their hands in despair or try to ram their ideas through to completion. But such top-down decision-making is likely to lead to failure or lingering resentment from the rest of the community, making the next problem even more difficult to solve. Token efforts to involve the public, which only amount to informing citizens after decisions have already made, don't work either. Citizens still feel left out; they feel no ownership in the decision.

However, in a small but increasing number of communities, the "movers and shakers" are working toward local decisions from the bottom up. Beginning in the early stages of an effort to solve a particular problem, this new breed of leaders involves citizens from all walks of life. As a result, citizens contribute constructive ideas and understand and support the eventual solution. Trust is born and nurtured.

When widely divergent interests, ages, temperaments, and histories are represented from the beginning, citizens become better informed about community issues. Participants have a chance to understand one another's

Discussions in comfortable settings can be the basis for more civil discussions in public meetings.

concerns and appreciate the complexities of real-life community decision-making. They learn that solutions to community problems can't be found on bumper stickers.

The practical problem with this bottom-up approach is that it takes time. Most community leaders attend too many meetings already and can't bear the thought of more. But many leaders have found that the brawl that results from avoiding genuine public involvement takes even more time than a few meetings that might lead to consensus. They're looking for methods to fully involve the community without the rancor often found at public hearings.

The process described in this guide is one of those methods. It's a comfortable way to bring together community inhabitants, start from scratch, and determine what the community should do about development. Using this process, citizens don't just comment on someone else's proposal at a public hearing, they work together to create their own.

For this process to be effective, the people leading it must be genuinely committed to a bottom-up approach. They probably have their own ideas about what path the community should take or what kinds of economic development projects the community should pursue. But if they attempt to impose their notions on the ER process, disaster is likely to result, no matter how well-meaning they are. Other participants will understand what's going on and will either drop out or disrupt the process. For Economic Renewal to generate projects that will work best, its leaders must be willing to allow it to lead to results supported by consensus of the participants, even if those results are different from their own. (Consensus doesn't mean unanimous agreement—it means a decision that just about everyone can live with.)

Community Politics

Here's an example of the way community politics often works. Say we live in the hypothetical town of Zorchton, where the president of the Downtown Business Association (DBA) decides that a revolving loan fund would be a terrific help to local businesses. She publicizes a meeting downtown, invites several local organizations, and brings in a speaker to talk about revolving loan funds.

At first glance, this sounds like an open and reasonable way to get some development going. But in Zorchton, as in many communities, the economic development people are suspicious of the downtown people. The Zorchton Economic Development Association (ZEDA) doesn't get along too well with the DBA. ZEDA members start wondering, "What are they trying to pull this time? They probably want to bolster their downtown shops and beat our outlying businesses. They're trying to capture that state loan money for themselves." At their Tuesday breakfast meeting, ZEDA members decide to boycott the DBA meeting. Some belittle the meeting to people they see around town. The result: poor attendance at the DBA meeting and, eventually, a failed attempt to improve the local economy.

It may seem ridiculous that something as innocent as a meeting about a loan fund would turn into a local controversy. But it happens everywhere. If your community is normal, you can probably recall a local political battle that seemed equally absurd. The issue between ZEDA and DBA isn't the loan fund, it's trust. Various groups in your community—longtime residents and newcomers, perhaps, or the municipal and county governments—may distrust one another. Local rivalries may be so bad that many creative and capable people have given up on community affairs. "I can't

COLLABORATION REDUCES CONFLICT

In the fall of 1992, the city council of Aspen, Colorado held a referendum asking voters to allow the city to buy a vacated school and renovate it for various community uses. When the referendum was approved by a narrow margin, Mayor John Bennett wasn't satisfied. He took a big political risk by calling a day-long meeting between proponents and opponents to revisit the issue. His allies were angry. "What's to talk about?" they asked. "We just spent our time and money to win the election, and we won. Let's just get on with it!" But Bennett respected the interests and fears of those who had held opposing positions on the issue.

The position of each person at the meeting was well known: roughly half were in favor, half were opposed. But a few hours into the meeting, all had stated their interests, which were heard for the first time by their adversaries. Surprisingly, virtually everyone agreed more or less with the proposed use of the old school.

The immediate value of the meeting was that it exposed the real point of disagreement: finances. Proponents trusted the city to do the project in a fiscally sound manner; opponents didn't. Thus it became clear that they had an important common interest: a financially sound project. The meeting concluded successfully when the mayor asked opponents to serve on a financial oversight committee. Participants left the meeting largely satisfied and talking about ways to collaborate on the next issue *before* it became adversarial.

CHAPTER 3

deal with the politics any more," they've said. "I'm wasting my time." These individuals just wanted to accomplish something constructive and go home to their families, but now they're fed up.

Their frustration is understandable; what they don't recognize, though, is that politics is simply public relationships. Whether it's getting something done at work or keeping family members from strangling one another, everyone must deal with relationships on a daily basis. Why should it be any different at the community level? If you regard community politics as something to avoid or endure, then your participation will be uncomfortable, ineffective, and infrequent. In contrast, if you regard it as nothing more than the public aspect of all human relationships, then you'll be able to take comfort in the knowledge that, as with most relationships, the difficulties are outweighed by the rewards and, with some work, can usually be overcome.

If you recognize that community politics and jealousies can be a mine-field, you stand a much better chance of avoiding explosions. The shortest distance across the minefield is not a straight line. To avoid unpleasantness, you'll have to turn this way to discuss things with one group and that way to collaborate with another.

Collaboration Versus Cooperation

Though local politics may never be a dream, it need not be a nightmare. An effective way to move toward constructive local politics is through collaborative problem-solving. "Wait a minute," you might say, "isn't that what Zorchton's Downtown Business Association tried to do?" Well, yes and no. The DBA president was headed in the right direction, but didn't go far enough. In effect, she asked for *cooperation*, not *collaboration*. Cooperation is working together to implement an idea that's already formulated. Collaboration starts much earlier: it's working together to create the idea in the first place. When people have a hand in creating an idea, they're far more likely to support it, or at least be willing to live with it.

When one trusted friend seeks cooperation by asking another, "I've got this great idea, why don't you help me put it into action," the second friend will probably help. But if the same words are said by the leader of one group to a competing group's leader, the question may sound more like, "Why don't you come help *us* look good and get *our* goals accomplished." Though that's not what the Zorchton DBA meant, it's what ZEDA members, in their mistrust of the DBA, may have heard. It's no wonder they didn't show up for the meeting.

Collaboration is an easier, more reliable path to consensus. When community politics becomes more collaborative, it becomes more constructive, less messy, and more comfortable.

It's important to remember that a collaborative process such as Economic Renewal is not an attempt to get others to do what *you* want. Rather, it offers a powerful means for citizens to get what *they* want by working with others. It's carefully designed to hear and respond to the needs of all participants. Of course, this doesn't mean that ER will give everyone everything they want. Rather, it provides a forum in which everyone's needs can be considered.

Taking Positions Versus Exploring Interests

Most everyone involved in community decision-making is accustomed to taking *positions*. When an important local issue comes up, each side typically stakes out its position and prepares to defend it. This may be a conscious tactic or it may just happen in the course of informal discussions. The ZEDA, for instance, certainly wasn't opposed to improving business,

Collaboration is a challenging art. It often means talking seriously with people you don't know, agree with, or even like. It means dealing with people you may fear or those you think have power over you. To make your collaborative efforts more successful (not to mention more fun and less stressful), review the following principles. They're guaranteed to help.

➤ **Hear their concerns and ideas before telling them yours.** In important discussions, many of us tend to blurt out our own ideas. But you're far more likely to be heard if you first listen to the ideas of others. Once they've said their peace, their minds are clear to hear your ideas.

➤ **Understand their interests before describing yours.** Look for the interests, fears, and values that underlie the things they're saying. Repeat what you think you're hearing. Ask if your understanding is correct.

➤ **Describe your interests instead of defending your position.** Most of us have a good idea of how our interests can be fulfilled. That's our "position." If, instead, we talk about what we want—our problems, needs, and interests—before seeking solutions, the discussion may lead to alternative ways of fulfilling those interests.

➤ **Join them before asking them to join you.** Look for ways in which their interests are consistent with yours. Then work with them to focus on how you can both get what you want.

➤ **Set aside differences and disagreements to solve mutual problems.** If you're talking with people with whom you've disagreed in the past, don't ignore those differences. Instead, clear the air by acknowledging them. Agree to disagree respectfully on certain points, but keep in mind that what's most important is that you're part of the same community and you're eager to collaborate on this particular effort, regardless of past differences.

➤ **Employ active listening.** Acknowledging, empathizing, and clarifying: described on page 88, these are the most valuable skills that can be brought to any important communication.

➤ **Pursue easier issues first.** Your collaborative effort may go smoothly, but if it's a highly charged discussion and the issues are difficult, tackle the easiest one first. That success will give you confidence and momentum to take on the more difficult issues.

but when its members saw what the DBA was "up to," they concluded that the DBA had established a position in favor of the loan fund. So the ZEDA staked out its opposing position to protect its "turf." Once positions have been established in this way, it's difficult to change them without loss of face. Whatever the outcome, one side ends up losing.

At first glance, the situation may appear hopeless. The losing group will get frustrated and angry. It will become even more distrustful of the other side, take tougher positions in the future, and work even more belligerently to beat the other side. But a closer look reveals real hope for similar situations in your community. Underlying any person's or group's position are various *interests*, which include both fears and reasons for their position. Looking at the interests of the ZEDA and the DBA, it becomes obvious that they have at least one important interest in common: strengthening local business.

To resolve this conflict and avoid senseless battles in the future, they should explore their common interests (and perhaps fears) rather than arguing about their particular positions. The loan fund is too closely associated with the DBA's apparent position—why not instead frame the discussion as "exploring finance problems of local business"? Participants could talk about their respective difficulties in obtaining start-up capital and inventory financing. In the course of that discussion, the loan fund could be suggested as one of several options. The result of such a meeting might be a decision to create a revolving loan fund. Then again, the process of finding common interests might spark an idea for a joint project that no one anticipated. Both groups would support it because they created it together. Neither side loses; both win.

Your initial attempts to focus more on the other party's interests and less on your own position may be a bit difficult. You may have put in plenty of time trying to convince others how terrific your ideas are. One way to help yourself get the hang of it is to ask a lot of questions and listen carefully to the responses before saying what you think the answers are. This cautious approach can lead to powerful results, although it may not always be possible. In a case where there's only a limited window of opportunity in which to make a decision, you'll have to work fast to explore all parties' interests, bring them on board with the proposal, and not miss the deadline.

But as former adversaries get used to collaborating and exploring interests, they'll find they no longer have to deal with one another at arm's length. One group can bring forward a specific idea without members of the other group assuming they're being attacked. Trust will have been established.

Building Bridges

But there are times when trust doesn't come easily. Suppose the relationship between the DBA and the ZEDA has so eroded over the years that a deep chasm separates the two. To begin serious discussion about mutual interests, they need a *bridge*.

The best bridges are trusted friends. Though two organizations may distrust one another, an individual in one group may be close to someone in the other group. To call the meeting about business finance, the DBA president could talk to the ZEDA board member whom she's known for twenty years. He's her bridge to the ZEDA. They've got a long history that transcends any squabble between organizations. She could ask him to ask his group to participate in the finance meeting. If things go well at that meeting, she might request that the ZEDA co-sponsor the speaker on revolving loan funds.

To be even more effective on an important project, the DBA should begin a concerted bridge-building campaign. The DBA president should first gather members

Friends can bridge the gaps between factions.

of her organization to list all local groups that might wonder what the DBA is "up to." They should also list all groups whose involvement will be valuable, and those that might be upset if a project goes ahead without their knowledge and participation. They should be sure to include the organizations they regard as adversaries.

Next, the DBA should list key people in each group and other creative people who aren't part of any organization but who may be interested. Then, the DBA should identify which of its members are closest to each person on the list. These "bridge-builders" should contact their friends from the other organizations to seek their involvement and, eventually, their co-sponsorship.

In some cases, there may not be friends or acquaintances to serve as bridges. If not, you'll have to build bridges from scratch. Many of us would rather be audited by the IRS than make an appointment with an unfamiliar person who's part of another (possibly hostile) organization. But after the initial awkwardness, bridge-building can be easy and even fun. When your interest in others is sincere, the fact you took the time to call begins the bridge-building process. Distrust won't disappear immediately, but neither will it withstand a genuine effort to make respectful contact.

Building bridges will enhance communication and build collaborative relationships in every community endeavor and in each step of your development process. Each time bridges are built and used, progress becomes easier; community politics becomes less frustrating and more constructive.

When former adversaries work together on a project that is potentially controversial, the community will find the idea far more interesting and acceptable. Former adversaries working together is big news. It's positive grist for the rumor mill. The idea no longer appears to be controlled by one interest group—it's on the way to being owned by the entire community.

Warriors and Diplomats

Many community organizations have spent much of their energy mobilizing to ensure that their position prevails. When a controversy arises, they bring out their "warriors" to do battle. The warriors' goal is to defeat the enemy. Often, these dedicated people see issues as black or white and right or wrong. They think that considering the other side's interests is a sign of weakness. High-profile individuals who enjoy the limelight, they sometimes anger even their allies. You may know one or two of these people.

These warriors have served their organizations so well that they generally represent them in town meetings, which may work well in some circumstances. But a collaborative effort like Economic Renewal isn't just another community battleground for the warriors to fight over. It requires respectful public discourse. Therefore, the people who have fought your adversaries most valiantly in the past may not be the right ones to lead a collaborative process.

For collaboration, you need someone who's tactful and skillful in handling delicate situations, someone who listens carefully to all points of view and seeks mutually satisfactory solutions. In short, you need a diplomat.

In community politics, diplomats take bigger risks than warriors. Admired by their allies for hanging tough, warriors can feel righteous and confident; diplomats risk losing allies for the sake of community cohesiveness. Diplomats see the big picture: they know that if they win this issue by ignoring their adversaries' concerns, the adversaries will come back stronger and more angry the next time, maybe looking to even the score. Instead, diplomats build trust and build bridges for the long-term benefit of the community. It's an unusual person that can serve well as a warrior and then, later, as a diplomat. It's tough to fight adversaries one year and work with them the next.

We've gotten very good at making war in our communities, but to build for the future, we also must learn to make peace. If you send your warriors to meetings that were intended to make peace, you might end up with another war.

In the mid-1990s, the relationship between local leaders in the Western states and federal land management agencies is at an all-time low. After years of land-use conflict, especially regarding logging, mining, and grazing, at least 35 counties are so angry that they've declared sovereignty over federal lands inside county lines. In a few places, federal officials have been shot at, and offices and vehicles bombed.

Southern Oregon's Applegate Valley, historically a logging area, has been one of the areas racked by conflict. But more recently, residents have been dealing with these issues in a remarkably collaborative way. In 1992, people from the community, industry, and environmental groups came together informally to create the Applegate Partnership. The partnership has no legal authority; no politician appointed its members. No one officially represents a particular faction or interest group. It's just a network of committed community inhabitants seeking practical solutions to problems on which many other towns have given up.

Because it's innovative and doing things people care about, the Applegate Partnership has successfully found common ground on a number of divisive local political issues. It supported and secured a timber sale when virtually none were surviving the federal review process. Environmentalists, who had routinely appealed virtually every sale, didn't challenge this one. As a result, approximately fifty loggers went back to work.

The partnership is so well trusted by government agencies that the feds have allowed it to develop a watershed plan and the state allocated it over $500,000 for forest restoration. Fifteen people were put to work controlling erosion, improving irrigation headgates, planting trees, installing fish screens, and fencing stock out of riparian areas. The county allowed it to review potential gravel pit sites with its own community-based effort.

At a time when many local leaders are searching for someone to point their fingers at, the Applegate Partnership is getting the job done.

Collaboration Isn't Easy

Collaboration, though simple in concept, can be challenging in practice. If you're new to it, it may not come easily. But if, as your try your new collaborative skills, you tend to revert to your old adversarial ways, don't dismay. Keep at it. You are, in effect, teaching yourself and the people around you a new way of doing politics. It will make community controversy less destructive and more constructive, but it'll take time.

Collaboration creates ethical dilemmas. For instance, is holding to one's position to the bitter end noble and virtuous? Or is it self-serving and even irresponsible? When you "hang tough," you don't have to concern yourself with the outcome. You can say, "Whatever happens, I was right. I'm not responsible for the outcome." In contrast, diplomats seek solutions satisfactory to all sides. They risk the anger and resentment of friends and allies. They take full responsibility for the outcome by offering shared responsibility to the other side.

Controversy will never disappear, nor should it. Collaboration may work more on one issue, less on the next, but gradually the old adversarial approach to politics will be minimized.

This chapter is written to describe politics and relationships in a community where controversy, ill will, and distrust are widespread. Things may not be so difficult in your town. But even if decisions are reached relatively smoothly, these ideas for exploring interests, building bridges, and using diplomats will significantly improve the quality of local decision-making.

> **Collaboration doesn't mean giving up your principles or setting aside your interests.**

The Limits of Collaboration and Consensus-Building

By now you're probably asking yourself, "How far do I go with this collaboration stuff? Do I keep trying to build consensus with people who intend to take what they want, community be damned?"

These questions have no easy answers. But when you ask them, the first thing to do is question yourself. Did you sincerely make every effort to set your position aside for a while and consider the other party's interests? Are you genuinely committed to finding a solution that's in the community's long-term best interest? If your answer is yes, and the other side won't budge, then for this situation, your efforts to collaborate have probably reached their limit. You probably won't achieve consensus.

Collaboration doesn't mean you have to give up your principles or set aside your interests. It may not even necessitate compromise. Rather, it requires a good-faith effort to set aside your position, fully consider the other side's interests, look for ways in which your respective interests intersect, and seek mutually satisfactory solutions.

If you attempt to collaborate with people who believe, like you, that the long-term viability of the community and its environment are paramount, then you have the best chance of finding consensus. But if you're dealing with people who spout those values while their actions indicate that short-term personal or corporate gain is their number-one goal, then consensus will be more difficult. The time-worn example of this disparity in goals is the community that attempts to work with a large, absentee-owned company that has a financial interest in the community. Though there are exceptional companies that genuinely want to operate in ways that are compatible with their hosts, many use their power to run roughshod over communities. At their worst, they intimidate local leaders, manipulate laws and regulations, and essentially buy local elections. At best, they're ethical people who simply care more for their company's success than the long-term viability of the community.

Collaboration may also be difficult if you're dealing with someone whose fundamental goals are different from yours. In that case, you may have to return to the old adversarial ways of resolving differences. If you do end up in conflict or litigation, however, your effort to collaborate and build consensus will have established your credibility, and will have attracted strong allies to your side. You will be stronger and command more respect.

When dealing with a more powerful adversary, you're embarking on a challenging quest that is not the subject of this guide. Though a thorough exploration of the problem of unequal power in local politics could fill a small library, it's worth mentioning a few ideas here.

One effective way to deal with powerful opposing interests is to expose their deeds to the light of day. Pass information to the local newspaper. If the paper won't print it (often the case in a small town), print a thoroughly researched fact sheet independently and distribute it around town.

If the company is pushing a damaging project, force it onto the local ballot through petition. A major landfill developer, well known as a polluter, proposed a dump in a small West Virginia town where unemployment was over 25 percent. The jobs were badly needed, but local people initiated a petition and forced the dump onto the ballot. In the campaign that followed, local citizens were outspent by the polluter 200 to 1, yet the citizens won the election by a 2-to-1 margin. They're now working collaboratively to create businesses and jobs compatible with community values.

However, it would be naive to say that exposure, disclosure, and ballot initiative are sufficient to solve the problem of unequal power. It requires at least one additional ingredient: courage. Sometimes the risk of standing up to these people is one's reputation in the community. In some communities, controlled by a handful of people, the risk may be one's job or worse. Don't stand alone unless you must. That takes extraordinary courage and is usually less effective than standing with a crowd. Look for support; get organized. There's strength in numbers. Even Gandhi recruited folks to stand with him. If you need help getting organized, consider taking a course on community organizing at the Highlander Center (see page 216).

One last note about organizing to challenge the powerful: even if you think they don't deserve it, treat them with respect. It will pay off in the long run. Just because someone tries to do something contrary to community interests doesn't necessarily make them bad. In some cases, they're just decent people doing what they believe to be right. Gandhi, who spent most of his life trying to get the British out of India, said, "We want the British to leave, but we want them to leave as friends."

Getting Started

If you're serious enough about developing a more sustainable economy to have read this much of the book, you're probably anxious to get started. But there's important groundwork to be laid before the Economic Renewal process begins. For example, you'll need to assemble people to organize, initiate, and conduct the process. These early arrangements are crucial to the success of your work. The more you put into this preparatory work, the less time you'll need to put in later, and the better results you'll see.

You probably know at least a few people who are keenly interested in doing something to strengthen the local economy, and who want to ensure that actions taken to improve the economy also benefit the community and its environment. But you and they may not be sure what to do next. To help, this chapter discusses the roles that they and others can play in the Economic Renewal process, how to recruit volunteers and keep them interested, and how to run an ER organization.

Assembling the Key People

Three groups of people move ER from beginning to end. The core group gets the ball rolling; the coordinating committee is the link between the community and the ER process; and the program team organizes and conducts the process. You might think of these three as the starters, the coordinators, and the doers. Though they're described separately in order to distinguish among various roles that need to be filled, some individuals may participate in more than one group. For example, some core group members will probably serve as members of the coordinating committee, the program team, or both.

You may choose different names for these groups. For instance, you might use "renewal team" or "program directors" instead of "program team," or "executive group" instead of "coordinating committee." Use terms that work best in your town. None of these is any more or less important than another; they're simply roles that certain people choose to play.

The Core Group

Almost invariably, Economic Renewal starts with a loose-knit group of people who begin talking to one another about bettering their community. They're clear that something must be done and they're committed to making it happen. They may be locally powerful people, such as the mayor or president of the chamber of commerce, or they may be less prominent. Often, one person—the "spark plug"—brings the group into being through sheer enthusiasm and tenacious commitment. Soon, this informal "core group" becomes the engine that moves the community in a positive direction.

Your core group need not be large—three to ten people is plenty. It may already exist, in a loose sort of way. Maybe you've talked in the past about getting the local economy on the right track. Maybe you've worked together on other projects. Now you've bought this book, you like the sound of ER, and you're wondering how to get started. Your first step is to think how Economic Renewal might work in your community. Talk among yourselves about the ideas explored in Chapters 1, 2, and 3. Think about how each principle and lesson might be applied in your community.

Your core group's main task will be to assemble a coordinating committee (see below)—once it has done that, it can disband. Begin by introducing ER ideas to your friends, neighbors, and associates. Make a list of others who should be involved at this early stage, including thoughtful people on the other side of the political fence.

You needn't be an expert in Economic Renewal to talk to others about it. Just let them know why you're enthusiastic about it. See page 208 for a suggested summary presentation of ER. Establish a positive tone from the beginning. Acknowledge the community's past successes, whether or not the outcomes were to your liking, and emphasize the community's potential. And read the rest of the book: it will answer most of the questions that come up.

The Coordinating Committee

Before going public and fully involving the community in ER, you'll need to create a more formal coordinating committee, whose primary tasks are to build community trust in the effort, select the program team (see below), and raise money. (If the committee is successful in this last task, it should seriously consider hiring a paid assistant to organize and possibly run the ER process and creating a community fund—see sections later in this chapter.) The committee will probably be involved in mobilizing the community to participate in the ER process (see Chapter 7). It may also schedule meetings, spend funds, resolve impasses, and deal with political problems so the program team can concentrate on its duties. Much later in the process, the coordinating committee will probably reconstitute itself as a new organization to make ER an ongoing community effort (see page 177).

A good size for a coordinating committee would be ten to fifteen members, but its size is less important than its composition. Enlist members who are well respected in the community. Some may be individuals you don't agree with, even people you regard as adversaries. Every group, faction, or "side" in local political issues must be pleased with at least one person on the committee—otherwise, members of those groups may wonder what you're up to and assume that, whatever it is, it must not be in their interest. If they do, you'll be compelled to spend a lot of time later correcting misimpressions and rebuilding trust. The ER process will fail if it's perceived as being one-sided. On the other hand, people will really take notice and respect your effort if they see former adversaries working together.

To keep the size of the committee manageable, find individuals who are respected by more than one group. Make an extra effort to recruit a representative from each local government—if not an elected official, then someone who will report back to them on a regular basis. Consider involving a school board member and people who have been central to earlier economic development efforts. Some of your core group members will probably make excellent coordinating committee members, too. Having identified who you'd like to see serve on the committee, determine who in the core group is best suited to act as the "bridge" (see page 49) to each prospective recruit.

Members of the coordinating committee should read and discuss at least Chapters 1, 2, 3, and 7 of this guide.

At this stage, your Economic Renewal effort hasn't yet been announced in the paper—so far, it's just friends talking to friends. But keep your ear to the ground. Controversy about who is controlling ER could kill the program before it starts. If you hear that some people are concerned about the effort, contact them, explain what you're doing, and ask them to participate when the process begins. If they're constructive people, ask them to join the committee. If that doesn't work and significant numbers of people are becoming suspicious, you may have to go public with the process sooner than you'd planned.

The Program Team

The program team is responsible for the day-to-day operations of the ER process. Its four to seven members recruit and manage volunteers, work with the media, handle meeting logistics, and facilitate meetings.

The coordinating committee, which will advise the team throughout the process, should carefully consider who might make good team members; the success of the entire ER effort depends in large part on getting the right people. They need not be economic-development or government professionals. Some may already be members of the core group or coordinating committee. One may be that rare and extremely valuable volunteer who's qualified and can work full- or part-time for free, such as a retiree. It may even be possible to get a team member on "loan" from local government, the chamber of commerce, or a bank or corporation. Such an arrangement, if it comes with no strings attached, can be spectacularly beneficial, so don't be shy about pursuing potential lenders of staff. (Be sure to acknowledge the loan publicly.)

WILL THE REAL COMMUNITY PLEASE STAND UP

Before launching a community development effort, you have to know what your community is. This isn't always as straightforward as it sounds. "Community" shouldn't be confused with political jurisdictions, which may have nothing to do with the support networks, shared interests, and common affinities that make up what we call community. Your community might be the town or city you live in, but it might just as easily be a neighborhood, a school district, a twin-cities area, a county, a valley, or an island. Your effort will work best when participants feel somehow connected to one another, and where they feel they're "in the same boat."

There may be compelling reasons to bring together a group of neighboring towns to conduct Economic Renewal. For instance, if they have declining populations or economies, cooperation may be necessary for survival, and ER can serve as a flag to rally round. It can even help unify neighboring towns that feel a strong rivalry. ER can be conducted for an entire county if residents identify with the county and feel that it's their community—however, if they identify with their town and resent the county, this will be a fast ride down a rocky road. In cities of more than about 50,000 people, where it can be more difficult to get a representative group of people involved, it may be advisable to conduct the ER process in each identifiable neighborhood; then, representatives from each neighborhood could assemble and go through the process on a city-wide or multi-neighborhood basis.

A community may not be based on physical proximity at all. There are many "communities of interest" whose focus can be occupational, political, economic, educational, social, or environmental. Organic growers in Saskatchewan discovered they constituted a community of interest in 1992, when Mark Gimby of the Saskatchewan Research Council convened them for an ER process. More recently, Gimby has used ER to work with timber communities in Saskatchewan and Costa Rica.

A successful program team consists of people who are savvy self-starters, are interested in new ideas, and have a larger vision of what's possible. They must be flexible and willing to adapt to changing circumstances. They must be credible in the community. They should be sensitive to both genders and all races, religions, and factions within the community, and should not have burned any bridges (i.e., created any permanent enemies who are influential). If a prospective team member is known for taking one side in a controversial issue, his or her presence on the team should be balanced by someone representing the other side.

Team members' skills will tend to complement one another. Some may feel uneasy in front of groups of people, but comfortable coordinating volunteers one-on-one. They know how to demonstrate their appreciation and respect for volunteers, inspire commitment, do follow-up to ensure the work is complete, and find back-up volunteers to complete unfinished work. Some team members may be competent marketing people who can garner support from around the community. Others may be good organizers who can be relied on to prepare materials, be on time, set up for meetings, and so on.

But at least a few of the team members—those who will stand up and conduct the town meetings—should be comfortable speaking before groups and good at running meetings. Most importantly, they must be good listeners. Every meeting will be facilitated by at least two team members; depending on the mix of skills in your team, you could designate two people to facilitate every meeting or rotate the task among several people. Team members must be able to fully communicate with one another and must be prepared to deal constructively with conflict during the town meetings and within the team.

Although their primary motive must be community service, team members may be able to justify more complete involvement if they gain personally in some way. For example, someone stuck in a low-level job may see the opportunity to demonstrate his or her capabilities to potential future employers by serving on the team. Community recognition of someone's hidden talents can be a strong motivator. Discuss these advantages frankly. It's no sin to help yourself while you're helping others.

Serving on the ER program team is a big commitment. The team can expect to spend approximately 300 hours organizing the effort over a period of three to six months, starting a couple of months before the first town meeting and ending at the last meeting. Members will need to have a working knowledge of the ER process, so they should read and understand this entire guide, paying special attention to the facilitation skills described in Chapter 6. After all members have read the guide, discuss the ideas in Chapters 1, 2, 3, and 6.

The program team will probably accomplish its tasks more efficiently if team members each assume responsibility for broad functions. You'll need a team member or two to manage volunteers (see page 61), direct publicity (page 72), handle meeting logistics (page 93), and head up the community-mobilization effort (page 101). In addition, two to four team members should be put in charge of facilitating the meetings (see page 86). Discuss frankly who can best fill these roles. If team members feel they need more preparation, they can ask the coordinating committee to invite Rocky Mountain Institute to conduct an ER training seminar (see page 214).

Conducting the Economic Renewal process is an exciting challenge that will test the skills and patience of team members. Those who are chosen should be honored.

Paid Staff

The coordinating committee may decide that the responsibilities of the program team are too much to be fulfilled entirely by volunteers. They may decide to hire a part-time assistant to manage the program and ensure that all volunteer tasks are completed or to fulfill secretarial-type responsibilities.

Unlike volunteers, people who work for you have a vested interest in getting the job done; you can fire them. However, hiring someone has two potential drawbacks. First, it costs money. But if the largest institutions in your community—government, business groups, large employers, etc.—are serious about this effort, they should be willing to pitch in enough to pay a part-time staffer for, say, six to eight months. Second, hiring someone tends to diminish your volunteers' sense of responsibility. It can make them feel that Economic Renewal is someone else's program, and give them an excuse for not volunteering for various tasks. This problem can be avoided by explicitly limiting the role of the hired person to certain prescribed tasks.

Separately, the coordinating committee may choose to hire a professional facilitator to conduct the town meetings. In addition to the cost, the drawback of this approach is that an outside facilitator won't understand the local politics, personalities, and subtle undercurrents of the meetings. But hiring outsiders to run the meetings has several advantages. Outsiders may be more willing to say things in the meetings that a local would be uncomfortable saying. They may attract more participation because they're different and unknown. Also, they won't be associated with past controversy. Consider all these factors before deciding if paying for help is appropriate in your case.

Variations

This chapter has described a neat sequence of events: first you assemble a core group, which recruits and establishes a coordinating committee, which in turn finds people to serve as a program team. Though this is an excellent way to get Economic Renewal started, it's not the only way.

For instance, the core group could lay all the groundwork described in this part of the guide (Chapters 4–6), and not form the coordinating committee until first public step of the ER process (Chapter 7). One town manager invited Rocky Mountain Institute to train a program team before a core group had been formed—in fact, before anyone else in town even knew about ER. In that case, the team doubled as a core group and recruited the coordinating committee. In another town, the program team performed the functions of the coordinating committee in addition to its own functions. Team members were generally trusted in the community and accomplished their tasks in an open way, so the political distinction of the coordinating committee wasn't necessary. In yet another variation, citizens of three rural counties joined forces with staffers from a community economic development agency to create a program team that oversaw a regional Economic Renewal effort.

Maximizing Volunteer Involvement

The program team is responsible for carrying out ER, but to do so its members will depend of the efforts of many other volunteers. The team's role is not to do every task, but to ensure that each is completed. If it does a thorough job of recruiting, inspiring, and managing volunteers, most of its work will be volunteer coordination, meeting preparation, and facilitation.

You may be thinking, "Where are we going to get all these volunteers?" or, "I've been involved in volunteer work before and it seems like groups

PLAY ER BY EAR

The various exercises and tasks that comprise the Economic Renewal process are divided into steps, not meetings, to give you greater flexibility in conducting your effort. Though each step is designed so that it will require one meeting in most cases, you're not "most cases"—you're your own unique case. With this step-by-step format, you don't have to rush to finish a series of exercises by the end of a certain meeting. Conversely, if you complete one particular step well before the end of a certain meeting, you can move straight into the next. For instance, though Steps 4, 5, and 6 are described in separate chapters, they may or may not require three separate town meetings. You might complete them in two.

Other creative variations are possible. The Kentucky Local Governance Project, working in rural Harlan County, conducted separate meetings for Steps 2 through 4 in each of seven small towns in the county. Project leaders then brought participants from all seven towns together in an all-day work session and picnic for Steps 5 and 6. Leaders of this effort had sufficiently familiarized themselves with the ER process that they felt this format was most appropriate for their community.

Food attracts better meeting attendance.

usually blow up or peter out." Though community leaders are often burdened by excessive volunteer work, ironically, they seldom do much to get and keep others involved. Often they're heard to say, "It's just easier to do the task myself than to get volunteers to do it." That's true if you're talking about a single task, but not for a larger effort. In fact, the most effective community leaders are those who spend most of their time recruiting and coordinating volunteers, doing only a few of the actual tasks themselves.

How do they do it? Not by accident. Successful volunteer efforts are the result of concerted effort. Here's a whole list of tips for recruiting, coordinating, and retaining volunteers. The next time you find yourself whining about lack of help, ask yourself how many of the following you are pursuing.

➤ **Make time to recruit.** Set aside specific meeting time to decide who to recruit and how to do it. Don't regard recruitment as some secondary task that you hope you'll get around to. Make it a major portion of your effort—it'll save you a lot of time in the long run.

➤ **Market volunteer opportunities.** Don't assume that, just because your program is terrific, everyone will come running to help out. Get the word out through personal contacts, fliers, and media announcements. See if you can get a professional marketer to donate time to promote your program—it'll be good PR for them, too.

➤ **Actively welcome new volunteers.** This one may sound obvious, but ask yourself if deep down inside you really want other people involved when you've put so much into this effort. Or do you unconsciously treat them like intruders? When newcomers ask questions or make suggestions that have been covered earlier, how do you respond? Do you impatiently dismiss their ideas? Do you take them aside to offer history and background, or do you let them sink or swim? Assign someone to familiarize and update volunteers, and even court people who are considering joining the effort.

➤ **Ensure productive activities.** Few volunteers will tolerate their time being wasted. Make sure each meeting and volunteer activity is well run and accomplishes something.

➤ **Restate the purpose.** At every meeting, say why the effort is under way. Refer to the group's goals or mission. Remind each volunteer how he or she is contributing to the goals and is part of a larger cause.

➤ **Appoint a task manager.** Assign a team member to coordinate and oversee all volunteer tasks. He or she should maintain a list of tasks, people responsible for each, and the date by which each is to be accomplished. If a volunteer doesn't come through, it's the task manager's job to find someone else to complete the work. The task manager doesn't carry out any tasks, but ensures that they're completed. A task manager must be especially respectful of others; someone who merely issues orders will doom the program.

➤ **Define tasks clearly.** No one likes to volunteer for an open-ended task. When you ask for a volunteer to do something, describe the task and how long it will take.

➤ **Emphasize short-term projects.** Most worthwhile volunteer efforts take a while. To keep volunteers motivated, involve them (especially new ones) in relatively short-term projects. People will stick with the program when they get a sense of accomplishment.

➤ **Accommodate limited participation.** Don't make people feel guilty for not attending every activity. Many would rather be assigned tasks than be expected to attend meetings.

➤ **Accept non-participation.** To you, finding a volunteer to perform a particular task may seem paramount, but the person you approach to do it may have other priorities. People serve the community in different ways. They may deliver meals on wheels, volunteer at the hospital or church, or serve as a volunteer firefighter or planning commissioner. Just because they don't want to help with ER doesn't mean they aren't good people.

➤ **Accommodate individual work preferences.** Does the volunteer prefer organizing or detail work? Would he rather make phone calls or stuff envelopes? Does she like planning projects or implementing them? Tasks can be assigned based on preferences.

➤ **Use volunteers' best skills.** Different people have different skills. When clearly identified, these skills can complement one another to produce much more productive and enjoyable volunteer work.

- ➤ **Avoid volunteer burnout.** If volunteers are worked too hard for too long, they may become frustrated or dissatisfied. When you think someone is doing too much, find another volunteer to help.

- ➤ **Offer leadership training.** In virtually every region, programs are available to improve the skills of local volunteers, many of whom will make terrific leaders. Classes and workshops on running meetings, fund-raising, problem-solving, leadership techniques, mediation, organization management, coalition-building, and many other topics are available from colleges, governments, consultants, and nonprofit groups. These programs often cost money, but given that one of ER's functions is community leadership development, this may be a justifiable expense.

- ➤ **Contact volunteers before each activity.** It's simply the most effective way to ensure attendance. Establish a phone tree to streamline the process. A phone tree is a system in which one person calls five group members, each of the five calls five others, and so on, until everyone has been contacted. A newsletter can be useful for conveying more detailed, but less timely, information.

- ➤ **Feed 'em.** One effective way to get people to show up to a meeting is to let them know that food will be served, even if it's just coffee, donuts, and juice. Occasionally, make a full meal available. Get local restaurants to donate food in return for recognition at the meeting and in the media. Some people who are uncomfortable with other tasks will help with food service.

- ➤ **Get to know one another.** Mutual respect amplifies group effectiveness and makes activities much more enjoyable. Spend plenty of informal time discussing why each person volunteered to participate. Understanding one another's motives leads to respect for differing opinions.

- ➤ **Acknowledge volunteers.** Thank each volunteer for each task they accomplish. Do it within the group and, when possible, do it publicly. For example, you might run an ad in the newspaper listing all who are helping. When a volunteer does something special, difficult, or time-consuming, celebrate her or his contribution. Acknowledgment not only makes people feel good, it also publicizes their skills, which for many volunteers will be a tangible benefit.

- ➤ **Celebrate success.** Make a big deal out of everything that might remotely be regarded as a success, such as good attendance at a meeting. Brainstorm ways of acknowledging and recognizing victories and successes, however small.

- ➤ **Adjust your attitude.** If you seem burdened, upset, self-important, or overwhelmed, volunteers will "catch" your attitude as if it were the latest flu bug. If you're upbeat, eager, and respectful, they'll catch that condition instead.

➤ **Don't tolerate destructive people.** Respect, but don't put up with self-indulgent or abusive individuals who injure the work of the group and drive away conscientious members. If they persist, politely show them the door. Make it clear that such behavior, if allowed to continue, would defeat the group.

➤ **Have fun.** An entertaining event or meeting is more attractive to potential volunteers than one heavy with significance or controversy.

Starting an ER Organization

Outwardly, your ER effort will look a lot like an election campaign: you'll be contacting as many community members as possible, volunteers will need materials and places to work, handouts will be typed and copied, money will be spent and must be carefully accounted for, and a temporary office may be required. And like an election campaign, the process described in this book is really only the beginning—it's only when the campaign is over that you can begin on the long-term effort to create a more sustainable economy. For that, you'll need to create a permanent organization. But that's covered later in Chapter 13.

For now, focus your efforts on creating an organization capable of coordinating the ER effort. Previous sections described the people you'll need to run the organization; this section highlights some of the more mundane logistical matters associated with starting up.

Necessary Arrangements

Virtually every community that has used ER has found that the following arrangements are minimum requirements for success. Those who didn't complete each item ran into problems later.

Coordinating Committee Responsibilities

➤ **Name the program.** Come up with a name for your community's version of ER. You could call it Economic Renewal, of course, but a name that celebrates your community's history, people, or places may do a better job of attracting attention and enthusiasm. When Carbondale, Colorado used ER, participants called it the "Pioneer Project." Skagway, Alaska, called it "Beyond '98," to celebrate the Yukon gold rush that began in 1898 and used Skagway as its jumping-off point.

➤ **Accounts.** Open an account at a local bank so you can deposit donations and write checks for expenses. Decide who can sign

Outwardly, your ER effort will look a lot like an election campaign.

checks and for what amounts. All program expenditures should be accountable to the coordinating committee: you don't want any questions about inappropriate use of money to come up. Also establish accounts with an office-supply store and with someone who does copying. You'll need paper, pencils, and possibly binders and other office supplies, and you'll be copying lots of pages from this guide.

Program Team Responsibilities

➤ **Schedule.** Establish a schedule for introductory presentations (optional—see page 108) and town meetings (Chapters 8–14). Be sure dates don't conflict with important community events, meetings, holidays, and sporting events such as high school games or Monday Night Football. Develop a tentative schedule first, then seek the advice of active people around town (government, church, school, and business leaders) before finalizing it. Try not to interrupt

DON'T WRITE AN ECONOMIC RENEWAL PLAN—YET

Economic Renewal is carefully designed to ensure planning for results, not just planning to write a plan. The process focuses mainly on verbal dialogue, and entails only minimal writing until the creation of specific project action plans in the final step.

Nevertheless, there may be circumstances in which writing a separate, overarching Economic Renewal plan is beneficial. For instance, a foundation or government agency may require it as part of a request for financial assistance. The purpose of such a plan, essentially, would be to explain what you decided to do, how you decided to do it, who's going to do it, and how. Equally important, it would document your community's collaborative decision-making process, and prove that the proposed actions are supported by the community and not just a small group. The plan could include a community vision statement, lists of sponsoring organizations and process participants, action plan(s) developed for chosen project(s), and letters and resolutions of endorsement from key local organizations and individuals.

All of these elements will emerge as a matter of course during the Economic Renewal process. For now, all you have to do is set up a record-keeping system that captures this information should it be needed later. You may or may not need an ER plan, so don't actually write it unless you're called upon to do it.

the process with the long Thanksgiving–Christmas holiday season, which can sap momentum.

In considering the scheduling of any series of meetings, judge how often you can hold meetings without wearing participants out. A one- or two-week interval between meetings often works well, although more frequent meetings are possible (Indian Lake, New York, conducted Steps 2, 3, and 4 on three successive evenings). A three-week interval may be so long that participants lose track of what's going on, or forget to attend.

➤ **Records.** Start a program binder to record relevant news articles, ER press releases and public service announcements, program endorsements, public comments, and suggestions for improving Economic Renewal (please pass ideas on to Rocky Mountain Institute!). Also keep on file a written record of all decisions made and actions taken during the ER process, along with anything else that might help later in writing project action plans, grant or loan requests, or an Economic Renewal plan (see box).

➤ **Sponsor list.** Keep track of all individuals and organizations who donate equipment, materials, and money to your ER effort. Write them thank-you letters, invite them to all events, and publicly acknowledge them whenever possible.

➤ **Supporter list.** Keep track of all individuals and organizations who endorse the ER effort. This is your proof of credibility. Make this list available to anyone who's considering becoming involved.

➤ **Participant list.** Keep a list of all people who participate in the ER town meetings, along with their phone numbers and, if possible, their skills.

➤ **Volunteer list.** Keep a separate list of everyone who's volunteered to carry out tasks. Don't forget to note what the task was, and the deadline.

Optional Arrangements

The coordinating committee should use its best judgment to determine which of the following arrangements will be necessary or beneficial in your situation. For example, an ER office can help, but it isn't absolutely necessary. In some communities the cost of storefront space is so expensive that the committee will probably find better ways to use limited resources.

➤ **Phone.** Secure a telephone line as a central communication point for the program. Publish its number on program materials. You might be able to use one of the program team member's phones, but it's usually best to set up a separate line. Arrange for an answering machine, which can be used to indicate what volunteer activities are taking place and when.

➤ **Cash.** Set up a petty cash account for small expenditures, and again, keep track of all money that goes out.

➤ **Office.** Secure a small office in a central location, which can serve as a place where the program team works and volunteers meet as well as a drop-off and pick-up point for program materials. If possible, try to get donated space—the chamber of commerce or local government may be able to spare a side office on a temporary basis. Much like an election campaign, your ER program will appear more serious to the community if it has a storefront and a sign.

➤ **Equipment.** Obtain office equipment including chairs, tables, a word processor, printer, and, if possible, a copier. If you don't establish an office, this equipment will probably have to be kept in a program team member's home.

➤ **Calendar.** Start a monthly calendar. Log all local meetings, ER meeting dates, speaking engagements, individual appointments, volunteer schedules, and media release dates.

PLAN AHEAD—START A COMMUNITY FUND

As you get people interested in becoming involved in Economic Renewal, seriously consider creating a community fund to provide seed money for the projects that will emerge at the end of the process. The money should be generated locally from business, government, and nonprofit sources, and might be enhanced by small grants from foundations, the state, or federal agencies. For advice on fund-raising, see page 198.

Start beating the bushes now, at the outset of the ER process, and you'll be ahead of the game when it's time to start implementing projects. Even a modest community fund can make a big difference. For example, a grant of $500 from the fund could help with the development of a business plan; $250 could be offered as a prize for the best idea for a festival or crafts marketing effort; $5,000 could pay for the development of tourist marketing materials; and $1,000 could bring in a consultant or other specialist.

The money would need to be held by a nonprofit organization such as a chamber of commerce or economic development commission. (See page 181 for examples of development organizations that might administer such a fund.) The nonprofit's governing board or advisory committee would be responsible for disbursing the funds based on explicit criteria created by the nonprofit. The "Project Idea Evaluation" worksheet on page 166 might be helpful.

- ➤ **Liaison.** Assemble a schedule of local meetings that are relevant to the ER program and begin to identify which ones program team members or coordinating committee members should attend. These meetings will keep you abreast of local events and issues that relate to the program. However, be selective; don't try to attend everything or you'll have time for little else. Call the person in charge of each meeting to determine if the topics to be covered are relevant to ER.
- ➤ **Nonprofit status.** If your ER organization decides to become permanent and to accept donations, it should seek IRS tax-exempt status (under section 501[c]3 of the tax code) as a nonprofit organization. This will allow donors to write off their contributions. In the meantime, if potential donors require that their contributions be tax-deductible, ask an established nonprofit group in the community if it would be willing to accept the donation and pass it through to your organization.

Taking Stock

Most rural towns and many urban neighborhoods have a clear sense of identity rooted in historical occupations and shared traditions. Just think of the ranching towns of the West, New England's fishing villages, logging towns in the Northwest, farming towns on the Great Plains, Appalachian mining towns, and the ethnic neighborhoods of many cities. In all cases, the traditions run wide and deep, and reflect strongly held beliefs about the way a community's culture should look and feel, and about the way business is done.

We can be proud of these identities, but we must take care that they don't blind us to today's realities. Montana economist Thomas Michael Power warns that when communities make decisions based on what they've been, rather than what they are now, they're like a driver who's looking at the road through his rear-view mirror. It's a ridiculous way to drive, and a dangerous way to lead a community into the future.

Many towns' local economies have changed profoundly over the past decade or two. Transformed through a series of often subtle and incremental shifts, these economies are no longer based on cattle, manufacturing, fish, timber, wheat, or coal. Instead, when such communities examine the data, they find that most of their income now comes from, say, tourism, retirement, second homes, retail trade, or wages earned in a nearby city.

Locals may or may not like these changes. They may want to slow, stop, or steer them; they may want to do things to preserve the old ways. All of these efforts are admirable when supported by community consensus. A problem arises, however, when the community deludes itself by ignoring the changes or refusing to examine the facts.

If your community is experiencing this dilemma, you might try taking stock by examining the economic trends that are affecting it. To get a clear idea of how the community is actually working, compile key data for the past twenty or so years. Some of the most useful indicators are: local income, employment, average annual wage by type of industry, investment income, number of businesses established and closed, county tax revenue by source, average family income, and population. The best tool for compiling this sort of information is a workbook called *Measuring Change in Rural America: A Workbook for Determining Demographic, Economic and Fiscal Trends* (see page 222). Note, however, that most economic data are available only for entire counties; very little is available for individual municipalities, and virtually none is available for unincorporated communities. Therefore, if your community's economy differs significantly from your county's, you may not have much luck.

You'll probably need help generating the information suggested in *Measuring Change*. This assistance might be supplied by a private consultant, or you might get it free or inexpensively through a state or regional development agency, a university, or a nonprofit community-development organization. The book's authors also provide consulting services.

Alternatively, invite a group of professionals in agriculture, tourism, retail, public works, or other relevant fields to analyze the trends affecting your local economy. You might use a mix of locals and experts from the private sector, state government, or university extension service. Ensure that different points of view are represented. If you use outside experts, find those who will work inexpensively or for free.

Offer them Chapter 2 so they understand the context within which they'll be offering information. Ask them to address issues directly affecting your community, and to steer clear of academic theories or technical analyses. They might also address their perception of the biggest challenges to community survival within their interest area, how towns should respond to the challenges, success stories, and available resources. This approach might actually be less expensive and time-consuming than the workbook approach suggested in *Measuring Change*, but beware: such experts tend to discuss what they know, which may or may not be what the community needs to hear, and they may have antiquated perspectives on economic development.

This stock-taking exercise, if you decide to do it, can take several weeks or more, so it's advisable to get started on it as soon as possible. The results should be presented to ER participants during or prior to Step 3, "Identifying What You Have to Work With" (Chapter 9).

Checklist: Getting Started

Develop a timeline for the following tasks, bearing in mind that some tasks will proceed simultaneously.

Core Group Tasks

☐ Read and discuss at least Chapters 1, 2, and 3.

☐ List and contact key people who should be involved early.

☐ Recruit a coordinating committee.

Coordinating Committee Tasks

Many tasks listed for the program team may also be taken on by the coordinating committee.

☐ Read and discuss at least Chapters 1, 2, 3, and 7.

☐ Talk informally about Economic Renewal with friends.

☐ Pick a name for your Economic Renewal effort.

☐ Recruit the program team.

☐ Set up a checking account.

☐ Raise money.

☐ Define the boundaries of the community in which you will conduct ER.

Program Team Tasks

Some of which might be taken by the coordinating committee.

☐ Read this entire book, and discuss Chapters 1, 2, 3, and 6 as a group.

☐ Assign general areas of responsibility to team members (e.g., volunteer task management, publicity, meeting facilitation, meeting logistics, community mobilization).

☐ Develop a schedule of ER introductory presentations and town meetings.

☐ Start and maintain lists of sponsors, supporters, meeting participants, and volunteers.

Optional Tasks

☐ Hire paid staff.

☐ Bring in Rocky Mountain Institute to conduct an ER training seminar.

☐ Arrange for a phone.

☐ Start a petty cash account.

☐ Establish an office.

☐ Secure office equipment.

☐ Start a calendar of community events.

☐ Assign a liaison to attend relevant local meetings.

☐ Secure nonprofit status.

☐ Take stock of local economic conditions.

☐ Offer leadership training.

Getting the Word Out

Economic Renewal is most effective when it involves as many people as possible in the community, so getting the word out is an important part of the process. Most of your publicity efforts will go into working with local newspapers, radio, and possibly television. Media coverage of ER builds momentum, boosts participants' morale, and keeps them excited about the program. It also keeps non-participants in the loop, which is important in any democratic process and ensures more broad-based support (or at least less opposition).

If local editors assign someone to cover your ER effort, communicating with the community will be easy. You may not have to do much more than notify the local media of meetings and other developments. However, it doesn't always work that way. To increase the chances of coverage—and to retain more control over the message that goes out—you'll need to mount a well-thought-out publicity campaign.

Much of the work described in this chapter will occur primarily during Step 1 (see Chapter 7), when you'll be mobilizing the community for the first Economic Renewal town meeting. However, each subsequent meeting and event will entail some further media-handling and publicity.

Approaching the Media

Your first task is to create a complete list of local media outlets. You may be surprised to discover how many there are in your community, even if it's only a small one.

Once you've identified likely outlets, call to find out who is the best person at each to contact about ER events. Ask each contact when their deadlines are and when you should deliver information to them so that they can comfortably meet their deadlines. If you talk to a reporter for a weekly newspaper published on Thursdays, for example, she may need information by noon on Tuesday to complete her stories by a Wednesday afternoon deadline. The form on the next page suggests a simple way to keep track of media contacts. It's useful to jot down notes after each conversation, especially if the job of media relations is split among several members of your program team.

Most media outlets make money from advertising, so don't be surprised if they try to steer you toward the advertising department. With a grassroots effort like ER, however, you should be able to get lots of publicity without having to pay for it. Advertise sparingly, and only as a last resort.

Media Contact Form

Media outlet name: _____

Contact person: _____ Position: _____

Phone #: _____

Deadline(s)/Best time to call: _____

Advertising rates: _____

PSA procedure: _____

Dates Contacted: _____

Responses: _____

Newspapers

If your local newspaper is circulated primarily in your town, it can be an ideal medium for promoting community collaboration and Economic Renewal. Its editor will probably care about the community and be happy to print notices of upcoming meetings and to report on what happened afterwards. However, if your local paper is very small, it may not have the resources to cover ER very well, or if it has a large circulation area, it may regard your effort as a minor story. In such circumstances you'll just have to be more resourceful, persistent, and professional in publicizing ER. (The residents of one small community in Colorado were so disappointed with the lack of coverage their community activities were receiving from the paper—a regional daily published in a city forty miles away—that they decided to start their own. The new paper has become a focal point for the community's Economic Renewal program.)

To start off on the right foot and avoid possible negative impressions, contact the newspaper very early. Approach local newsletters, too—many companies, school districts, and other organizations distribute their own newsletters or bulletins. Spend as much time discussing ER as the editors and reporters are willing to spare, and give them a copy of Chapter 2. Their interest might waver initially when they learn that you don't yet have an event for them to cover, but explain that you're offering background information now so that they understand the concepts when the town meetings begin. They'll appreciate the heads-up.

Later, when your ER process is under way, they'll be more receptive to the story ideas you suggest to them. The following pointers will help you package ER to make reporters' jobs easier and get yourself better coverage.

Set the Hook

Reporters and editors want "hooks" they can hang a news story on. A hook may be a significant event, decision, development, or milestone—or even a seemingly insignificant one that heralds the emergence of a new trend. Most of your press releases will probably report on such news items. But reporters are also always on the lookout for features, where the hook can be an individual or group doing something positive for the community.

In general, news is something new. Stories based on events should focus more on results, less on the process involved. When deciding what to emphasize, ask yourself: What does the public want to know or need to know? What do they care about? How does this action or idea affect local people?

Journalists are mainly interested in stories about current events, not general ideas or good intentions. Here are some suggestions for tying your efforts into their interests:

➤ **Sell the human-interest angle.** Gather local success stories from businesses, households, and government. Reporters look for human-interest stories that describe remarkable people.

➤ **Indicate ER's broad support.** Economic Renewal involves people from many walks of life. If applicable, indicate that people from very different backgrounds are working together.

➤ **Discuss the bottom-line benefits.** Discuss and promote Economic Renewal in terms of people's pocketbooks. You might use examples from Chapter 2 and speculate about what benefits similar projects might have in your community.

➤ **Emphasize hope.** When talking about ER with anyone in your community, including the media, emphasize that there is hope. This hope isn't based on blind faith but on local successes and the success stories in the ER materials.

➤ **Provide photos.** If possible, photograph something or someone who relates to your story. You'll stand a much better chance of seeing your story in print and it will attract more readers if you include the photo with it.

Press Releases

The press release is the opening gambit in most journalistic encounters. It isn't necessarily intended to be reprinted verbatim, and indeed there's no assurance that it will run at all, but journalists usually like to see "something in writing" before even considering doing a story. "Advances," which simply publicize upcoming events, stand a good chance of getting in print. Press releases reporting on the outcome of events are more likely to be ignored or rewritten (perhaps with a very different angle), but they can be a powerful tool for influencing the news agenda.

Press releases should be one or two pages in length, three at the very most. Use short, simple sentences—avoid flowery, descriptive language. Like news stories, press releases normally start with the most important points and then fill in the less important details. Be sure to include all necessary information: who, what, when, where, why, and how.

The lead paragraph summarizes what's newsworthy. Often the first sentence will explain the *who* and *what*, with a second sentence providing the *when* and *where*. If appropriate, the first sentence can be a "tease" to draw readers into the story, but the factual information must follow soon after. Subsequent paragraphs focus on *why* and *how*, preferably backed up by quotes from authoritative sources, which establish credibility and personalize the story.

Effective publicity generates support for your efforts.

Quotes can sum up progress made to date, express enthusiasm, or review good insights into the process or decisions made. Avoid giving your opinion, and don't exaggerate; just report the facts. Double-check any figures. Use full names and titles the first time you refer to people, but only last names on later references.

Some newspapers are more relaxed about the above conventions than others, so study your local paper before writing releases. Does it strictly follow the "who, what, when, where" formula, or does it also allow for a little spice, humor, and interpretation? Does it carry stories full of long, direct quotes from participants, or favor a summary of the action and a few quotes? Some editors like to lead with the conflict angle, such as: "At the meeting of the ER finance committee, disagreement erupted about whether increased property taxes or new city sales taxes should fund downtown revitalization." Then the story says who "won" the debate and why. Knowing your local paper will allow you to judge how the editor handles such situations and tailor your releases accordingly.

If your release concerns the results of a meeting, summarize what the group did or decided, unless there's something particularly interesting about the process (such as traditional adversaries working together). Follow up your reporting of the main outcome with a list of ideas that didn't quite make the final cut. Those who had minority opinions will then feel their participation was worthwhile.

When writing advances for meetings, be sure to state who's invited, who's organizing it, and why (your first few releases should also explain why the ER approach was chosen). Describe what kinds of things will be talked about or decided. If the meeting location may be unfamiliar to some readers, include directions on how to get there. When your ER process is in full swing, you should be able to produce dual-purpose releases that report what happened at the previous meeting and advance the next one.

Every release should end with a description of your organization and the name and phone number of a spokesperson readers can call for further information. Write the headline last. The purpose of a headline in a press release is mainly to get the editor's attention; it's rarely used in the paper.

Press releases should be printed on plain white paper (or letterhead with same-color second sheets). Put your organization's name and address at the top, as well as the contact person's name and phone number. You can also put the words "NEWS RELEASE" at the very top, but that's optional. The text of the release should be double-spaced or space-and-a-half. The margins should be 1" left, right, and bottom, at least 2" on top. If the release runs onto a second page, center the word "more" at the bottom of each page and the number "30" at the end of the release.

Follow-up

Distribute advances a week to ten days before each event. Be aware of deadlines, which are different for weeklies and dailies, and may be different again for a paper's calendar section. Be especially diligent in spreading the word about the first ER town meeting. If you give editors plenty of notice about an upcoming event, they may even publish two stories on it (especially if you have photos).

Since reporters may get dozens of press releases every week, follow up with a phone call to ask if they're coming to your event. Don't be surprised if they haven't seen your release. You may have to send another. To avoid confusion, don't send releases to more than one person at a given paper.

It may not be worth writing an after-the-event press release if you know that the journalist was there and plans to write his or her own story. If you do write one, submit it well before the reporter's deadline to have any hope of influencing the published story. If no reporter was present, take a little time when you submit your release to make sure the editor or reporter understands what happened and why, since it's likely your release will be rewritten.

Offer to be available to answer any questions or provide more information, but never ask to approve the copy before it's published. This will probably make the journalist mad. Given the correct facts, the journalist will probably get them right in the story.

If you find errors in a story, don't be upset. Everyone makes mistakes. Inform the reporter or editor of the problem in a pleasant and respectful way. You might try taking the blame by saying, "I'm sorry, I must have been unclear." If it will make any difference, ask for a correction or clarification.

There's little you can do if a story appears with an angle you don't like. Presenting information in a concise manner that stirs readers' interest is the journalist's job. At best, you can write a diplomatic letter to the editor explaining that the story's emphasis was misplaced or certain points were overlooked. Then thank them for running the story (warts and all). A poorly done story is often better than no story at all.

Radio and Television

Radio is another excellent way to get the word out, especially if there's a station based right in your community. Radio stations typically broadcast public service announcements (see below) free of charge, and they often co-sponsor community events. If you're lucky, your local station might be willing to broadcast your ER town meetings, or at least the first one. Public radio stations tend to allocate more time to local discussion programs, but even commercial stations usually have at least one community-affairs slot a week.

However, not all radio stations have their own local news broadcasts, and those that do usually air only short bulletins, which rarely give as much detail as newspaper articles. Moreover, there's really no radio equivalent to the small-town weekly paper: radio stations tend to serve larger markets, such as cities or multiple towns. All that means your ER effort will probably face stiff competition for airtime. To make sure your story gets the attention it's due, meet with station managers early and brief them in the same way as newspaper people.

Everything said about radio also applies to television. But because TV stations are so much more expensive to run, they usually cover even larger areas than radio stations, so it will be even tougher to get their attention. Even if you do, their coverage will be broadcast to a mass audience, which won't help very much in getting the word out to your particular community. A public-access station will be more accommodating, but its audience will be smaller, and probably no better targeted.

Public Service Announcements

Public service announcements (PSAs) are short, attention-getting items publicizing an upcoming event or ongoing effort. Most commonly PSAs are written specifically for radio stations, which read them on the air as a public service during their regular non-news programming.

Try to limit your PSAs to three or four sentences, or about fifteen to thirty seconds of reading time—see the box on the next page for examples.

Peak radio listening hours are 6–10 a.m. and 4–6 p.m., but you probably won't have any control over when your PSA is broadcast. Some stations will air PSAs as part of a regularly scheduled community bulletin board or calendar, but others may run them only rarely or relegate them to the graveyard shift. Therefore, you can't rely on PSAs to get the message out. They're only one of several outlets for your information.

You can also send PSAs to newspapers, which may use them as fillers or repackage the information in their events calendars. However, newspapers generally have more space than radio stations have air time, so for them you may want to rewrite your PSA into a full-blown press release.

Working with the Media

Press releases, public service announcements, and so on are just the start of what will hopefully be a two-way relationship with the media. If reporters start requesting information and interviews, that's a good sign. Most encounters with media people will be fun and positive, although a few may be hard work or downright unpleasant. Here's some general advice about how to make the most of the situation.

Designate Spokespeople

Pick someone from the program team to serve as spokesperson and someone else to serve as backup when the first isn't available. These representatives should be well-informed, articulate, and comfortable around microphones and even cameras. But don't pick a show-off or someone who likes to shock people with their words. This role is about ER and the community, not how terrific the spokesperson is.

Your spokespeople should develop friendly and frank relationships with media contacts, help them get the facts straight, establish clear news angles, and familiarize them with the intentions, procedure, and principles of your ER effort.

Give media contacts the home and (if appropriate) work phone numbers of your spokespeople so they can always be assured of a quick response.

Sample Public Service Announcements

The following are a few examples of the kind of PSAs you might want to run to ensure full participation in your meetings and workshops. Pick the ones you like and adapt them for your particular circumstances. Fill in the blanks as appropriate, and be sure to provide a "kill date" (the date when the spot should be pulled from the air).

The first three spots announce the start of the ER process. The last two pertain to specific meetings later in the process.

ANNOUNCEMENT OF ER PROGRAM

Economic Renewal is coming to (town name). The program offers an opportunity for you to get involved in grass-roots economic development. Help improve our future by assuring a healthy, diverse and stable local economy. To find out how you can get involved in the Economic Renewal program, call (contact person's name) at (phone number).

ECONOMIC RENEWAL DECISION-MAKERS NEEDED

WANTED: People with ideas, energy and an urge to improve the local economy. No previous experience necessary. Skills needed include a love for the community and a desire to see it prosper, an ability to work with others and a vision of a better tomorrow for all of us. It's volunteer work and the rewards will be well worth every minute. For information on how you can become a grass-roots economic developer, call (contact person's name) at (phone number).

ECONOMIC RENEWAL DECISION-MAKERS NEEDED (#2)

The Economic Renewal program is looking for a few good volunteers interested in improving our local economy. Even if business is not your business you can help generate ideas to strengthen local jobs and businesses, encourage new local business start-ups and generally make our local economy stronger. For more information on how to get involved, call (contact person's name) at (phone number).

WHAT OUR COMMUNITY HAS TO WORK WITH

The next Economic Renewal program workshop will be on (date) at (time) in the (place). It will focus on local economic problems, needs, and assets to help us identify what we have to work with as we search for ways to strengthen our economy. For more information, call (contact person's name) at (phone number).

NEW IDEAS FOR LOCAL DEVELOPMENT

The next Economic Renewal town meeting is coming up on (date) at (time) in the (place). All members of the community are invited to come help brainstorm a wide range of potential projects aimed at strengthening the local economy. For more information, call (contact person's name) at (phone number).

Interviews

Interviews are good opportunities to broaden the media's and the public's understanding of Economic Renewal. You can use an interview to bring people up to date with the process, dispel or confirm rumors, plug upcoming events, inspire participation, solicit help and ideas, or clarify points that you think haven't been fully understood. You can also help personalize ER for people—seeing your comments in the paper or hearing your voice on the radio reminds them that this is an effort that's being carried out by ordinary people just like themselves.

But there are risks. If the interviewer is hostile toward you or your effort, or if he's just trying to make a name for himself, he may play "attack journalism" and attempt to embarrass you or get you to say things that make ER look bad. Maybe the guy has seen too many TV news magazines with reporters chasing people accused of dastardly deeds. Whatever his motive, you need to be on your toes.

If a journalist calls to ask a few questions, don't feel you have to answer on the spot. After all, you're a volunteer, not a pro. If you're not the group's spokesperson, ask if you can have the spokesperson call him back. If you are the spokesperson, ask the reporter what the questions are about. Then, if you feel you're not entirely prepared to respond, ask if you can call him back in a few minutes. No need to be mysterious about it. Tell him you'd like to get your thoughts together. Then take a few quiet minutes to think about the answers, maybe write down a few thoughts, take another moment to relax, take a couple of slow deep breaths, and then call him back.

There will probably be instances when you're the one requesting the interview. If you think you have an interesting story, call the reporter with whom you're most at ease, tell her your idea, and ask if she's interested. If she says yes, make yourself available at her convenience. You might ask if you could bring along one or two key members of the coordinating committee (the ones that are good talkers).

Do your homework before any interview. Practice saying what you want the public to know, and have your facts down cold. The best way to influence the final story is to talk about what you think is important. Make a list of points you want to stress and make sure you mention everything on the list, in addition to responding to the reporter's questions. Be ready with several concise, quotable comments. Provide written background on ER, such as a copy of Chapter 2.

Use short sentences. If you say more than necessary, your main message may be lost. If you don't know an answer, don't fake it. Instead, say you don't know and that you'll attempt to get the information and call it in. If the reporter begins to ask tough questions, take as much time as you need to think through the answers. There's no hurry. Don't refuse to answer a question—it will just arouse the reporter's interest in that topic.

TIPS FOR A SUCCESSFUL INTERVIEW

1. Don't panic when a reporter calls.
2. Return a reporter's phone call immediately.
3. Be prepared to discuss three or four specific "talking points"—the main ideas you want to get across.
4. Practice saying the talking points in several different ways.
5. Role-play to prepare for the interview.
6. Take your time answering questions. Think before you speak!
7. Don't be afraid to say you don't know.
8. Never, ever say "no comment"!
9. Speak in English…not technical jargon.
10. Be honest. Don't bluff or exaggerate. The reporter will know.
11. Realize that some reporters are inexperienced.
12. Don't go "off the record," unless you know and trust the reporter (see page 82).
13. Assume that you're on the record and being quoted anytime you talk with a reporter, even casually on the street.
14. Talk in short, complete sentences for radio or TV interviews.
15. Don't answer defensively. Don't argue over the question. But do clarify.
16. Put your conclusion first.
17. Don't be evasive.
18. Don't answer hypothetical questions.
19. Don't ever ask to see the story before it's published.
20. And remember…
    ➤ Advance preparation is the key to a successful interview.
    ➤ You have a choice in what you say and how you say it.
    ➤ You can control a major part of the outcome.

    —*Jeannette Darnauer*

Broadcast interviews call for special speaking skills in addition to those mentioned above. Speak slowly and clearly on the air. Speak into the microphone and not to the interviewer. Don't be afraid to speak up; someone will adjust the volume as your voice goes out over the air. Radio transmission flattens out most voices, so ham it up a little, overemphasize your inflections.

Pack all the information you can into your comments. Remember, punctuation doesn't count in radio; run-on sentences are fine. The reporter will normally tell you when you're speaking for broadcast. If not, ask. You don't want offhand comments to air instead of your reasoned responses.

Off the Record

There may be only one absolute rule of journalism: nothing is off the record. This is a confusing issue that can cause problems. The journalist is the one who can offer to keep something off the record; you can't suggest it. Just because you declare something off the record doesn't necessarily mean your comments will never see the light of day.

Once the information is in the journalist's head, there are several ways it could appear in a story. It could pop up unconsciously when she's working on subsequent stories. It could appear in an opinion column or editorial without attribution. If the journalist is determined to get the information in a story, she could call another source, put the information in the form of a question, and then print the other source's response to the question.

Once you develop a working relationship with local journalists, you'll learn how each handles off-the-record comments. But if you don't want to see it in print or hear it over the air, just don't say it.

Community Journalism

It's no secret that there's a trend in journalism away from in-depth reporting and toward superficial, "sound-bite" coverage. No one is more concerned about this than responsible journalists. A few are bucking the trend by heading in the direction of community-oriented journalism—reporting that gets involved in the community, asks important questions, and seeks serious answers.

Your challenge is to give local journalists the opportunity to report on ER—not as just a bunch of meetings, but as a new way of thinking about the community and its future. You won't be able to do this in a press release or a phone call. It will require spending some time exploring the ideas of ER face to face with reporters. It will require an approach using many of the collaborative techniques described in Chapter 3, where both parties—you and the journalist—set aside their positions and instead work together to produce coverage that's in the best interest of the community. That coverage may turn out to be more critical than you'd like, but if it generates constructive debate about economic development then it can only be for the good. It may even suggest ways your effort could be improved.

Leaders of a community development effort in Ketchikan, Alaska developed such an excellent relationship with the newspaper editor that the paper featured a series of articles about community economic development in the weeks leading up to the first town meeting. Each article was identified by a standing logo, which later accompanied meeting announcements and stories about the progress of the planning effort. There are many other ways to collaborate with the media. Suggest special features on people involved in ER who have interesting stories to tell, or notable projects

Your challenge is to give journalists the opportunity to report on ER.

resulting from the effort. Your local radio station might be willing to broadcast one or more of the ER town meetings. The newspaper could print the results of the preferred-future exercise (see Chapter 8), allowing others in the community to participate indirectly. Either the newspaper or radio station might consider co-sponsoring the first town meeting, providing publicity that leads up to it.

Creating Your Own Publicity

Take some creative time with the program team, willing members of the coordinating committee, and other inventive locals such as actors and artists. Make big pot of spaghetti and brainstorm ideas to make ER more visible and exciting to the community. Let the ideas flow. These ideas are especially important in communities where there's no hometown radio station or newspaper.

Whether or not the media are covering ER, the single most effective publicity technique is to develop a one-page leaflet which will also serve as a poster. Print it on brightly colored paper, add eye-catching illustrations, then distribute and post it anywhere residents pass or congregate. This leaflet/poster will be most important for the first town meeting, but you may choose to print updates for subsequent meetings. It must include where and when the meeting will take place, the name and phone number of your organization, and what the meeting will be about.

Posters should be attractive and of sizes appropriate for the places you hope to hang them: shop windows, notice boards, power poles, etc. Small ones usually get placed in more locations than larger ones.

Here are a few more thoughts to seed your brainstorm:

➤ **Create photo ops.** Much of the ER work will take place in meetings. With few exceptions, photos of meetings are boring. Therefore, create photo opportunities and media events. Kick off the first week of ER activities with a picnic, farmers' market, craft display, talent show, or other special event.

➤ **Use community events.** Time the ER process to coincide with an existing annual event such as a parade or a fair. Put an ER float in the parade or set up an ER booth at the fair. Photos and news coverage from these events will help promote the effort.

➤ **Create your own event.** Organize an Economic Renewal Week or a Community Economy Awareness Week. Ask for economic information from state or regional government agencies. Assign a different theme for each day. The first ER town meeting could cap the week. Hold a press conference.

➤ **Seek endorsements.** Ask newspapers and other media outlets to endorse and promote Economic Renewal. If one of your coordinating committee members is an advertiser, she could make the request.

➤ **Use props.** Consider all the possible visual means to attract people to ER: posters, banners, pins, buttons, leaflets, displays. Involve local artists, crafts people, and school children, especially those in art classes. A big banner over Main Street is always a great idea if you can get permission to put one up, someone to make it, and someone to hang it.

RADIO ACTIVITY

Leaders in Ketchikan, Alaska, found an interesting way to work with local media to develop interest in their community development effort. For about ten days preceding their opening town meeting, they invited various experts—some local, some from outside—to speak on community issues and economic development. The talks were broadcast on the local public radio station at the same time each day so that residents got used to listening at that time. The radio shows significantly increased local interest in the effort and contributed to an excellent turnout for the first meeting.

CHAPTER 5

Checklist: Getting the Word Out

Develop a timeline for the following tasks, bearing in mind that some tasks will proceed simultaneously.

- ☐ Designate spokespeople.

- ☐ Recruit volunteers to help with your media campaign.

- ☐ Inventory all local media outlets.

- ☐ Complete a media contact form for each outlet.

- ☐ Meet with the editor or publisher of the newspaper and reporters or managers of radio and TV stations.

- ☐ Offer written materials and in-depth discussion about ER.

- ☐ Decide whether to buy advertising, and if so, develop an ad budget.

- ☐ If you need help writing press releases, find a good local writer who'll volunteer.

- ☐ Write public service announcements and press releases for the first few town meetings. Create a schedule for sending them out.

- ☐ Gather creative people to brainstorm publicity ideas.

- ☐ Very important: Develop your ER leaflet/poster. Be prepared to distribute it well before the first town meeting.

- ☐ Request interviews with each local media outlet. Schedule them to coincide with the first town meeting.

- ☐ Call all your media contacts before the first meeting to inform them of it.

Conducting Effective Meetings

Getting anything accomplished in a community or an organization requires meetings. Many people who attend meetings don't fully participate because they're bored, frustrated, or shy; others dislike meetings so much that they simply stay away. The group loses the benefit of their participation and creativity. Valuable projects and tasks can fail simply because meetings don't work well.

Yet meetings need not be dull or intimidating. They can be productive and efficient, even fun—and you can be someone who helps make them that way, whether you're facilitating or just sitting in the audience. You no longer need to sit passively through a poorly run meeting. Instead, you can ask questions and offer suggestions that will help the meeting along.

This chapter contains general suggestions that will be helpful for any meeting and more specific tips for running Economic Renewal town meetings. Much of it is common sense—ideas you've already experienced and seen in action. It will remind you of what works and doesn't work in meetings. Try skimming it before any meeting.

The Art of Facilitation

One of the reasons that so many meetings are run poorly, or not run at all, is that many people think nothing needs to be done to make them run well. They think that good and bad meetings just happen naturally. They might say, "You go to the meeting, you talk awhile, you go home. What's the big deal?" Too often the person who feels that way is the one running the meeting.

Facilitation—conducting meetings—is a subtle art that encompasses people skills, listening skills, sensitivity, and the all-important ability to distinguish between the content and the process of a meeting. Not everyone is born with these skills, but you can acquire them through practice.

Your Role as Facilitator

The best facilitators are positive, energetic, assertive, and respected. They work well with a wide variety of people and are well organized. They're willing to manage the group process and the flow of information without taking over or manipulating the group's decisions.

Arguably the most important thing you can do as a facilitator is to set aside your needs in favor of the needs of the group. Though you may want a particular result from the meeting, your responsibility is to ensure that the group gets what *it* wants. You're not a superior who tells the group what to do, you're the leader of a group in which all members share decisions and

Well-run meetings are effective, productive, and fun.

responsibilities. This kind of leadership helps groups perform more effectively by harnessing the skills and potential of all members. When members of a group fully participate and share in decisions, they'll commit to the results.

Have fun! Establish an atmosphere of friendly, open sharing of ideas. Encourage participants to take risks by taking risks yourself.

When in doubt, check with the group. It's not your responsibility to know everything. If at any point you're not sure how to proceed, ask participants what they'd like to do. Offer options, but leave the decision to them. Be open to criticism from the group; you're there for their benefit. It's their right to hold you accountable.

When facilitating a meeting, it's crucial that you be aware on two levels: content (the subject being discussed) and process (how group members interact). As you prepare the agenda and define expectations with the group, focus mainly on content. Once the meeting is under way, though, it's your responsibility to concentrate primarily on process. Be careful not to let your interest in the content distract you from the workings of the group. If the group allows you to participate in the discussion (by asserting positions, offering alternatives, taking sides, etc.), carefully assure participants that the group process is your first priority. Your interest in influencing the outcome should be secondary.

Keep things moving at a lively pace. Each time you explain anything, ask participants if they have any questions. But phrase your question in a way that doesn't imply that they've misunderstood. Rather, ask if anything you said was unclear. This way of phrasing the question puts the "blame" for misunderstanding on you, and therefore makes it a little easier for shy people to ask questions.

Make sure participants understand the purpose of each exercise. They'll often want to take shortcuts, push the process, and move too quickly to solutions. "We already know what the community's economic problems are," someone may say, "let's just pick a project and get on with it." Yet inadequate understanding of local economic conditions is a common cause of project failure. Explain to participants that during the Economic Renewal process they'll gain new insights into the community and its economy.

If, despite your efforts, one or two people continue to question an exercise or complain about a particular aspect of the process, spend personal time with them. Get them aside during a break, before or after a meeting, or outside of the normal meeting time. Listen to their concerns and frustrations. Make sure they know you're listening (use the active listening techniques described below). After they understand that you've heard their concerns, help them to understand the process—how each exercise leads to the most effective decisions about projects, how jumping to conclusions too quickly tends to alienate people and foreclose opportunities.

Employ Active Listening

This may be the most potent and important section of this manual. Active listening is the basis for all effective communication. When people understand that you're listening to them, they'll listen to you and others; they'll want to work with you and the group.

Active listening is based on three skills: acknowledging, empathizing, and clarifying. These skills are easy enough to understand; in fact, you probably already have them. But to use them, you must practice.

As you work with your group, look for the positive. Then, during discussion, *acknowledge* people for making perceptive comments, going out on a limb, showing a willingness to volunteer or to work with an adversary—whatever positive you find. There's no need patronize; just make sure people are clearly acknowledged for what they've said or done.

Don't, however, gloss over difficulties. Rather, when people indicate they're having a problem, *empathize* by letting them know that you understand what they're going through. You might note similar difficulties that you've had.

Empathy isn't sympathy. For instance, "I get the feeling that you're angry" is an empathetic statement. It acknowledges important feelings, it confirms that what is being said is being heard. In contrast, "He shouldn't have done that to you" is sympathetic. It supports negative feelings and judges who is wrong or right—an inappropriate position for a facilitator.

When people talk about issues that are important to them, their statements can become a bit jumbled. One excellent way to help them find their way through the tangle is to *clarify*—say what you think you heard them say. Carefully reframe, rather than interpret, their statements. That is, don't color the clarification with your values, needs, perceptions, and assumptions (even if you think you're right). Another way to clarify is to summarize. For instance, when several points are made over the course of a long statement, you can help by summarizing the points and checking with the speaker or speakers that your summary is correct.

You'll find that some people repeat their points, sometimes endlessly. Usually, they repeat themselves because they think no one has heard them. As facilitator, you can eliminate most repetition by summarizing and clarifying. If they hear you say it, they'll feel less need to repeat it.

These active listening techniques are important to any communication. They may seem obvious, but they're easier said than done. Many of us tend to talk and not listen. Practice acknowledging, empathizing, and clarifying with your friends and family. You'll be amazed at the results you get.

Defuse Conflict

Before any important meeting, identify potentially divisive issues and statements that may come up. Be prepared to respond to them in ways that (a) are respectful of the person making the statement and (b) defuse the situation. For example, if you think a logger may say that the town's problem is "all those radical environmentalists trying to shut down the industry," then someone (probably a core group member) who's respected by loggers needs to be prepared to respond diplomatically. Your "diplomat" should acknowledge (though not necessarily support) the concern and say something like, "Though that's an important issue, this is not the place to deal with it. This is where we work together to find solutions we can all live

BRAINSTORMING

Finding solutions to problems can be a chore or it can be a lot of fun. Brainstorming can make problem-solving fun and maximize creativity. It's a technique that may come in handy while facilitating any ER meeting, and it's central to Step 5, "Generating Project Ideas." A few guidelines:

➤ **Be open to new ideas**—even those that seem impossible.
➤ **Avoid criticism or objections**—there are no wrong ideas. (Combining or adding to ideas need not imply criticism.)
➤ **Listen to the full explanation of each idea**—don't interrupt. (But the facilitator should encourage participants to make their comments short.)
➤ **Encourage one another's participation**—everyone's ideas are necessary for success.

with." Similarly, if an environmentalist is likely to begin harping on the "rape of the forest," then someone respected by environmentalists should be prepared to defuse that anger.

This is an important skill to develop for all community gatherings. However, some people may not accept this approach. They may keep attacking their perceived enemies and disrupt the session. In this case, consider asking a mediator to intervene. This type of intervention could go a long way toward resolving deep-seated community conflict.

Keep the Group Focused

It's easy to become absorbed in the details of discussions. Keeping people focused on the topic retains their interest and involvement, and avoids frustration. You may need to clarify (or ask for clarification) and summarize discussions to bring them into focus.

Make sure everyone understands the subject and the purpose of the discussion. If there are awkward silences when everyone seems to be waiting for someone else to say something, it could be that they don't know what they're supposed to be discussing or how to approach the subject.

If the discussion wanders, remind participants of the subject and steer them back to it. But allowing for creative discussion while keeping the group on purpose is a delicate balancing act. If a digression seems useful, ask participants if they want to continue on that path or get back on the main road. If the discussion becomes circular, say something like, "Has this subject been thoroughly covered? Should we move on?"

Trust your intuition. If you think the discussion should change direction or move on, others probably feel the same way. Check with the group, then make the change. They'll probably be pleased, and you can't go wrong if you check with them first.

To avoid discussions that drift from one topic to another, assure that each item has been resolved before moving on to the next. As decisions are made, note the actions required. Sometimes the discussion will begin to drift, particularly regarding complex topics, and no specific closure is possible. Summarizing the issues or points being considered will often lead to a prompt end to the discussion.

Find Consensus

Consensus isn't unanimous agreement—it's a decision just about everyone can live with. Voting is quicker, but the problem with voting is that it creates winners and losers. Rather than disappearing, losers tend to come back angry and stronger next time. Consensus may take a little longer in the short run, but it averts conflict and saves time later.

When, in the course of discussion, it appears that participants are relatively comfortable with a decision, ask if everyone can live with it. If no one

> Consensus
>
> isn't
>
> unanimous
>
> agreement—
>
> it's a decision
>
> just about
>
> everyone can
>
> live with.

speaks up, you have a consensus. But make sure that shy people don't feel they've been railroaded into submission. If there are dissenting voices, you can return to discussion to resolve remaining issues.

Let's say you're conducting a meeting to decide how to lease space in a city-owned building to nonprofit groups. City manager Jones says, "All nonprofit lessees must obligate one or more board members to pay if the group cannot." You're thinking: "The nonprofits will never agree to this. If I call a vote, one side will win and the other will lose. The losers will walk out and the whole project will go down the chute." Your task is to seek some way to achieve Mr. Jones' goals without injuring the nonprofits.

You might suggest a specific alternative. For instance, you guess that Mr. Jones isn't trying to torpedo the nonprofits (although they may think so), and his only concern is that bills get paid. So you say something like, "Mr. Jones, would you be comfortable if all leases were let by standard business practices?" He says sure; the nonprofits are relieved; and everyone breathes easier. You've averted a battle. You didn't find a compromise in which somebody "gave up" something. Rather, you found a mutually satisfactory alternative that everyone could live with.

However, like most humans, you may not possess the wisdom of Solomon. In many cases, you won't know what the mutually satisfactory alternative is. That's OK. There's plenty of help in the room—ask for it. You might respectfully ask Mr. Jones about the interests that underlie his position. Ask why he thinks his proposal is necessary. His response is likely to be that he just wants a businesslike operation. "Sounds reasonable," you say. "Can anyone think of a way to achieve this goal in another way?" Someone makes a suggestion. You say, "Can everyone live with that?" If no one says no, you have consensus with very little effort.

Anyone can call for a vote. It takes skill and patience to find consensus.

Ensure Fairness and Respect

Make sure everyone gets their turn. If several people want to talk at once, quickly create a verbal list of who will talk and when. You might say, "OK, we'll hear from Sharon next, then Bill, Jim, and Peg." While one person is speaking, if someone else is anxious to talk, catch their eye and nod to let them know that you know they wish to speak. Then call on them when it's their turn. These techniques help participants listen more carefully instead of worrying about whether they'll get to speak.

People who have useful things to say may not feel comfortable saying them. Conversely, those who talk a lot may have little to say that's useful. At the beginning of the meeting, you might remind the group that some people tend to talk a lot in meetings and, though their full participation is definitely welcomed, their responsibility is to help provide the opportunity for others to participate. Gently "tame" those who speak too much or too often. Careful diplomacy is required. For instance: "Thanks for your comments, and let's see if some of the others have ideas to offer." The words you say are less important than your intent as you say them. If you're respectful, people will know it. Ensure that shy people are given ample opportunity to offer their opinions and ideas, but don't force their participation.

Respect is probably the most critical ingredient of constructive group process. Many people become frustrated, even angry, when they feel that others aren't listening. They may feel that they aren't respected. Therefore, you must ensure that each participant feels she or he is being heard.

If participants' opinions are trivialized or demeaned, many will run for cover. As facilitator, you must establish the meeting as a safe place to voice ideas by preventing or deflecting disrespectful responses to people's comments. A cheerful and optimistic attitude is critical to maintaining the enthusiastic participation of everyone in the group. For instance, if someone makes a point that's off-base, don't criticize. Acknowledge the value of the point and indicate that it doesn't seem to contribute to resolving the issue at hand. If you're sincere, you won't sound patronizing.

If you must be critical, speak in terms of your own experience or feelings rather than making a universal statement. Instead of saying, "Your calculations are wrong," you might say, "Your numbers don't correspond to mine." The first approach asserts that the other guy's numbers are inconsistent with the whole world's. The second approach is less threatening: it doesn't say that his calculations are wrong, only that they're different from yours.

Deal with Conflict

Until everyone agrees on everything, conflict will be part of group process. It's a necessary and creative part of a democratic group working together. But disagreements need not involve bad feelings—they can lead to constructive change and growth. Therefore, create an atmosphere of trust so that disagreements can be aired and resolved before they fester.

Unresolved disagreements can hurt feelings and destroy efforts to move toward a common goal. Group members become afraid to express opinions, or fear being misunderstood or ridiculed. Unresolved conflict discourages participation and is often the basis for a group's dissolution.

There are at least five ways participants can deal with conflict:

➤ **Avoidance.** One or both parties can withdraw from the conflict. They may refuse to deal with it, or they may decide this isn't the appropriate time to cause disagreement.

➤ **Smoothing over.** Emphasizing agreement and avoiding disagreement can preserve the relationship, but it can also be a form of giving in. People who try to smooth over can be taken advantage of.

➤ **Compromise.** Many conflicts are resolved through bargaining, where each party gives a little and gets a little. However, people often compromise without exploring the alternatives. They assume that "splitting the difference" is the only acceptable solution.

➤ **Forcing.** One side may force the other to give up, thus getting what it wants at the other's expense. The trouble with this approach is that the losing side probably won't soon forget it was beaten; it may gather support for a more effective fight next time. Ongoing conflict may result.

➤ **Problem-solving.** The parties can agree to find a solution that will meet each one's needs so that neither feels like a loser. Both parties' needs are identified to determine if all or most of them might be fulfilled by a mutually agreed-upon solution.

The last approach is usually the best, but it's not always possible. Your choice will depend on the situation. However you handle conflict, create an atmosphere of trust and respect so participants will be willing to bring out disagreements that would otherwise remain beneath the surface.

Preparations

Many meetings are dead on arrival because nothing was planned ahead of time. Every meeting requires at least a little thought and groundwork. More complicated sessions, such as Economic Renewal meetings, require serious design work to be successful.

Use the following checklists to ensure the effectiveness of your meetings. The first list enumerates tasks that might best be carried out by the program team, the second those that could be delegated to other volunteers. The "Preparations and Materials" sections in Chapters 8–14 give further advice specific to each meeting in the Economic Renewal process.

CONSIDER 'CROSS-FACILITATING'

People are often more receptive to new ideas if they come from someone from outside the community—particularly if that someone is a guy in a suit with a briefcase from very far away. When they hear an idea from a local person, no matter how practical it is, somehow it's just not as good. They know him too well. They know about his problems, his weaknesses, even how he did in school twenty years ago. You may run into this problem in your community. One way to deal with it is to just keep plugging away until people come around. Another way is to "cross-facilitate." Ask your counterparts in other towns to conduct ER meetings in your community while you conduct ER meetings in theirs. Besides defusing suspicion, you'll also reap other benefits such as learning from one another and enabling your communities to work better together.

Program Team Preparations

> **Location.** Inventory all available meeting rooms. If you're working with more than one town or settlement, consider rotating meeting locations among them. Choose the most suitable meeting room based on size, lighting, desirability of possible seating arrangements, and availability of a public address system (if you think it will be needed). Use locations that are "neutral turf"—that is, places that aren't closely associated with one side in the community's controversies. (Note: Step 4, "Discovering New Opportunities"—see Chapter 10—will require very large wall space; a high school gym is ideal.) Reserve chosen rooms for the appointed dates, and ensure that no other distracting activities will be taking place during the meeting.

> **Who'll do what.** Determine the role that each program team member will play. For instance, good speakers should make the presentations; experienced facilitators should conduct group discussions. Alternatively, you might divide team members into sub-teams who each organize and conduct one or two meetings. Dividing portions of the agenda among different people adds variety to the meeting.

> **Tag teams.** One way to move through the agenda efficiently and keep participants alert is to use two program directors as "tag-team" presenters. As one presenter finishes an item, he doesn't have to wonder whether everything has been covered or fish around in papers to figure out what's next. The second presenter steps in to begin the next item. Also, she may offer additional thoughts, remind her partner of an omitted item, or recognize participants whose hands are up.

> **Agenda.** Write out the agenda on a flip-chart sheet or blackboard, and make sure it's clear in your mind to avoid confusion during the meeting. Familiarity allows flexibility so that the agenda can be modified if necessary.

> **Prepare yourself.** Know your material well. Before each town meeting, study the chapter that describes it. Make sure that you know exactly what you're going to cover so that you can move through your part of it quickly. Otherwise, the session will take longer and participants will begin to wonder if they're wasting their time. You may want to identify expendable agenda items that you can drop if you run short of time.

> **Visuals.** Secure visual aids such as flip-charts, chalkboards, or an overhead projector. Later chapters of this book refer only to flip-charts, since they tend to work best for the ER process: sheets can be detached and taped up on a wall so that participants can see all their comments at once. If you use flip-charts, make sure they're supported by substantial easels or attached to the wall. Writing on flimsy

easis is awkward and can delay meetings. (Tip: If you can't afford flip-charts, go to the nearest newspaper printer and ask for "roll-ends." Because they normally discard these rolls of blank newsprint, they'll probably donate them. You can make your own flip-charts by cutting sheets of newsprint and mounting them on plywood or cardboard.)

➤ **Outline.** Write an outline of the ER process on a flip-chart sheet to be posted at the front of every ER town meeting.

➤ **Meeting summaries.** Prepare brief summaries (not minutes) of each meeting to hand out to all participants at the next meeting. This keeps everyone feeling involved even if they miss a meeting, maintains momentum and continuity by reminding people of results of past meetings, and demonstrates that this is a serious effort.

➤ **Participant list.** Circulate paper pads or 3x5 cards at the beginning of each meeting to collect participants' names, phone numbers, addresses, and occupations. An alternative method is to have participants sign a pad of paper at the greeting table, but this is likely to create traffic jams. The participant list enables you to ensure adequate participation by calling people prior to each meeting. (Tip: You might also ask participants to list "additional skills." You'll be amazed at the useful talents hidden among people you've known for years. This information may come in handy when you're looking for volunteers.)

➤ **Phone coordinator.** Assign one person to ensure that all participants and prospective participants are called before *every* meeting. Each call is just a quick reminder, but a crucial one. This is by far the most effective way to ensure good meeting attendance. Participation will certainly suffer if you don't use it. The coordinator should assemble a team of volunteers to make the calls and should check back with all volunteers to ensure they've made them.

➤ **Role-play** (optional). Practice conducting portions of the meetings, with program team and coordinating committee members playing the roles of community participants. They can offer suggestions and supportive criticism.

Volunteer Preparations

➤ **Scribes.** Find two people with good handwriting, particularly those who have experience writing large notes in front of groups. Ask them to serve as scribes to keep records during meetings.

➤ **Room details.** Recruit a small team for room set-up, clean-up, operation of lights, etc.

➤ **Child care** (optional, but important). Find a volunteer or group of volunteers to offer child care during meetings. Without child care,

> **Ensure that all prospective participants are called before *every* meeting.**

many community residents won't be able to participate. (When you publicize ER meetings, be sure to mention that child care will be available.)

➤ **Greeting table** (optional). Set up a greeting table where participants will pick up name tags and materials for each meeting. Copies of handouts from previous meetings should be displayed with a sign indicating, "Old Handouts." Copies of handouts for the current meeting should be displayed with a sign saying, "New Handouts."

➤ **Name tags** (optional). Provide name tags. Make first names very large and legible.

➤ **Refreshments** (optional). Arrange for refreshments—juice, coffee, cookies, whatever seems appropriate. They make the meeting more pleasant and provide a subtle incentive for participants to return to later meetings. Several communities have had excellent results when they scheduled their ER meetings around potlucks.

➤ **Marker** (optional). Develop some means to recognize all Economic Renewal participants. For instance, when ER was conducted in Alamosa, Colorado, each participant was given a little pin that said, "Alamosa Economic Renewal."

Making Meetings Work

Facilitation is a science as well as an art. The following procedural tips will help ensure that your meetings run smoothly.

Setting Up

Make sure you have what you need to keep the meeting moving smoothly. Working materials need to be in the right place at the right time. Know the location of the restrooms and know how to control the temperature of the room. It shouldn't be too warm, especially following a meal.

If possible, each participant should be able to make eye contact with everyone else. It's especially important for the facilitator to have eye contact with everyone: traditional classroom arrangements, with you at the front and everyone facing you, tend to put you in the position of authority and separate you from the rest of the group. A circle of chairs is an ideal configuration, since it puts all members on an equal footing and encourages rapport and common purpose. If the group is too large for a circle and a classroom arrangement is unavoidable, emphasize to the group that, although you happen to be in the front of the room, you have no more authority or responsibility than anyone else in the room.

Even if the room is fully set up, arrive at least thirty minutes before the start of the meeting to handle unforeseen problems and greet early arrivals. Take time to be alone before the session begins, even if it's for only a minute

---

> It's especially important for the facilitator to have eye contact with everyone.

or two. Clear your mind, leave other activities and concerns of the day behind. Take a few deep breaths and relax.

Out of respect for those who arrived on time, begin each meeting punctually, no matter how many people haven't yet showed up. If you begin late, participants will be later for each successive meeting, until it becomes nearly impossible to know when to start.

Introductions

Introductions are a great ice-breaker. Ask participants to introduce themselves and say what they expect of the meeting. Each participant might also indicate personal, special, or community interests. Provide an example by introducing yourself first. Following introductions, everyone will have a better idea of who's there and why. The loose gathering of people will begin to recognize common interests and feel like a group or team. The division between the speaker and the participants will tend to dissolve.

Introductions are particularly important for meetings in which participants will initially have little opportunity to participate verbally—where they must sit and listen a while. Under these circumstances, introductions reassure them that they are, in fact, participants and not just observers. Introductions tend to release their tension, and having been heard, they can then listen.

Larger meetings require shorter introductions per person, otherwise they'll dominate the agenda. (However, that may be appropriate if the meeting is the first of a series with the same participants—in fact, introductions could be the primary purpose of that first meeting.) In a group of more than thirty people, you may want to limit comments to name and position. In a very large meeting, you might not have time for any introductions, though another approach is to break the group into small groups or pairs for introductions.

Meeting Considerations

> ➤ **Purpose.** Identify the purpose of the meeting, the particular issues to be covered, and the intended outcome. Always ask for questions.

> ➤ **Agenda.** Ask participants if they'd like to make any changes to the agenda, and be genuinely open to suggestions. Then, ask for agreement and commitment to the agenda. This may sound overly elaborate, but it only takes a minute or two and it gets everyone focusing their creative energy on the tasks at hand. Involving the group in setting its own course encourages cooperation. Groups are usually much more committed to their activities when they decide themselves what those activities will be.

> ➤ **History.** Early in the meeting, summarize your perception of the facts that led to it, then ask if anyone sees it differently. This is a

powerful technique that establishes a common understanding of history. When participants remember events differently but aren't aware of the differences, the result may be misunderstandings, arguments, and wasted time. Don't leave controversial or emotional events out of your summary: if they're not acknowledged, they'll become barriers to progress.

➤ **Timing.** Participants find it reassuring when you guarantee a specific ending time. An evening meeting should take no more than two and a half hours; two is better. Be conservative in your estimates of time required for each item. Resist the temptation to unrealistically shorten the time for a certain item to fit it into the meeting time frame. Set a crisp pace so that participants know that something is happening, and that the meeting is worth their time.

➤ **Record-keeping.** Use a blackboard or flip-chart to record participants' ideas and comments as they say them. This acknowledges the value of each person's contributions and can give a clearer idea of the direction the meeting is taking. The record must be neutral, without editorial comment. Decide what sort of record should be preserved for possible later use (see page 66). Is a detailed record needed? Who needs it and when? Will the flip-chart sheets be saved? Ask volunteers to help in typing, duplicating, and distributing the record when needed.

➤ **Ground rules** (optional). You may want to propose that the group establish ground rules such as those on the next page.

➤ **Task instructions.** When conducting group exercises, keep instructions simple and give deadlines for tasks one at a time. If you try to give instructions for several tasks at once, participants will probably get bogged down in the first few, and never get to the last ones.

➤ **Lost leader.** If, as facilitator, you lose your place and can't remember what comes next, take your time. If you need more than ten or fifteen seconds to find your way, calmly ask the group to wait for a moment. They'll start talking among themselves while you search.

➤ **Breaks.** Try not to go more than ninety minutes without a break. No matter how much time you ask participants to take, breaks usually require more time than you allowed. Fibbing is one approach to getting everyone back in a reasonable period of time. For instance, if you want a break to last fifteen minutes, tell them you'll allow ten. Announce the end of the break at least five minutes before you intend to have participants back. But remember, breaks aren't wasted time: important work is accomplished informally in small groups and one-on-ones.

➤ **Wrap-up.** At the end of the meeting, summarize the decisions that were made, actions to be taken next, and who will do what and

GROUND RULES

While the facilitator does everything possible to make meetings fun and productive, participants must help. Agreement on basic ground rules minimizes disputes, increases participation, and expedites the meeting.

Missoula, Montana Mayor Dan Kemmis worked for several years with towns interested in community economic development. He suggests the following ground rules:

Openness, Outreach, and Ongoing Activities

➤ Sessions are open to anyone in the community.

➤ Newcomers are welcomed. To help them become part of the process, summaries of what has already taken place are provided.

➤ Those groups and interests that haven't participated so far are actively encouraged to participate by everyone involved.

➤ An agreement that has already been reached will not be lightly overturned. Anyone wishing to challenge settled decisions is free to do so, but preceding work must be respected. This group intends to make things happen.

Decision-Making

➤ Consensus process is used as much as possible in order to assure maximum agreement. Consensus doesn't mean complete agreement; rather, it is reached when almost everyone can live with the results.

➤ Where consensus cannot be achieved but agreement is necessary, a vote will be taken and the majority will prevail.

➤ In such cases, the minority view will be recorded.

Participation

➤ All participants will check their old disputes, feuds, and ideologies at the door.

➤ Participants should speak in ways that achieve the broadest and deepest consensus, rather than seeking to win debating points.

➤ Those who know they tend to be dominant in a group should make a sincere effort to encourage shy folks to participate.

➤ When responding to other people's points, participants should identify agreements with them as well as disagreements, and try to understand their intentions before deciding to disagree.

➤ It's assumed that no one has the entire answer, and everyone has part of it.

It's up to you whether you want to have ground rules at all, and what you want them to be. These are merely suggestions. If you do choose to use them and if someone breaks one of the rules, offer a gentle, light-hearted reminder rather than a hard-nosed notice of violation.

when. Never, ever end a meeting without determining what's next and who will do it! Great ideas have fallen flat because a meeting was ended with no future direction. Assign a program team member to follow up with people who volunteered for tasks. You might also ask how well expectations were met.

➤ **Afterwards.** Extremely important: convene the program team for a few minutes to discuss what worked, what could have been done better, if the turnout was sufficient, and what, if anything, should be done to ensure better turnout. Discuss who wasn't there and should have been. Decide who will conduct the next session and who will carry out the various preparations for it. Most importantly, celebrate the success of the meeting.

Step 1: Mobilizing the Community

In laying the groundwork for Economic Renewal, you've already accomplished a lot. You've organized your coordinating committee and your program team. You've begun to recruit additional volunteers for specific tasks. You've made contact with the media. You're now ready to carry out the actual Economic Renewal process. This chapter details the first step: mobilizing the community to participate. The remaining steps are covered consecutively in Chapters 8 through 14.

Mobilizing the community is a full-scale campaign based around the big kickoff event, the first ER town meeting (described in the next chapter). Build a ground swell of excitement and support for the first meeting, and your effort will be off to a running start. In part, this will draw on the media and publicity techniques already described in the previous chapter. But in this first step of Economic Renewal, more than in any other, you and the other members in your team will need to talk to people directly, through one-on-one contacts and group presentations.

You'll talk to as many people as possible from as broad a cross-section of the community as possible. You'll court people whose participation will add to your effort's credibility, whose ideas will enrich the process, whose knowledge of local history will inform it, and whose endorsement will up the chances of success. You'll contact these key leaders to enlist not only their support but the support of their constituents. You'll also reach out to the rest of the community to bring in new ideas, encourage new leaders, and avoid getting stuck in the old ways of doing things.

There are good reasons for mobilizing so many community interests. First, community residents get behind decisions they had a part in creating. When you collaborate with others to make a decision, you "own" it and are more likely to support it. Second, the resulting decisions are based on a wider range of community experience and wisdom. Diverse people bring forth more and different ideas, giving the community more options to choose from. Third, this approach builds community leadership. It offers traditional leaders a more effective means to seek solutions to community problems, and it opens the leadership door to new people. Many citizens—those who are tired of seemingly endless meetings and those who've never been involved—find this process is a comfortable way to get involved. Feeling more competent and comfortable, they increase their involvement. Because they've been heard and treated equally, they become more interested in helping solve problems than pushing a point of view. Many even run for office.

Identifying Your Community Leaders

Start with the leaders in your community. People will be more likely to support your Economic Renewal effort if it's associated with leaders they respect.

You've probably already spoken to some local leaders about ER when you were recruiting for the coordinating committee and program team (see Chapter 4). They include those in obvious leadership positions, such as elected government officials and chamber of commerce members, as well as leaders of civic, cultural, ethnic, religious, and neighborhood organizations. Some may lead groups that aren't formally organized; some may not lead groups at all, yet are widely recognized within certain segments or factions of the community. They may simply be individuals who are respected by the community at large—maybe the retired woman who taught everyone sixth grade, or the long-time local pharmacist. Neither is part of any formal group, yet you know they'll contribute a lot to your economic development effort.

When looking for leaders, notice people who communicate with lots of other people and those who get the job done. Think back over the last several years: when a community problem came up, who was there to help find a solution? Many leaders don't think of themselves as such. When you ask them, they may say, "Me? Are you kidding? I'm just working with my neighbors to get the speed limit reduced," or, "I'm just a business person who talks to a few people about getting the community moving." Don't let 'em fool you. They're leaders.

The sections that follow will help you identify the leaders in your community. Your list of likely contacts might end up being anywhere from ten to seventy names long, depending on the size, diversity, and dynamism of the community. The length of the list isn't as important as its inclusiveness. Your goal is to ensure that all groups in the community feel they have an ally who's involved. For each leader who isn't involved, there may be a group of people that feels left out of the process or even threatened by it.

As you're compiling your list, don't make the mistake of thinking "she doesn't have the time," or "he'd never get involved in something like this." Never assume that certain people won't come; don't make the decision for them. Time after time, RMI staff have heard program team members say, "It's a miracle that so-and-so got involved—we never thought they would, but boy did they make a huge contribution."

For each leader who isn't involved, there may be a group that feels left out.

Established Leaders

Some kinds of people are virtually always involved in economic development. Easy to find, they're often the community's most powerful members:

➤ Government officials
➤ Business people
➤ Chamber of commerce members
➤ Realtors
➤ Real-estate developers
➤ Newspaper editors and publishers
➤ Industry representatives
➤ Political party representatives
➤ Service group leaders

Many of these people are experienced in dealing with economic development issues and have plenty of ideas. Many have access to and knowledge of sources of capital. A few are "gatekeepers"—people who can open or close the "gate" to people and resources. For example, the town manager is often the gatekeeper to the town council. The person in charge of a regional development agency often keeps one of the gates to state resources.

Such leaders are often accustomed to getting their way. Some may not be thrilled with this new bottom-up approach, and may be inclined to oppose your effort if they feel threatened by it. Yet, whatever their interests, they're important players who must be directly involved in ER, or at least kept informed.

Frequently Overlooked Leaders

Many community segments have historically been kept on the fringes of decision-making, or allowed only token representation. Here's a partial list (you'll probably be able to think of others):

➤ Women and minorities
➤ Retirees
➤ Young people
➤ Teachers
➤ Health and social-service professionals
➤ Religious leaders
➤ Newcomers
➤ Loggers, fishermen, and miners
➤ Farmers and ranchers
➤ Environmentalists
➤ Neighborhood activists
➤ Laborers
➤ Artists and craftspeople

Yet many members of these groups have valuable knowledge and experience quite different from those who usually make the community's development decisions. Many have creative new ideas. And, despite frequent assumptions to the contrary, they're often concerned with issues that have a direct bearing on community development. The Economic Renewal effort in Colorado's Plateau Valley was initiated by high-school seniors, who wanted the option to stay in the community and felt they had the most to win or lose in its future. The directors of a health-planning organization in Sitka, Alaska initiated a community economic development effort because they understood that health and development issues were interrelated (as when, for example, spouse abuse tends to increase with unemployment). The leaders of such groups will probably become enthusiastic about your effort when you explain it in terms of their special interests.

Some of these groups won't have obvious leaders, but the important thing is to bring on board at least one person who's respected by each group. This may not be easy. Some may say they've tried in vain to get decision-makers to listen. Having been ignored in the past, they may be frustrated. In some cases, you may need to make a special effort to deal with their anger and resentment (see pages 88-93 for suggestions). Assure them that this time, they'll have just as much say as anyone else involved in the process.

Making Personal Contacts

Having identified and listed your community's leaders, contact them to familiarize them with Economic Renewal and seek their commitment to participate in the process.

This is a personal campaign consisting of people talking to people. You may wish to precede your contact with a written invitation (see page 213), but don't leave it at that; letters don't mean what they used to. The only effective way to get people to actually attend the meeting is to contact them personally. Start contacting leaders as soon as possible to give them plenty of time to make room for the ER process in their schedules.

Divide the Labor

One person shouldn't accept the burden of making all the contacts: try to distribute the work among as many members of the coordinating committee and program team as possible. Read out each name on your list of leaders and determine who on the committee or team is most likely to successfully recruit that person. Where possible, assign contacts to people who have already built bridges to those organizations (see page 49).

Too often, people volunteer for tasks at meetings but never get around to doing them. A group that operates this way will fail. Contacting community leaders is a crucial task. Those who volunteer must clearly commit

The only way to get people to actually attend the meeting is to contact them personally.

to making their contacts by a certain deadline. Don't volunteer to contact people if you actually mean: "I'll call 'em if I have a chance."

Cold-calling people about community economic development isn't everyone's cup of tea. If some team members are reluctant or shy about it, you might call a brief meeting on making contacts. At the meeting, make sure each person is clear about what they're supposed to say (see below). Then talk about how you feel when you make contacts such as these. Are you uncomfortable? Say why. Ask others if they feel a little uncomfortable, and have them talk about their reasons. Ask them what they'd do if they got responses that you think they're likely to encounter. Try role-playing to get over the awkwardness.

What to Say

Call or visit contacts, whichever is most comfortable and convenient. Create a positive overall impression. Don't base your presentation on the negative: warnings that "We're all going to be in deep trouble unless we do this" will turn people right off. Instead, make it clear that *there is hope*. You might want to refer to some of the hopeful examples in Chapter 2. Celebrate past local successes and acknowledge those who made those successes happen.

Your intention shouldn't be to persuade people to do what *you* want, that is, participate in Economic Renewal. Remember that you're offering something—ER—that will help them get what *they* want.

Here are six main points to get across:

Their Concerns Matter

Let contacts know that their ideas are wanted and needed. Even if they don't become involved in ER, they'll feel better about it because you were sincerely interested in their participation.

Ask them what their concerns are regarding the local economy. Listen carefully to what they say. In fact, listen *actively* in the ways described on page 88. Unless they know you hear them, they won't listen to you and they may not participate in ER.

Describe Economic Renewal

Here's a brief summary you could work from: "Economic Renewal is a different approach to economic development. It doesn't depend on the government or some big corporation to come save us. And it won't try to make us like everyone else. Instead, it will help us tailor our economic development efforts to our unique situation. We'll conduct a series of meetings in which we'll focus on our common interests rather than our differences. Then, we'll seek solutions that everyone can live with." The appendix contains longer scripts that will give you more to go on (see page 208).

Before contacting anyone, become familiar with Economic Renewal by reading Chapters 1, 2, and 3. But you need not be an expert on economic development to make an effective contact. The most persuasive thing you can do is to make it personal. Say why you decided to get involved in this effort and why you think it will help the community achieve its goals. Portray ER not as a bunch of meetings but rather a series of exciting events that offer the community great opportunity. If a contact wants more detail about ER than you feel comfortable providing, give him or her a copy of Chapter 2. Ask if there's anything about ER that hasn't been made clear.

If your contact says the community has already done economic development, acknowledge those efforts and indicate that economic development isn't a one-time quick-fix and that success requires ongoing work. You may need to distinguish ER from other programs or approaches the community has tried in the past.

Secure Their Commitment

Don't make people feel like they've got to buy into the entire Economic Renewal process, but do gently try to get them to agree to come to the first town meeting. Since very few people are comfortable being the first to try something, it helps to indicate who has already committed to (or expressed an interest in) the program.

Don't be discouraged if they're initially coy about agreeing to participate, since that may just be the way your community operates. Some folks may wait to gauge their neighbors' reactions and then come to later meetings. Others may be reluctant to participate because they fear it might compromise their leadership position or because they're uncomfortable representing their group. Ask them to sit in on meetings as observers or advisors; as they become more comfortable with the ER process, they'll probably participate fully. Assure them they're not expected to speak for their group, and that you're inviting them because they understand the goals and intentions of their group.

Don't Push Them

Plenty of people simply don't like to attend meetings. That's OK. Tell them you'd still like to make sure their views are considered in the process and that there are important pieces of information they're uniquely qualified to provide. For instance, what has gotten people through tough times in the community? What do they know how to do that might help themselves and the community? What is most needed by their friends and neighbors? And don't let them disappear from your radar: keep them informed of ER's progress and consult them on specific questions.

Harness Their Influence

Ask contacts who else should be involved in ER—friends, neighbors, allies, colleagues, coworkers—and if they'd be willing to recruit these people to participate in ER. Ask for an endorsement of the ER effort to help influence others to participate. Ask what can be done to involve their constituents. For instance, where and when should meetings be held? Who should invite them?

Suggest a Group Meeting

Finally, ask if you could talk about ER at the next meeting of the group or groups with which your contact is affiliated. You'll be more persuasive with that group when you're introduced, and thus effectively endorsed, by your contact. Such connections can have a positive domino effect in your effort to mobilize the community.

Mobilizing the Rest of the Community

Once you've got a representative group of leaders on board for the first Economic Renewal town meeting, it'll be a lot easier to get other members of the community to come. The leaders will open doors for you to make presentations to groups they're affiliated with, and their endorsements will help persuade their friends and followers to participate.

It's now time to go public with your ER effort. Use whatever means seem appropriate in your community: the following sections discuss individual, group, and community-wide approaches. Time your activities so that momentum builds and the community perceives an increasing level of intensity and excitement that culminates in the first town meeting. Presentations, posters, media coverage, and other publicity should begin early enough that residents have time to plan ahead, but not so early that they regard the meeting as some distant event that they then forget about.

Personal contacts ensure full participation.

Personal Invitations

Obviously, you and your fellow team members will personally tell friends and associates about the upcoming meeting. In addition to these and the leaders you've already contacted, there are other residents who probably deserve personal invitations.

For instance, seek out the quiet, creative people who do their homework, but who are shy and dislike public meetings. The quiet ones often have the best ideas. Recruit the natural networkers in your community, those whose daily contacts make them influential: mail carriers, cashiers, waitpeople, bartenders, firefighters, police, receptionists. When they're involved in ER, they can keep others informed and encourage them to participate.

The lists on page 103 may suggest other people to invite. For example, retirees—both old-timers and newcomers—can play an important role in ER. They often have plenty of time to volunteer, and they're usually committed to building community and enhancing quality of life. Carol Lamm of Kentucky's Mountain Association for Community Economic Development says that retirees "bring a broader perspective and often considerable skills" to community development efforts. They become involved "from a more public-spirited perspective than is common. When they are local-folks-returned-home, they tend to be readily accepted and appreciated by the community." Bart Kennedy, manager of community development for Alabama Power, notes that retirees who move to town bring commitment, outside experience, and financial independence from local "ol' boys," and are less encumbered by a town's social-structure baggage.

Finally, nearly every community has crackpots who participate in community meetings. You probably won't want to invite them, but they're going to come anyway. If you don't invite them, they may arrive mad.

Group Presentations

Though optional, group presentations can be very effective in mobilizing the community. Not only do they enable you to address many people at once, they also let audience members hear each other's questions, discuss ideas together, and pick up on each other's enthusiasm.

The leaders you contacted earlier will be the bridges to the main groups in your community, but there may be other groups worth addressing as well. Again, refer to the lists on page 103 for ideas. Young people, for example, are easily reached through school assemblies. To the peril of most communities, young people are nearly always left out of decision-making processes; when invited to participate as equals, however, they can be a vital source of good ideas and volunteer help. You may also see fit to schedule one or two community-wide presentations, which should be announced in the media.

Group presentations can be as big or as small as you want them to be— Economic Renewal will be most effective when you find ways to talk about it that fit with your community. For instance, the Kentucky Local Governance Project launched ER by first holding a series of informal "kitchen-table meetings" in local homes. The project team there felt that residents wouldn't attend the larger meetings unless they first became familiar with ER at these more intimate introductory sessions.

FEEDBACK

It's likely that only a few people from each community group will be able to attend Economic Renewal meetings. These participants can significantly assist the process by serving as links between the ER process and their group. Though they may not speak *for* their group, it's vital that they speak *with* it. When they let their group know what's happening at the meetings, and when they talk about their group's concerns in the meetings, they provide a feedback loop that makes community consensus-building possible.

Therefore, as the process gets under way, urge participants to report ER meeting results to their groups, and to bring their group's concerns and ideas to the meetings. Some of this feedback will occur naturally. For instance, chamber of commerce members who participate in ER will probably talk about it at chamber meetings. In most cases, however, participants will need to build these feedback loops. Fortunately, this won't be wasted effort: the improved communication created by this process will help all community decision-making.

In effect, your group presentations will serve as "teasers" for the opening town meeting, and shouldn't be allowed to upstage it. Their purpose is to preview the basic concepts of ER, which aren't always easy to appreciate in one sitting; unlike the town meeting, these presentations generally won't include any exercises. (Of course, rules are made to be broken. To mobilize its youth, one community conducted the preferred-future exercises outlined in Chapter 8 in local schools prior to the first town meeting, then presented the results at the end of that meeting. This enriched the preferred-future results, generated excitement in the ER effort from an unusual source, and increased young people's involvement in the process.)

Team members who were designated as meeting facilitators will probably be the most appropriate people to lead these gatherings. One painless technique is to let two or three people tag-team the presentation. If you're a presenter, this will be a good opportunity to ease into your public-speaking role.

You'll make most of the same points that you made in your one-on-one contacts with community leaders (see page 105). Your role is simply to lead a discussion of Economic Renewal ideas—don't worry about justifying ER or convincing anyone that it's the best approach. The most important thing you can do is leave people with a positive impression of hope, opportunity, and the community's potential. As you describe each aspect of ER, ask for participants' reactions and ideas. Allow plenty of time for discussion. At the close of the session, indicate that you're available to discuss the process one-on-one, and ask who can be counted on to participate in the first town meeting.

Give a copy of Chapter 2 to each participant in every session. You might also offer copies of Chapters 1 and 3. (Note: Rocky Mountain Institute is available to conduct one or more of these sessions.)

General Publicity

Publicity—in the form of media coverage, posters, banners, and so on—is the most visible aspect of mobilizing the community for ER. It's less personal and therefore less effective than direct contacts, but it's the only way to get the word out to the silent majority of the community. Publicity techniques are discussed in detail in Chapter 5.

Everything you can do to involve people in Economic Renewal at this early stage of the process will pay big dividends later on, and publicity is no exception. How much of a buzz you can create around the first town meeting is a pretty good predictor of participation in the entire process. Of course, the majority of residents won't attend, but that's all the more reason to publicize what you're doing. Though they're not involved in ER, many non-participants want to stay *informed*. If you keep them well informed through the media and other publicity, they'll probably support your efforts.

And don't be discouraged if you don't get a huge turnout for the first meeting. A relatively small number of people can find creative solutions and put them to work if they stay in communication with the rest of the community.

Finally, stay positive. A man in Holly, Colorado, called a community development meeting to which almost no one came. When later asked about it, he said it was a really terrific meeting and a lot was accomplished. He called another meeting and the turnout was excellent.

Checklist: Mobilizing the Community

Develop a timeline for the following tasks, bearing in mind that some tasks will proceed simultaneously.

Leader Contacts
- [ ] Identify all relevant local groups.
- [ ] List individuals who may be regarded as leaders of each group.
- [ ] Add to the list other leaders who aren't part of any group.
- [ ] Assign program team and coordinating committee members to contact each person on the list.

ER Presentations (Optional)
- [ ] Designate one or more people to serve as presenters.
- [ ] Brainstorm and list groups and places for possible ER presentations.
- [ ] Request an audience with each relevant local group.
- [ ] Schedule one or two community-wide presentations. Develop and distribute PSAs and press releases (see Chapter 5) to announce these sessions.

Preparation for Step 2 (First ER Town Meeting)
- [ ] Read Chapter 8.
- [ ] Secure a large meeting hall and other necessary facilities (see page 112).
- [ ] Decide which program team members will conduct the meeting; enlist a "host" to introduce it (see page 113).
- [ ] Distribute PSAs, press releases, leaflets/posters, and other materials to publicize the meeting (see Chapter 5).

Step 2: Envisioning the Community's Future

This is the first Economic Renewal town meeting—the big kickoff. It's when things start getting fun and the process begins to take on a life of its own. The meeting has four main purposes:

➤ **Explain what will take place and why.** Community residents may have heard a lot of different things about ER in the past several weeks. A thorough introduction starts everyone on the "same page." By beginning with the same information, they'll work more effectively as a team on subsequent steps. It offers an innovative perspective on local economic development that opens doors to creative and sustainable ideas. Also, it gives participants a firm basis for recruiting their friends and neighbors.

➤ **Envision the community's "preferred future."** Three guided exercises will focus participants on the big picture—how they want the community to be in the future. Because many conventional economic development efforts focus only on business, they lose sight of, and often conflict with, basic community values. These three important exercises establish the reasons for the ER effort so that these community values become the goal.

➤ **Build trust.** The preferred-future exercises also develop rapport and a sense of common purpose among participants, building the trust that is essential for effective community economic development.

➤ **Create a lot of hoopla.** Finally, the meeting provides an event that generates publicity and excitement at the start of the process, creating momentum that will carry through to later stages.

Preparations and Materials

Study this chapter thoroughly. Refer to page 93 for general advice on preparing for meetings.

Schedule this first town meeting for no later than two months after the start of your community-mobilization effort. Delay may result in loss of momentum and decreased participation.

Choose a meeting location. You'll need someplace big, since this first meeting will probably be the most heavily attended one of the series. A school auditorium works well. A room where conflict often takes place, such as the city council meeting room, is less ideal because many residents will associate it with disagreement and bad feelings. A room owned by or perceived as the "turf" of a particular group may also put some people off.

You should have already designated two or more of your program team or coordinating committee members as meeting facilitators. They'll conduct the main part of this meeting, but it's a good idea to let a separate "host" make the opening remarks. The host should be a widely respected member of the community who isn't associated with any particular faction. He or she may be a member of the coordinating committee. If you can't find a host who would appear relatively neutral, then ask representatives of conflicting factions to jointly open the meeting. It makes a powerful statement when adversaries support the same effort.

Make copies of Chapter 2 and the "Our Preferred Future" worksheet (pages 118-9), one for each person you expect to attend. The worksheet can be copied on two sides of the same sheet of paper. Make the chapter available at the entrance to the meeting room; you'll distribute the worksheets during the meeting. Also have enough pencils on hand, plus "lap desks"—pieces of cardboard to write against—if participants won't be seated at tables.

On a flip-chart sheet or blackboard, write the following headings:
➤ Arts
➤ Built Environment
➤ Business and Jobs
➤ Community (Social Capital)
➤ Education
➤ Government
➤ Health
➤ History and Tradition
➤ Natural Environment
➤ Recreation
➤ Skills and Talents

Prepare flip-chart sheets that list the principles and tools of Economic Renewal (see pages 17-33) in large, bold letters. Post these sheets at the front of the meeting room for this and future meetings.

AGENDA

➤ Opening remarks *(10 minutes)*
➤ Exercise: "What I Love About My Community" *(15 minutes)*
➤ Introduce Economic Renewal *(45 minutes)*
➤ Exercise: "What I Would Like to Change" *(15 minutes)*
➤ Exercise: "When These Things Have Changed..." *(15 minutes)*
➤ General discussion *(10–15 minutes)*
➤ Wrap-up *(5 minutes)*

Use this as a guide to create your own agenda, indicating what time each item is expected to begin. Post your agenda in the meeting room.

The Meeting

Since this may be your first experience in facilitation, this chapter is more heavily scripted than later ones. Passages in italics are simply suggested wordings, which you can take or leave. As you gain more experience, you'll probably find that you quickly become more comfortable leading meetings and workshops and can create your own scripts.

Fully involving participants as soon as possible reassures them that the session is theirs, not yours. That's why this meeting plunges right into the first of the three preferred-future exercises. However, many participants may not have received any background information on Economic Renewal. By the end of the first exercise they'll be wondering what ER is all about, so you'll then move into a full introduction to ER. After that, you can return to and complete the second and third exercises. (Variations on this agenda are possible—see page 124.)

Opening Remarks

The host should welcome participants, refer to earlier community successes, say what led to the meeting, thank everyone who helped, and introduce the facilitators. This opening must be brief, not an opportunity for the host to make a speech. If any organizations or individuals paid for or donated services or goods to the program, they should be acknowledged at this time. The host should orient participants to the facility and indicate the location of the rest rooms and smoking area.

The host might say: *"A group of local residents who understand the Economic Renewal process has agreed to organize and conduct this series of meetings. We call them our program team. A couple of them will serve as facilitators and help us in moving through the town meeting process and getting our work done."*

Ask the facilitators to identify themselves. *"They're not leaders who'll try to tell us what to do. Rather, facilitators help a group in which all members share decisions and responsibilities. This kind of leadership will help us perform more effectively by using all of our potential."*

If this meeting isn't the first development effort in the community, the host should mention the valuable efforts that preceded it and indicate that ER will build on those earlier efforts.

Have the host read or display the list of organizations who endorse your effort. It gives participants the clear sense that Economic Renewal is broadly supported and isn't being directed by any particular group. You might ask representatives of organizations to stand as they're named. (But don't invite them to talk—there's no time for speeches!)

Finally, the host should introduce the agenda and offer a one-minute overview of ER, just to give participants a sense of what's coming. Keep in mind that you'll thoroughly explain the program later in the meeting. All the host has to say is something like:

"We're about to embark on a community decision-making process that involves people from all walks of life in finding sustainable development solutions. It's called Economic Renewal, and it helps communities help themselves economically while preserving community and environmental values. We'll inventory our unique conditions, analyze what to do with our assets, problems, and needs, then identify projects to strengthen the community and its economy. We'll describe the program in detail in just a few minutes, but first we want to hear from you."

The Preferred-Future Exercises

There are many ways for your community to establish a vision of its "preferred future," some of them quite involved. For instance, you could consult with key community people and groups, hold public meetings, and conduct surveys. A committee could then distill the results, publish a draft version, solicit public comment, and finally publish the community's preferred future.

But this could easily take a year or more, by which time many participants would have dropped out. They'd leave shaking their heads and mumbling something about, "Why can't these people just get on with it!" Even if you convinced a group of people to participate, once the process was complete and you were ready to begin actually *achieving* the preferred future, most participants wouldn't want to hear about another meeting, let alone attend one.

The visioning technique described in this chapter takes far less time. The result, while not as conclusive as what a more elaborate process might generate, is a list or statement defining what the community wishes to preserve and create. For the purposes of Economic Renewal, this approach is quite adequate.

The first preferred-future exercise identifies what the community wants to *preserve* by asking participants what they love about their community. The second and third exercises identify what people want to *create*, by asking what they'd like to change about the community and what the community would be like when those changes have been made.

These exercises encourage participants to see that economic development is more than just "improving business and jobs." Economic Renewal seeks to strengthen the entire community, including business; this broader scope will attract more and different people than conventional economic development efforts. Also, projects chosen through the ER process are more likely to be compatible with the community's values because participants will use the preferred future as one basis on which to judge them.

Visioning also establishes a basis upon which residents can work together. In many communities, the very idea of working together seems impossible. Quarrels can become so bitter that some people on one side of an issue won't even talk to those on the other side. In the midst of such controversies, people focus on disagreements. But most of the time the subjects of those disagreements represent only 5 percent of the whole. Certainly they're important, but during the battles people tend to forget about the other 95 percent. The preferred-future exercises focus primarily on the 95 percent that just about everybody agrees on—that the community should be friendly and safe, that it should be a good place to raise kids, that it should retain and enhance certain unique characteristics, etc. There's always plenty of time later to deal with the last 5 percent. Once residents begin to understand that they want pretty much the same things for themselves and their families, they begin to trust one another. Community conflicts don't disappear, but they become more constructive and less personal.

Exercise: 'What I Love About My Community'

At this point the host will hand over the meeting to the facilitators, who can begin the first preferred-future exercise. As you begin introducing it, have an assistant distribute copies of the "Our Preferred Future" worksheet.

Be careful not to drag on too long with your introductory remarks. Say just enough to clarify the purpose of the exercises and what will take place. Allow time for questions. Take no more than ten minutes, but don't hurry; make yourself clear.

Say: *"One thing that distinguishes this approach to economic development from others is that it's driven by the values and goals of the community. It's not driven exclusively by business considerations, but by all community values, including those related to business. So we're going to do three exercises to help us identify those values. They'll help us envision what you might call our 'preferred future.' In a later meeting, we'll use the results of these preferred-future exercises to decide which projects the community should pursue. While we're doing these exercises, notice how your values compare with those of other residents, especially people with whom you may disagree.*

"The sheets that have been handed out contain three questions, one for each of the exercises. Your answers will remain anonymous. At the end of the meeting we'll collect your sheets and the results will be compiled by volunteers into a single list of common interests, which we'll distribute at a future meeting.

"In a moment you'll respond to the first question and write down things about the community that you love. Not just the things you like, but those you feel strongly about. One way to think about this is to imagine that you're talking to your favorite cousin or an old friend who knows nothing about the area. You want to persuade her to move here. What would you tell her?

> **Visioning establishes a basis upon which residents can work together.**

"We want to strongly suggest that, for the time being, you not list specific projects, programs, or activities. There will be plenty of time later for specifics. Rather, for this session, indicate broad aspects, values, characteristics, and other things that you love.

"At the front of the room is a list of categories to remind you of the kinds of things you may want to list." Point to the list. *"You might say such things as: 'safe streets, enough income for a decent standard of living, clean air, don't have to lock your doors, jobs for young people, supportive neighbors.'*

"Are there any questions?

"Before we start writing down our thoughts, let's brainstorm for a moment. In brainstorming, there are no wrong ideas. One person says her idea, the next person doesn't criticize her thought, he just says his idea.

"What would you mention about the community to convince your cousin to come?"

If people don't raise their hands right away, call on someone who's outgoing. As people begin to respond, also call on those who appear to have something to say but aren't raising their hands. The purpose is to get people thinking broadly about the question. If a participant suggests a specific project or activity, don't negate them in any way. Rather, acknowledge the suggestion by, for instance, indicating that it's an interesting idea. Then ask what reasons, interests, or goals underlie the specific project. Ask why this specific thing is important, what it would achieve, or what it would do for the community.

Brainstorming in this way ensures that the group understands your instructions and, more importantly, allows each participant to hear what others value. This experience builds trust.

In some communities, people are just plain quiet; they may not say anything when you ask the group a question. That's OK, just move on to the written portion of the exercise.

Brainstorm with the group for two or three minutes. Then say: *"One more thing: you may be concerned that the results of these fast-moving exercises are superficial or incomplete. Don't be. There will be plenty of time later to develop complete ideas. OK, you'll have ten minutes, start writing now!"*

After they've been at it for a couple of minutes, say: *"If you're racking your brains for the best idea, consider that someone else may think of it. So just write whatever important things come to mind."*

Warn the group two minutes before time is up. If participants complete their work before time is up, you'll notice that they're looking up or talking. If not, simply announce that time is up. Then say:

*"This list tells us what we want to **preserve** about our community. We've begun to build our preferred future. To complete it, we'll look for what we want to **create**. But before we do that, let's spend about 45 minutes hearing about how other communities have developed themselves in more sustainable ways."*

Worksheet: Our Preferred Future

What I love about my community:

_____

_____

_____

_____

_____

_____

_____

_____

_____

_____

What I would like to change about my community:

_____

_____

_____

_____

_____

_____

When the above things have changed, the community will be like this:

_____

_____

_____

_____

_____

_____

CHAPTER 8

Introduce Economic Renewal

Responsibility for this presentation should be divided among at least two members of the program team. The presentation must be clear and concise. Prior to the meeting, speakers should carefully develop their presentations and practice in front of other team members, accepting constructive criticism.

You can use the speech offered on page 209, or you could derive your own from Chapter 2. Your address will have two major elements: the content of ER (the principles and tools) and the process (the series of town meetings and workshops). Emphasize the content; spend only enough time on the process to make it clear. Consider beginning your presentation like this:

"Economic Renewal is different from the consultant approach to economic development. A consultant would analyze our community and recommend what we should do. But we know best what our community is and what it ought to be. We're the most qualified people to determine our needs, identify our problems, and figure out what to do about them. Economic Renewal offers us the experiences of other towns, but allows us to decide for ourselves what ought to be done.

"However, in taking the responsibility for making our own choices, our role in these meetings must shift from passive observers to active citizens. We can't be couch potatoes. We must use Economic Renewal to spark our own ideas. Without a serious personal effort by each of us to think creatively, we'll just be going through the motions with these meetings.

"Carefully consider each principle and tool in this presentation. Think about ways in which each applies in our community. And please don't stop thinking about them when you leave this room. If you haven't already done so, please pick up a copy of the handout titled "Introduction to Economic Renewal" on your way out. Don't just read it—study it and think about what the community might do differently in light of these ideas."

In your presentation, indicate that Economic Renewal has five purposes:
➤ To develop several projects to improve the local economy.
➤ To improve the community's "can-do" attitude—the feeling that local people can solve local problems.
➤ To expand participation in the community's development effort.
➤ To improve the skills and knowledge of participants.
➤ To ensure that the town's development effort becomes ongoing.

Central to the content of ER are the four principles and nine tools (see pages 17-33). These are best understood through real-life examples, not theory. As you describe the principles and tools, you might ask participants if they can think of local projects or ideas that demonstrate them. This will drive your points home even better, and remind the community of past progress. If it seems appropriate, ask if anyone would like to participate in a

While discussing the community's preferred future, two general themes often come up. First, when participants discuss what they love about the community, they'll often talk with great feeling about the importance of respecting and protecting the traditions, values, and landmarks of the community. Tradition is the glue that binds the community, the things we think about when we're far away.

A second common theme is the need to be open to new ways and new ideas. Participants will point out that change is inevitable, and that the community must either move with the times or risk being passed by.

Sometimes these two themes will be in conflict. For instance, many people may want to keep downtown just the way it is, while others want to change it, maybe add new street lights. If this split arises during your discussions, acknowledge it. Concede the potential for tension, but point out that it can be creative tension. Invite participants to seek ways in which traditions can be preserved while at the same time accepting and accommodating positive change.

A community that views change cautiously is smart. Change for change's sake, or for the benefit of only a few, can damage a community. But a successful community embraces and guides inevitable changes to maximize positive effects. A community is not likely to find success if it accepts any proposal for change that comes along. Neither will it succeed if it automatically rejects new ideas and newcomers. A successful community cautiously and seriously considers new ideas. It encourages people to suggest them, then picks and chooses the changes it wants and makes change work for the community.

CHAPTER 8

discussion group, outside the ER process, to study the principles and tools. Pass around a sign-up sheet for those who indicate interest, and assign a team member to set up the first meeting. You could even have each participant "adopt" the principle or tool that they find most useful or interesting, and talk about it with their friends and neighbors. They'll have plenty of chances to look for ways to apply it during future town meetings.

Look for ways to liven up this presentation. Carol Lamm of the Mountain Association for Community Economic Development, a nonprofit community development corporation in Kentucky, recommends using props to illustrate the four principles in an entertaining way. She uses a leaky bucket to demonstrate "plugging the leaks" and a deflated basketball to portray "supporting (or pumping up) local business." A cheerleader acts out "encouraging new local business." Someone with a fishing pole depicts "recruitment of new businesses by using the right kind of bait to catch the right fish."

Exercise: 'What I Would Like to Change'

By this time, participants will probably be ready for a change of pace. This exercise will get them back in action. For it, they'll be using the flip side of the worksheet used in the first exercise.

Say: *"When we listed what we love about the community, we were, in effect, saying what we want to preserve. Next, to identify what we want to create, we start by saying what we would like to* **change***."*

You might play this next part a little comically: *"Imagine that your in-laws just called. They told you they're thinking about coming to visit. You never much liked your in-laws, but you don't want to offend your spouse by putting them off. Since you want to discourage their coming, think of things that you might tell them—negative, but not unrealistic, impressions of town. If you like your in-laws, think of somebody else you're not crazy about.*

"Think broadly about the things you'd like to change. Include not only more obvious things such as what the community looks and feels like, but also how it makes decisions and deals with conflict. List **what** *about the community should be changed, not* **how** *it should change. For instance, 'High school graduates can't find jobs,' or 'Downtown looks run-down.'*

"For the time being, work just with the top half of your sheet. We'll get to the bottom half in a moment. Any questions? Let's begin writing. You'll have ten minutes."

If you think the group isn't clear on how to proceed, you might want to brainstorm a little, as you did in the previous exercise. Again, give a two-minute warning before announcing time is up.

Exercise: 'When These Things Have Changed...'

Move straight into the third and final preferred-future exercise.

"Now, to identify what we want to **create** *in our community, let's look at the positive side of each of our answers to the previous question. What would the community be like or what would happen if you could change the things you listed? Consider them in order, and list these positive things on the bottom half of your worksheet. When you're done, there will be a close correspondence between the top and bottom halves of the worksheet—for example, if your first answer to the previous question was 'not enough affordable housing,' then your corresponding answer to this question will probably be something like 'adequate affordable housing.'*

"Again, we want to strongly suggest that, for the time being, you not limit yourself to specific projects, programs, or facilities. Rather, consider broad aspects and characteristics of the community.

If you have a specific project in mind, ask yourself why you want it.

*"It's natural to want to focus on specific projects. The problem is that if you jump from your problems to solutions without carefully considering a range of options, you might miss the one that will be successful. It's like saying, 'Ready, fire' instead of 'Ready, **aim**, fire.' The aiming part is essential to avoid shooting yourself in the foot.*

"If you have a specific project or facility in mind, look deeper by asking yourself why you want it. For instance, people in one town were thinking about listing 'parking lot at the corner of Mill and Main,' but then they asked themselves why they wanted it. They ended up listing 'convenient access to downtown business.' Later in the process, someone suggested a new idea for a cheaper, easier way to improve access. If, early in the process, they'd limited themselves to the lot on the corner, then they probably wouldn't have discovered the new idea.

"The arguments that take place in a community are usually about specific projects and proposals. In contrast, people generally agree on most goals and values. If those are identified first, it can lead to projects and programs that no one thought of before and that most people can agree on.

"Any questions? Then let's complete the sheet."

Again, give a two-minute warning before calling time.

General Discussion

At this point a few leading questions can prompt a very positive discussion: *"Did anything come up this evening that surprised you? Do you feel any differently about our potential as a community?*

"Let's hear your ideas about what the town will be like when things have changed for the good."

If a significant number of participants are shy about speaking in a large group, consider breaking them up into smaller groups of perhaps six to twelve people each. In small groups, participants may be less reluctant to speak. They should then report their findings back to the larger group. This extra step adds time, but it allows participants to discover their common ground with others in the community.

At the end of the discussion, tell participants where they should leave their completed handouts. Emphasize: *"Your responses will be incorporated into a single list that will tell us what we want to preserve and what we want to create to achieve our preferred future. We'll bring it back to you at a future meeting for your review."* If you decide to create a vision statement (see page 127), tell participants that you'll bring that back for their review, too.

Wrap-up

Finish the town meeting on an upbeat note. Thank everyone for coming. Talk a little bit about what will happen at the next meeting. Encourage everyone to come. Here's one way to twist their arms:

"There are three groups of people here: those who have decided not to participate further in Economic Renewal, those who are undecided, and those who know that they want to participate, at least in the next meeting. Because we need to plan for that session, can I have a show of hands of people who intend to participate? Let's find out how many want to work together for a better future.

"Great, we'll look forward to seeing you. Remember, when you agree to participate in the next meeting, you're committing only to attend that session. You can decide later whether you want to go further. Please raise your hand if your schedule doesn't allow you to attend the next session, but you'd like to attend later meetings."

Enthusiastically acknowledge and thank those who will attend future sessions. Remind the group that those who don't attend the next meeting are still welcome to participate in later ones. Most important, state the date, time, and location of the next meeting.

After this and all future ER meetings, convene the program team for a quick debriefing—see page 100).

Alternative Agendas

As mentioned earlier, design your ER program to fit your community's particular circumstances. Here are some variations on the standard Step 2 agenda that you might find appropriate.

Make Time for Introductions

Having participants introduce themselves is an excellent way to start off a meeting (see page 97), and this is especially true for the first ER town meeting. Unfortunately, this meeting's agenda is already packed. Squeezing in introductions will probably add a half-hour to an already long meeting. However, you may feel this is an appropriate tradeoff to help get ER off to a smooth start. Maybe recent controversies have made meetings a little awkward, or maybe many participants are newcomers who aren't well known and don't know old-timers.

If you add introductions to your agenda, keep them brief. If each person says much more than name and occupation, the meeting will go on all night.

Two Meetings

If you think participants in your ER process need more time to get to know one another, consider spreading Step 2 over two meetings. The first would consist of an extra-long round of introductions followed by the introduction to Economic Renewal. If you're going to take this extra time, you may wish to ask each person to say, for instance, one thing they love about the community; their statements could be recorded and included in the first preferred-future exercise. The second meeting would include the three preferred-future exercises and, optionally, the "What Will Shape the Community" exercise (see page 128) as an opener. This approach also would allow for more time to discuss the preferred future.

No ER Introduction

If introductions of participants aren't necessary and if everyone has heard enough about Economic Renewal during the mobilization effort, you could dispense with the ER introduction. That will free up enough time to add the "What Will Shape the Community" exercise at the start of the meeting, and enable you to run through the three preferred-future exercises consecutively.

No Preferred-Future Exercises

If your community has conducted some kind of visioning process in the recent past, then you need not conduct the preferred-future exercises. In their place, do the "What Will Shape the Community" exercise. Since you'll still have time to spare, during the introductions you could ask participants to say how the community would be if it were just the way they wanted. This will provide the opportunity for participants to hear one another's values and begin building trust without the complete three-exercise process.

Two Preferred Futures

If your community is so deeply divided by controversy that it's difficult to get rival factions together in the same room, conduct the preferred-future exercises separately with each "side." Next, with the help of a few diplomatic volunteers from each side, unify the preferred-future lists of each. Then, develop two lists—one noting the similarities between the two factions, the other noting the differences. You'll probably find far more similarities than differences. Last, call a meeting of both factions to report your findings. Follow your report with a group discussion of the similarities. Ask participants if they find the results surprising, and if they think they might be able to work together to achieve the goals that they agree on, temporarily setting aside their disagreements.

Small-Group Meetings

If you'd like to enable participants to envision the community's preferred future in a more thorough and memorable way, schedule about ten separate small-group meetings in advance of the town-wide meeting. The composition of the small groups might be based on neighborhood location, political affiliation, association with some way of thinking, or a cross-section of views. Conduct the three preferred-future exercises with each group and unify their responses into a draft preferred-future list to be presented at the first ER town meeting. Town meeting participants could then suggest what to add, remove, or emphasize. This approach requires a skillful facilitator who can deflect confrontation without angering people. It also entails a greater time commitment by the program team and other volunteers.

Before the Next Meeting

There's a lot to do before the next meeting. Volunteers can do most of it, but it's the program team's responsibility to make sure the tasks get done.

Get More Responses for the Preferred Future (Optional)

In all likelihood, your preferred-future exercises generated a healthy range of responses. But if you feel you could use some more input, consider soliciting additional responses from individuals and groups who didn't attend the town meeting.

Don't make too much work for yourself—stick to groups that are relatively easy to contact, such as teachers, students, and downtown business people. Distribute copies of the "Our Preferred Future" worksheet at their meetings or assemblies, and give at least a minimal explanation of the exercises' purpose. Invite members to attend future ER town meetings. Don't forget to report back to each group with the final preferred-future results.

Unify the Preferred-Future Lists

The main task that must be accomplished before the next meeting is to unify all the individual responses to the three preferred-future questions into a single list. This procedure will take roughly one hour for each twenty worksheets. Three competent volunteers will be needed.

Start with thirteen blank sheets of paper, one for each of the eleven categories you displayed during the meeting ("Arts," "Built Environment," etc.) plus two extras, "Miscellaneous" and "Project Ideas." Divide the category sheets between two of the volunteers. Have the third volunteer read out each response from the participants' worksheets. As each item is read, one of the two volunteers will write it under the appropriate category. Responses that don't fit clearly in one of the original eleven categories should go under "Miscellaneous." Those that relate to specific things that someone believes the community should build or do should be listed separately under "Project Ideas."

Each item should be worded to indicate the way participants want the community to be. The resulting master list will consist primarily of things people want to preserve (responses to the first preferred-future question) and the things they want to create (responses to the third question). Responses to the second question will tend to drop out. Some responses will have to be reworded. For instance, "more positive feeling in town" or "people shouldn't be so negative" might be reworded to read "positive community attitude." Both "clean up downtown" and "sweep the dirty sidewalks" might be reworded to read "clean downtown."

Take your time. When you get stuck on an item, discuss the range of possible ways to say it. During the exercises, participants correctly wrote things that came to mind without carefully considering them. Therefore, there will be many items that may not belong in the preferred future. You'll need to judge whether to include these. They may be items that advocate a particular position or are funny, sarcastic, or trivial. You might want to enter some on a separate list for a record of items that are "Probably Not Part of Our Preferred Future." But be careful: don't eliminate items just because you disagree with them.

Look for ways to reduce the total number of items to a manageable list of, say, thirty or forty. Eliminate duplication: when you come across an item that you think you've already covered, don't write it again. Your preferred-future list will consist of all the items listed under the first twelve categories. (The "Project Ideas" category shouldn't be included in the preferred-future list, but should be saved for Step 5, "Generating Project Ideas.") When it's complete, present this draft list at a future ER meeting and ask participants to ratify it. The ratified list will serve as a distillation of residents' shared vision for the community, and an inspiring foundation for the next meeting. Later, in Step 7 (see Chapter 13), it will provide guidance for the selection of project ideas.

Create a Vision Statement (Optional)

A well-written and concise "vision statement" (or "preferred-future statement" or "community goals statement") can be a powerful unifying force in a community, and provide the philosophical basis for the rest of the ER process. It can be the rallying point for greater and more collaborative citizen participation. People who've never been involved can become enthusiastic players in community affairs.

If you decide to translate your preferred-future list into a vision statement, find one or two local people who are good wordsmiths and willing to take on a challenge. Ask them to read the preferred-future list and compose its overarching ideals in a single statement, which can be any length from a paragraph to several pages. The vision statement for Fort Mill, South Carolina is five pages long and covers eight topics such as culture, education, and housing. A shorter vision statement may be more difficult to write, but it also may be more effective for inspiring community action.

Here's an excellent example of a short vision statement created in 1995 by a cooperative effort of 25 neighborhoods in inner-city Atlanta:

A Vision to Create an Urban Village Within Atlanta

Our vision is of an "Urban Village" working cooperatively to improve the quality of life and conditions of our neighborhoods, with an emphasis on "sustainable development" that is economically and ecologically sound. We seek to empower and inspire members of our neighborhoods, especially our children and youth, to develop effective responses to the needs of our community and to promote cooperation, collaboration and partnership with social service agencies, government and the private sector to create livable communities. We also seek to positively impact the social, economic and spiritual development of our neighborhoods and city. A priority of our zone is providing safe, decent and affordable housing. Our vision can become a reality when our community becomes a cooperative village, an extended family, that is self-reliant, self-sufficient and self-determined.

Ask program team members to review and comment on the draft statement. When the program team is comfortable with it, offer it to ER participants for approval at a future ER town meeting. Once approved, it can be distributed to participants and displayed at the front of the meeting room. You could also try to get it published in the newspaper or ask important local organizations such as the town council and the chamber of commerce to adopt it as community policy.

Publicize the Next Meeting

You'll probably have to work just as hard to ensure good attendance for the second meeting (and all remaining meetings) as you did for this one. Again, personal phone calls work best. Distribute news releases, public service announcements, and (optionally) leaflets and posters to publicize the next meeting and any others already scheduled.

Other preparations for the next meeting are detailed on page 130. Be sure to recruit the extra facilitators that will be needed.

EXERCISE: 'WHAT WILL SHAPE THE COMMUNITY' (OPTIONAL)

This optional exercise is fun and moves very quickly.

Distribute copies of a single sheet of paper headed, "What three things will shape the community over the next ten years?" The only other writing on the handout should be lines below the question for participants to fill in their responses. To help this exercise begin efficiently, distribute the sheets to participants as they come in the room.

Say: *"Let's do an exercise that will focus on the future of our community. It will also be fun. It's intended to get your first impressions, so it'll be done quick-*

ly. You have in front of you a sheet titled 'What three things will shape the community over the next ten years?' OK, I want you to quickly jot down the three things. Begin now!"

Give them one minute to write. Then say: *"In a moment, you'll pass your sheet to the person on your left. Then take the sheet from the person on your right and quickly circle the one factor on their sheet that you believe is most likely to shape the future. You'll have five seconds. OK, pass the sheet."*

Give them five seconds to circle. The room will be chaotic, but that's OK. Then say: *"Now pass the sheet to your left again. Take the sheet handed to you and again circle the factor that you believe is most likely to shape the future."*

Some participants will want to take longer. In a good-natured way, insist that they move along. Again, give them five seconds.

"Now return all papers to their original author. You have seen two sheets in addition to your own. On these sheets you and your neighbors have begun to focus on the strongest factors facing your community. What are some of the influences? Do most of these influences come from inside or outside the community? Did you find items on other people's sheets similar to your own?"

For just a few minutes, call on people who raise their hands in response to your questions. If no one raises a hand, spot some gregarious person and ask them to start the discussion. You might record these responses on a flip-chart. You might ask participants to raise their hands if they listed items similar to the ones stated.

Summarize the responses. People's ideas may diverge widely, but probably no more than half a dozen factors will be consistently mentioned. Acknowledge the common perceptions of influences on the community. Also indicate your thoughts as to whether the influences are primarily external or internal. They'll probably be largely external.

Say: *"The influences on any town's economy are both from outside and inside the community. We may be able to change the external factors, but that's tough. For example, it's very difficult to change the price of electricity—but we can definitely determine how much of it we use. That's why Economic Renewal focuses primarily on the things we can affect directly—the internal factors.*

"A big problem can be discouraging or challenging. It's discouraging when we think that we can't do anything about it. But it's challenging and exciting when we can get a grip on it—when we understand the problem and have the tools to solve it. Economic Renewal can provide the means to solve the problem.

"Recent studies show that the most important ingredients of any community's success are attitude and commitment. In contrast, conventional development thinking assumes that to achieve success, a town must first have such things as a railhead, a nearby interstate, brochures, business parks, and tax-incentive programs. Sure, these things can help, but knowing we can improve our community, and committing to act on that knowledge—that's the key to success. Healthy businesses grow out of a healthy community attitude."

Step 3: Identifying What You Have to Work With

This is an essential step in any community development process, but one that's all too often skipped over. Though participants may be chomping at the bit to get on with it, they have to identify problems before looking for solutions, and they have to identify assets before knowing what they can use to solve the problems.

This is the first serious analytical work participants will tackle. And though it generates crucial information about the local economy, this step is important for another reason: it sets the tone for the rest of the Economic Renewal process. When it goes smoothly, participants gain confidence in both ER and the community's prospects.

Though the procedure is straightforward, it takes a little getting used to. You'll divide participants up into seven small groups, each of which will look at the community from a different angle: access to capital, business environment, human resources, the informal economy, infrastructure, natural resources, and quality of life. Focusing on one of these seven community factors, each group will brainstorm to come up with all the community's problems, needs, and assets they can think of. This information will be used in the next step to determine what the community might do to strengthen itself. This work will require participants to take a good hard look at their community and overcome myths and preconceptions.

The seven groups will be guided by volunteer facilitators, whom you will train in a short session prior to the main meeting. They'll also draw on advice and leading questions given in a series of "factor summaries" at the end of this chapter.

Preparations and Materials

Study this chapter and the "Preparations" section in Chapter 6 before the meeting. Make sure that you know exactly what you're going to cover so that you can move through it efficiently. Otherwise, it will take longer and participants will begin to wonder if they're wasting their time.

Decide whether to provide flip-charts for each factor group. A flip-chart display assures participants that their comments are being recorded appropriately, but rounding up seven flip-charts and easels means extra work (newspaper roll-ends come in handy here—see page 95). Alternatively, recorders could write ideas down on a spare copy of the "What Our Community Has to Work With" worksheet, and participants could look over the recorder's shoulder for reassurance.

Make copies of the "What Our Community Has to Work With" worksheet and the factor summaries at the end of this chapter. You'll need

➤ Opening remarks *(20 minutes)*
➤ Introduce factors and the worksheet *(5 minutes)*
➤ Exercise: "What Our Community Has to Work With"
  (60 minutes)
➤ Discussion *(5–20 minutes)*
➤ Wrap-up *(2 minutes)*

enough copies of the worksheet to give one to every participant. Make as many copies of each factor summary as you think there will be participants in that group (bear in mind that some groups will be more heavily attended than others).

On a single flip-chart sheet, write:

Factor	Group Instructions
Group:	- Pick recorder
On your own:	- Read factor summary
	- Write your ideas
Group:	- Brainstorm ideas
	- Record ideas
Recorder:	- Transcribe to flip-chart

Prepare another flip-chart sheet that says:

Economic Factors
➤ Access to Capital
➤ Business Environment
➤ Human Resources
➤ Informal Economy
➤ Infrastructure
➤ Natural Resources
➤ Quality of Life

Assemble written examples of community economic success stories: *The Business Opportunities Casebook* (see page 220) is one excellent source. You may find additional sources in your own town or through your state's development office or university extension service. Look also in magazines such as farm, fishing, and rural-development periodicals (for example, *Small Town*). Make several copies of each and stack them on or near your greeting table with a sign that says something like, "Success Stories for Your Reading."

In both this step and the next, you'll ask participants to read these materials. But regardless of your persuasive abilities, people will have a strong tendency not to not get around to reading them. If leaving handouts at the greeting table seems too passive for your community, try a more active approach. Have members of the program team read the materials and pick fifteen or twenty examples that best fit your community. Then, at the end of this meeting, read out the title of each case and ask for volunteers to read them and report to the group at the beginning of Step 5 ("Generating Project Ideas"). These reports would form one basis for project ideas in that step. Program teams have found this approach to be particularly valuable in communities with high illiteracy.

The best space for this meeting is one in which chairs can be rearranged easily and the groups can be separated enough so they don't disturb each other. High-school gyms and cafeterias work well. Prior to the meeting, set up seven tables, each big enough to seat up to ten people. Have more tables and chairs on hand in case you need them. Prepare simple signs for each factor, to be placed on the tables when participants re-seat themselves in their small groups.

Choosing and Briefing Facilitators

Prior to the meeting, select seven to fourteen people to facilitate the factor groups. Seek out people who are good listeners and sensitive to others. Don't recruit people who have short tempers or who like to throw their weight around and tell others what to do. Facilitation is a good task for people with very limited time who want to be actively and publicly involved in Economic Renewal. Facilitator skills are described in Chapter 6 ("Conducting Effective Meetings").

Distribute one copy of this chapter and Chapter 6 to each facilitator several days before the session. If you can do so without making them feel overburdened, also give facilitators a copy of Chapter 2 ("Introduction to Economic Renewal"). Tell them it's essential that they read the materials before the session. In particular, call their attention to the instructions on pages 140-1.

Schedule a briefing session for the facilitators about one hour before the start of the main meeting. This session need not be formal nor particularly structured—all you need to do is review this chapter, giving special attention to the "Instructions for Factor-Group Facilitators" section. If you have more time, discuss Chapter 6. Ask people what worked in meetings they've attended, what didn't, and what could have been done differently. Everyone can contribute ideas about how to conduct more effective meetings.

The Meeting

A certain amount of flexibility and creativity is required to get through Economic Renewal meeting agendas. Because many people will have lots to say, each agenda item can easily go on for more than its allotted time. The facilitator's responsibility is to get the work completed without going into overtime, while at the same time ensuring that all participants feel as if they've been heard.

This meeting consists mainly of a single exercise, "What Our Community Has to Work With." Though you may decide that you don't need the full sixty minutes suggested for this exercise, do ensure that participants have sufficient time to creatively carry it out and say what's important to them. The more efficiently you run the early portion of the meeting, the more time you'll have for the potentially very valuable discussion at the end.

Opening Remarks

Welcome participants and briefly introduce everyone who will help conduct the meeting. Acknowledge everyone else who has helped make the meeting possible: volunteers, program sponsors, and program funders, if any. Review the agenda. Make any necessary announcements. Tell people the location of rest rooms, handle parking issues, etc. Indicate how long the meeting is expected to last.

Briefly outline what was covered in the first ER town meeting, review the ER process, and describe where this meeting fits into it. While you may have covered much of this information at previous meetings, it's a helpful reminder, especially for those attending for the first time.

Assuming your community carried out the preferred-future exercises during the previous step, you might say the following: *Take a moment and look around at the other people in the room, particularly those whom you may have regarded as your adversaries in the past. As a result of the last meeting, do you feel any differently about these folks? Do they seem less like your enemies and more like people you respect but just happen to disagree with on a few points? Maybe not, maybe you don't feel any differently. That's fine. But if you do, notice how it affects your reaction to their comments. Notice if you have a different per-*

Keen observation of your community generates rich information about what you have to work with.

spective on what they say. If you feel differently about them, then a trust is beginning to be built. That trust is a powerful basis for community problem-solving. It also makes this work we're doing a lot more productive and fun. One great thing to do when you get a chance is to tell them how your perception of them has changed."

Ask if anyone has any thoughts or questions based on the previous meeting's work. Indicate that you'd like the program team to assemble briefly following this session. Describe the purpose and procedure of this meeting. Allow time for questions.

Introduce the factor-group facilitators, explaining that they've volunteered to learn this step in the process in more detail to help ensure that the meeting is productive and short. Say that the session will work best if all participants help the facilitators keep the discussion moving and provide an opportunity for participation by everyone present.

Introduce the Factors

Say: *"By viewing the community through the 'lenses' of several community 'factors,' we'll create a pool of information that provides vital background for determining what the community needs to strengthen itself.*

"In a few minutes, we'll ask you to divide up into small groups, each of which will examine one of these factors: access to capital, business environment, human resources, the informal economy, infrastructure, natural resources, and quality of life. Think about which group you'd like to be part of. After we've divided up into groups, volunteers will hand out brief texts explaining each factor in more detail." Ask participants if they have any questions about the factors.

You may wish to ask certain people, or people with certain occupations or interests, to join particular groups. For example, local bankers are obvious candidates for discussing access to capital; the town manager could greatly help the infrastructure group.

Participants are divided into groups for three reasons: first, shy people participate more in small groups; second, it spreads out the work; and third, it's more comfortable to focus on one aspect of the economy rather than its intimidating whole. However, though this chapter assumes that you'll divide into small groups, you may wish to examine all factors as a single group, particularly if there are fewer than twenty participants. This approach, of course, will take longer.

Introduce the Worksheet

Hand out the "What Our Community Has to Work With" worksheet. It's a very simple worksheet, but it contains three terms that will require some explanation.

*"**Assets** are resources that can be put to work for a stronger community. They include physical resources, such as fertile soil or timber, as well as less tangible*

qualities, skills, talents, and unique characteristics that don't show up on traditional balance sheets. They may include the most precious and least quantifiable asset of all, 'social capital'—that is, a capacity to work together that is based on rich networks of community relationships.

"One way to think about our assets is to contrast them with those of nearby towns. This may reveal potential ways of maximizing the community's comparative advantage in terms of resources, assets, and skills.

*"By **problems**, we mean any kind of obstacle to a better community. Problems can be huge and fundamental, or specific and detailed; they may have to do with the way things are built or run, or the way business is conducted, or the way decisions are made. You probably won't have to rack your brains too hard over that one.*

*"For the purpose of this exercise, we'll be focusing on underlying **needs**, not the specific projects or programs that might fulfill those needs. For example, 'small-business management training' is a specific project idea that might come later—the underlying need is 'a way to improve local business management,' which might be fulfilled in various ways. This distinction is important because, if we home in on one particular way to fulfill a need at this early point in the process, we might overlook other, better options that would otherwise emerge in later steps."*

Another way to get this point across is to say: *"With this exercise, we inventory what we have now, not what we hope to get in the future. That will come later. When you identify a problem or need, try to look deeper to see what underlies it. Ask why a particular problem exists in order to attack causes, instead of merely treating symptoms."*

Exercise: 'What Our Community Has to Work With'

Place the signs on the tables, announce which factor will be discussed at each table, and ask participants to move to the table of their choice. The program team may need to help this re-seating process. If someone has trouble deciding, suggest that they join a group that has relatively few members.

Keep the groups small. If they include more than ten people, you should probably divide them into smaller groups, which will mean more than one group will discuss some of the factors. You may have to break out more tables and make more signs. If one group contains only a few people, request that others consider joining it.

During the re-seating process, deliver the appropriate factor summaries to each group.

As participants find their new seats, they'll start lots of side conversations. If you turn the groups over to their facilitators prior to re-seating, all the noise and confusion will make it difficult for facilitators to bring their groups to order. Therefore, as soon as the groups have formed themselves,

Worksheet: What our Community Has to Work With

Our Assets:

_____

_____

_____

_____

_____

_____

_____

_____

_____

_____

_____

_____

_____

Our Problems:

_____

_____

_____

_____

_____

_____

_____

Our Needs:

_____

_____

_____

_____

_____

_____

_____

ask for everyone's attention for further instructions. Amidst all the noise, you may need to do something funny or loud, like whistling, to get their attention.

Refer participants to the flip-chart sheet titled "Factor Group Instructions." Indicate that they can refer back to these instructions as they proceed with their work.

Ask the groups to choose recorders—volunteers who will record each group's ideas. Give them a minute to do it, then call them back to order. If progress is slow, you might have to intervene. For example, you could name a date and say that the person in each group with the birthday closest to it will do the task.

Next, ask participants to read quietly through the factor summary. Explain that the questions in the summary aren't meant to be answered, they're simply meant to stimulate creative thinking. Say that, when they've finished reading, they can use the worksheet to write down their ideas about the community's problems, needs, and assets specific to their chosen factor. Say that the ideas they write at this point are for their own reference. They'll be able to refer to their worksheets during the group discussion that follows. Then give them no more than fifteen minutes to quietly read, think, and write. This time helps focus each person's attention on the work at hand. Ensure that it remains quiet.

At the end of the quiet time, indicate a completion time for their group work, then turn them over to their facilitators.

As the groups proceed with their work, circulate around the room to see if each is running smoothly. If you think a facilitator needs help, ask her or him if you can offer a suggestion. The facilitator will probably say yes, but notice if he or she resents your intrusion and act accordingly.

Give ten- and five-minute warnings before you want the groups to stop. Make sure each facilitator is aware of your announcements. Then bring the work of the groups to a halt. You'll probably have to cut off some discussions while participants are still talking.

Feel free to call an end to the discussion ahead of your scheduled time if the groups have healthy lists of items (maybe ten to twenty in each section) and if participants seem to be straining to find new ideas. Otherwise, some participants will become frustrated or bored.

Say: *"Each group will transcribe its findings to flip-chart sheets for use at the next ER town meeting."*

Discussion and Wrap-up

If you have time left, conduct a discussion of the findings. For instance, you might ask participants what new information they learned or special insights they gained, what they found that was unusual or exciting, or how they think this exercise was useful.

To wrap up, thank participants for generating a solid base of information. Explain that it will be used in the next meeting to discover the hidden potential in the local economy. At that time, they'll look for ways that the assets they identified can help fix the town's problems or meet its needs. This explanation is very important. It reassures participants that their work is leading methodically to useful conclusions; it gives them a better reason to attend the next meeting.

Ask for a show of hands to see who will attend the next meeting.

Urge participants to take home and read one or more copies of the community success stories that are stacked on the greeting table. Indicate how crucial it is that they study at least one of these handouts and that they reread Chapter 2, which also contains success stories. You might say: *"We offer these readings, not just as a side dish, but as an essential ingredient to the main course that we're all working together to prepare. No one is going to hand us good ideas for developing our community. In order for this process to work, we must take an active role in finding our own ideas. These readings offer examples of successes elsewhere, some of which are probably adaptable to our situation. So read them and think carefully how they might apply here. We'll use your creative ideas in future meetings.*

"Talk about this meeting with your friends, neighbors, and co-workers. Encourage them to attend the next meeting." Announce the date, time, and place for the next meeting.

After the meeting, poll participants to see how they felt about its format and style, and take their comments on board as you prepare for the next one.

Before the Next Meeting

Sometime before the next meeting, the program team and factor-group facilitators will need to summarize each group's findings and transcribe them onto large sheets of flip-chart paper. (You could let the recorders or facilitators do this on their own, but if you go this route, follow up to make sure they bring the transcribed results to the next meeting—if they don't, you'll be up the creek.)

The success of the next step depends on the transcribed results being well prepared. They must be legible from ten or fifteen feet away. In small letters at the top, indicate whether each sheet lists problems, needs, or assets. There's no need to label the sheets by factor, because all sheets will be grouped as problems, needs, or assets, regardless of which group generated them.

Find points that can be summarized or grouped. The purpose of this important task is to reduce the lists to a manageable number of items and to highlight the less obvious and more interesting findings. Make note of common themes. For example, you might find that four of the seven groups noted "lack of funding" as a problem. This exercise will require judgment calls on your part.

Determine who will conduct the next ER town meeting and ask them to prepare for it. To ensure adequate attendance, publicize the meeting through the media and call all potential participants well in advance.

INSTRUCTIONS FOR FACTOR-GROUP FACILITATORS

Your responsibilities during this meeting are to serve the group, keep the discussion fair, organized, and on purpose, and ensure that the worksheets are completed. Before the session begins, develop a few of your own ideas for assets, problems, and needs so that you can offer these as examples if needed.

As soon as you sit down with your group, start thinking about who would make a good recorder. Look for a bright individual who can comfortably and competently record the findings of the group. Ask that person to volunteer to record when the main facilitator brings it up. It's generally not a good idea for you to do the recording, as you'll have your hands full facilitating the discussion.

The main facilitator will then ask participants to read through their respective factor summaries and begin writing down ideas. Your job begins now.

At a point in time suggested by the main facilitator, ask participants to stop working on their own and begin offering their ideas verbally. Be prepared to offer one or two suggestions if they don't respond right away. If they don't seem to be coming up with ideas, refer them to the questions in the factor summary. Ask the recorder to write group members' ideas on the worksheet, or on a flip-chart if one is provided. You may need to remind participants that the questions in the factor summaries aren't meant to be answered on the worksheet, they're only meant to stimulate thinking.

When considering needs, participants will probably suggest a few ideas for projects or programs. When someone offers this kind of suggestion, ensure that it's recorded on a separate "project ideas" list, but ask what community problem the project might solve or what need it might fulfill. Remind the group that the purpose of this exercise is to inventory what the community *has*, not what it wants or hopes to get. If, at this early stage, the group jumps ahead to focus on solutions rather than problems, then it may miss opportunities that might otherwise emerge. Don't be critical, but do encourage the group to dig deeper.

The group will tend to get bogged down in details or digressions. If you let them, they may spend twenty minutes discussing one point. Remember, it's up to you to keep the session moving. This is an inventory, not a detailed exploration. Get one idea down on paper and move on to the next.

When someone talks for a long time, the group will tend to lose direction and forget what it's supposed to be doing. If digressions occur, respectfully remind the group of its purpose and that it needs to get back to completing the task at hand. However, if it appears that digressions might lead to useful project ideas, make note of the ideas for future reference.

When participants offer complex or lengthy ideas, find a brief phrase that sums up the thought so that the brief version can be recorded on the worksheet. But check with the person who made the original suggestion to ensure that the shorter form is acceptable. Another volunteer can record the full idea to ensure its preservation.

As participants move through their worksheets they may indicate that they need more information about certain topics. Record these questions, then ask participants who would like to find the information and report back to the group.

Your group's list of ideas might not be as long as some had hoped or as long as those of other groups. That's fine. Participants shouldn't feel obligated to produce a comprehensive list. Their responsibility here is to be creative, not exhaustive.

From time to time, the main facilitator will announce how much time remains. When he or she calls ten- and five-minute warnings, start wrapping up the work of your group. This kind of discussion can continue indefinitely if you let it. Someone is going to have to cut it off sometime. Support the main facilitator in doing so.

CHAPTER 9

Access to Capital

The availability of money at affordable interest rates and terms has a major effect on development. Adequate seed capital and financing enable existing businesses to thrive, allow new businesses to start up, and attract expanding businesses from elsewhere in the region.

When a community keeps more money at home, the money recirculates, increasing the local "multiplier effect." It creates more value, pays more wages, finances more investments, and ultimately creates more local economic opportunity.

The projects that we identify during this development effort may require money. The people responsible for writing the checks—loan officers, foundation program officers, government agency people, investors, and private donors—all want to be winners just as much as anybody else. They win when they support winning projects. Economic development projects, whether private, public, or nonprofit, are far more likely to be winners if we've carefully scrutinized them and they're enthusiastically supported by the community. They stand a much better chance of securing funding than a project developed by one or a few people.

Use the following questions to help you fill out your worksheet, though not all will apply to our community. Don't fill out the worksheet with answers to the questions. Rather, use them to stimulate your thinking:

➤ Think about the checks you write regularly. How many of them go out of town?
➤ Where do most residents bank? Where do they deposit their savings?
➤ Does a lot of money leave the community for insurance premiums or investments in pension funds and municipal bonds?
➤ What are the financial needs of local businesses?
➤ Are business loans readily available in the community?
➤ Do local banks tend to support innovative projects, or only the kinds of projects they've always funded?
➤ What types of businesses tend to receive loans? Which do not? Are they starting up, expanding, or relocating?
➤ Do existing businesses use federal and state loan programs?
➤ What institutions provide capital?
➤ Are loan terms and rates better or worse here than other places?
➤ Is capital available through state or regional programs?
➤ Besides local banks, are there other sources of capital?
➤ Are private investors interested in investing in expanding or new businesses?
➤ Are venture capitalists interested in providing capital to types of business that the community might be trying to attract?

Business Environment

"Business environment" can be as tangible as local government regulations or as intangible as the attitude of the community and businesses toward one another. Stability and consistency form the foundation of any healthy business environment. A community with fair and predictable regulations will provide a far better business environment than one with only a few regulations that are applied erratically.

The excitement generated by efforts to strengthen the local economy is often contagious. Investment and reinvestment breeds confidence that often leads to more business development and a renewed commitment by existing businesses to stay. On the other hand, pessimism regarding the economy and business failures makes businesses hold back on most investment plans or consider relocating.

Though a supportive business environment often means reasonable commercial rents, business assistance, shared services, and links to financing sources, many business owners maintain that their business success is due largely to community support. Consumers are often loyal to reliable and friendly local business.

Use the following questions to help you fill out your worksheet, though not all will apply to our community. Don't fill out the worksheet with answers to the questions. Rather, use them to stimulate your thinking:

➤ What is the general level of business activity in the community?
➤ Are many businesses failing? What types? Why?
➤ What businesses have decided to relocate out of town? Why? What steps can be taken to correct the situation?
➤ Given current trends, do you foresee local employment prospects improving or diminishing for your children?
➤ Do local business people and entrepreneurs feel they have a supportive business environment?
➤ Are residents loyal to local businesses? Why or why not?
➤ Which community organizations support new business?
➤ How are relations between business and labor?
➤ Are local groups collaborating for better business conditions?
➤ What is the current attitude of local government toward business? Has it changed in the past few years?
➤ What local conditions impede new businesses formation?
➤ Do local business people have the skills necessary to succeed? What would help them acquire those skills?

Human Resources

More than any other aspect of a community, it's people that determine its success. A community made up of creative, educated, committed, enthusiastic, open-minded people who are willing to take calculated risks is unstoppable. It will succeed despite other major difficulties and deficiencies.

Creativity requires a willingness to discuss important decisions openly, to question basic assumptions, and to consider new ways to preserve the values and traditions that are so important to communities. Enthusiasm and commitment are maintained by the support and acknowledgment of volunteers and the encouragement of new ideas and leadership. Open-mindedness and risk-taking can be fostered by leaders who encourage alternative points of view. Community decision-making is at its most creative when it involves the broadest possible participation, careful consideration, and a minimum of name-calling.

Education and retraining of children and adults is crucial to community prosperity. It helps residents secure the jobs that result from economic success. It supplies business with qualified employees.

Use the following questions to help you fill out your worksheet, though not all will apply to our community. Don't fill out the worksheet with answers to the questions. Rather, use them to stimulate your thinking:

- ➤ Does the community encourage new leadership?
- ➤ Does the community support volunteers?
- ➤ What would it take to get more and different people involved in community affairs?
- ➤ Do local civic and interest groups work together? What services do they provide to the community?
- ➤ Are there residents—especially retirees—with valuable skills who aren't yet involved in the community's development, education, and training efforts?
- ➤ Are most residents working in jobs that take full advantage of their skills? What are the opportunities for advancement?
- ➤ What sorts of people are unemployed? Are they receiving job training? What skills are they learning? What other training might benefit them?
- ➤ What about the underemployed? What are their skills? How can they better employ their skills?
- ➤ How good is the match between job skills and job opportunities?
- ➤ What types of jobs are hard to fill? Can residents fill them?
- ➤ Can local schools play a role in supporting potential business people or in training workers?
- ➤ Do local businesses support employee benefits (child care, health insurance, maternity and paternity leave)?
- ➤ Are there any human-service needs that are unfulfilled?
- ➤ Have the beneficiaries of human-service expansions (for instance, expansions of police, fire, or school services) paid all the costs? Or have expansion costs been borne by residents who didn't require the expansion?

Informal Economy

The informal economy consists of all activities that exchange or collect goods and services without the use of money. Its foundation is subsistence activities—those that meet basic needs without being accounted on a ledger, such as hunting, fishing, gathering, gardening, clothes-making, home-building, carpooling, even solar heating. Barter—trading goods and services—is another important part of the informal economy in many communities. (The informal economy shouldn't be confused with the illegal economy, which involves illicit products and services, and the underground economy, which involves legal transactions that are illegally withheld from tax authorities.)

Informal commerce plays a far greater role in the local economy than is often thought. One researcher surveyed informal economic activities in Crown Point, New York, a town of 1,900 people. All told, the informal economy was economically equivalent to 100 jobs—a portion of the community's overall economy far too large to be ignored. Whether it's working on someone's car in exchange for them doing your taxes or trading beef for vegetables, the informal economy is an important part of many people's lives. It's especially prevalent in communities where residents have a history of working together.

The informal economy is sometimes erroneously identified with low-income people. In fact, it reduces the income needs of many middle-income people who, for instance, collect their own firewood or grow their own food. Even sharing vacation cabins is part of the informal economy.

In many cases, the informal economy builds self-worth, preserves culture, brings families together, reduces transportation requirements, reduces paperwork, augments retirement income, complements seasonal or intermittent employment, or takes up the slack when someone loses a living-wage job and finds only low-paying jobs.

Use the following questions to help you fill out your worksheet, though not all will apply to our community. Don't fill out the worksheet with answers to the questions. Rather, use them to stimulate your thinking:

> Is informal economic activity declining or increasing? Why?
> What products and services are traded or bartered in the community?
> What might be done to make informal economic activities easier?
> Are informal economic activities causing the unsustainable use of any local resources?
> Identify any barriers to informal economic activity (e.g. rules, ownership).
> In what ways can unemployed people more fully participate in the informal economy?
> Are there residents operating in the informal economy who would like to start their own businesses in the formal economy?
> If so, what barriers do they face?
> Do informal economic activities affect local businesses?
> Are there ways in which local resources were once used, but are no longer being used, for the informal economy? Could these be tried again?
> What educational opportunities are present in the community? Are they being used to help the informal economy?
> Is there any potential for people involved in informal economic activities to buy or trade cooperatively?
> Does the community encourage or discourage informal economic activities?

Infrastructure

Adequate roads, water, sewer, energy services, and communications systems are crucial to local business and residences. Sound and well-maintained infrastructure helps keep businesses in town and attracts new and expanding businesses. But it requires costly maintenance and replacement. Though some parts of a community's infrastructure may be privately owned (for example, electric utilities), most is built and maintained by local governments and districts. Knowing which parts of the infrastructure are most important to existing, expanding, and relocating businesses can help order capital improvements and maintenance priorities.

An emerging concern in expanding towns is that tax revenues generated by community expansion are often insufficient to pay the costs of the public services (including infrastructure) demanded by it. As a result, existing taxpayers often unwittingly subsidize much community expansion, especially the residential subdivision of unoccupied land. This is because local government spreads the costs of expansion among all taxpayers rather than charging only those who create the costs. This is often, in effect, a subsidy from the whole community to those responsible for the expansion.

Use the following questions to help you fill out your worksheet, though not all will apply to our community. Don't fill out the worksheet with answers to the questions. Rather, use them to stimulate your thinking:

> ➤ How does the cost and condition of infrastructure affect local businesses and families?
> ➤ What is the current condition of the community's infrastructure?
> ➤ Are certain elements of the infrastructure worse than others? Which ones?
> ➤ Which areas of infrastructure need the most improvement?
> ➤ In the last five years, how has the community invested in its infrastructure?
> ➤ Have the beneficiaries of infrastructure expansions paid all the costs? Or have expansion costs been paid by residents who didn't need expansion?
> ➤ Are your taxes increasing to pay the costs of someone else's infrastructure? Do you benefit in ways that compensate for your increased taxes?
> ➤ Do the local governments and districts who provide infrastructure understand the costs and revenues generated by expansion?
> ➤ Have any business people expressed concern over the community's public facilities? If so, which ones?
> ➤ How do the infrastructure needs of businesses and residents compare?
> ➤ Should the community borrow money for improvements?
> ➤ Is expansion of existing facilities the only way to maintain service, or would repair and renovation get the job done?
> ➤ Can demand on infrastructure be reduced through efficiency improvements?
> ➤ Can municipal workers assist in the design and construction of new infrastructure, instead of outside contractors?
> ➤ Is the community trying to attract businesses that will require the expansion of existing services or facilities? If so, who will pay the costs?

Natural Resources

Forests, wildlife, grasslands, minerals, soil, water, and air are the foundation of many community economies. The harvest of timber and wildlife, grazing of livestock, growth in the soil, removal of minerals and petroleum, use of water, and aesthetic appreciation of the natural world (i.e., tourism) are traditional sources of jobs and income.

For many years, these resources were carefully husbanded by rural people who lived and toiled with them, and understood their workings in detail. These people realized that if natural resources were used unwisely, the livelihood of future generations would be jeopardized. But more recently these resources have been depleted in many places, often by people who cared little for the communities that depended upon them. In some cases, depletion has been so gradual, and the effects of depletion so subtle, that even caring people haven't noticed that their community's foundation was slowly but surely eroding.

Even communities that have carefully managed their resources have suffered economic decline due to world markets that imposed tough and sometimes unfair competition. Volatile economic and political events have tormented many resource-based communities to the point that they feel they must fight just to stay alive. Unfortunately, many of them focus on who they can blame for their troubles rather than what to do to succeed in a rapidly changing world. Some communities have depleted their resources to the point of exhaustion and will surely decline. But other creative communities are learning how to harvest their traditional natural resources sustainably, and finding new ways to use their resources, add value to raw products, develop new products, and put resources to work that had previously been discarded.

The wise and sustainable use of natural resources builds communities. The unsustainable depletion of resources erodes and ultimately destroys those same communities.

Use the following questions to help you fill out your worksheet, though not all will apply to our community. Don't fill out the worksheet with answers to the questions. Rather, use them to stimulate your thinking:

➤ What are our community's natural resources and assets? Are they unusual or unique?
➤ Is anyone using, or thinking of using, local natural resources in unusual ways?
➤ Are there any useful natural resources not currently being used by businesses?
➤ How does local commerce or industry affect our town and its environment?
➤ Does the community currently consider the long-term health and availability of natural resources?
➤ Are there ways in which local resources were once used, but are no longer being used, to create jobs? Could these be tried again?
➤ Have any local natural resources been exhausted through unsustainable practices?
➤ Are any local natural resources being exhausted in ways that are not obvious?
➤ Is the community seeking constructive solutions to natural-resource conflicts, or focusing on who's to blame?
➤ If local resource users are involved in conflicts with environmentalists or state or federal land management agencies, has anyone attempted to mediate those conflicts?
➤ Are any local resources being used in ways that will eventually lead to their exhaustion?

Quality of Life

High quality of life makes a community a great place to live and do business. It attracts new residents, businesses, and possibly tourists. Cultural assets, strong traditions, safety, and clean air and water help sustain a healthy economy. Protecting natural assets, supporting the arts, and preserving historic buildings, for instance, will help maintain the economic and aesthetic vitality of the community. The things that make you feel good about living in this community will also attract new residents.

Use the following questions to help you fill out your worksheet, though not all will apply to our community. Don't fill out the worksheet with answers to the questions. Rather, use them to stimulate your thinking:

➤ What educational opportunities are present in the community? Are they being used to help business and labor?

➤ List artistic and cultural assets in the community. What facilities, traditions, landmarks, or activities are noteworthy?

➤ What is the effect of the arts on the local economy?

➤ Is our community a good place to raise children?

➤ How does safety in this community compare with other areas? What would make it less safe?

➤ Given current trends, do you foresee quality of life improving or diminishing for your children?

➤ How does the community's cost of living compare to the average for the state or the nation?

➤ What recreational opportunities are unique or unusual?

➤ What community assets keep businesses in town?

➤ What community assets attract tourists?

➤ What special amenities or assets might encourage new businesses?

➤ What amenities do residents want?

➤ Does the community have special cultural events or recreational facilities?

➤ Will improving local quality of life damage employment? Vice versa?

➤ Do the community's traditions tend to improve or damage the quality of life?

➤ How would you describe the community's way of life?

➤ What local characteristics detract from the quality of life?

➤ Will plans and proposals under consideration detract from the quality of life?

Step 4: Discovering New Opportunities

New ideas begin to bloom in this step, which marks the start of the exciting and creative part of the Economic Renewal process. In it, participants will look for ways in which local assets might help address the various problems and needs that were identified in the previous meeting. In doing so, they'll uncover new opportunities, many of which may have never been considered before. This exercise will create hope, especially among residents who may be feeling that there's not much hope.

Because anyone in the community can participate, and because it takes a little courage to step forward and communicate new ideas, this meeting tends to encourage new leadership. It has a way of eliciting creative ideas from people who previously may not have been regarded as leaders.

The main exercise of this meeting is designed to help participants make connections—literally—using the flip-chart sheets generated in the previous step. The sheets will be displayed on the walls of the meeting space so that everyone can view the community's assets, problems, and needs at a glance. Then, by writing items onto separate slips of paper and taping those up next to relevant items on other lists, they'll begin to form a picture of how the community can harness its assets to solve or fulfill its problems and needs—think of it as "Pin the Tail on the Opportunity." When participants get ideas for projects, the ideas will be listed on a flip-chart for use in the next session.

Because the procedure of this meeting is simpler than that of the previous one, you have even more opportunity to improvise. For instance, if participants exhaust ways to make connections, then you could start on generating project ideas (Step 5). The group will naturally tend to move in that direction anyway. For this reason, it's a good idea to read both this chapter and the next one and make all the necessary preparations for both steps before going into this meeting.

Preparations and Materials

Study this chapter and the "Preparations" section in Chapter 6 before the meeting.

This meeting requires a room with lots of wall space for attaching flip-chart sheets. A high school gym is ideal. You'll need two or three large tables and enough chairs to seat all participants.

Tape the flip-chart sheets summarizing the problems and needs identified during the previous meeting on a large blank wall. You'll need enough wall space for about fifteen columns of sheets, two sheets in each column. Space between the columns should be no less than the width of a sheet. The lists of assets should be grouped separately from problems and needs. You might arrange the sheets in one corner of the gym, with the "assets" sheets along one wall and the "problems" and "needs" sheets on the adjacent wall. If you have a big enough room, arrange the seats for the opening comments in one area of the room and display the flip-chart sheets in another area so that participants can move to that area to work on the exercise following introductory comments. Participants won't need seats during the exercise.

Set up two blank flip-charts or chalk boards, one at either side of all the columns of assets, problems, and needs. Print "Project Ideas" at the top of each.

Set up the tables about twenty or thirty feet back from the sheets. Place masking tape and lots of wide felt marking pens on the tables. The pens should be dark (light colors, such as yellow or pink, are very difficult to read). Tear several flip-chart sheets into fifty to seventy horizontal strips, two to three inches wide, and distribute them among the tables. If you run out of strips during the exercise, you can easily replenish the supply.

Using the information on the flip-chart sheets, prepare several of your own sample connections to help participants understand the exercise. Here are some examples of the kind of connections to be on the lookout for. One community using ER connected a need—"training in business skills"—with an asset—"successful local business owners"—to conceive of a mentoring program for fledgling business people. Another town linked several assets—high altitude, clean air, and a well-known local coach—to spark their idea of a high-altitude athletic training facility. In yet another town, participants identified an abandoned building as a problem and its bricks an asset; someone connected the bricks with a need—"no restrooms in town park"—and suggested the bricks be used to build the facilities. If your connections suggest ready-made projects such as these, so much the better, but at this point in the process all you need is the connections. Someone else will come up with the project ideas.

This is an active, noisy meeting. Consider bringing along some music to be played during the exercise when participants are milling around.

At your greeting table, set out more copies of the community economic success stories that you produced for the last meeting, along with handouts from previous meetings.

AGENDA

➤ Opening *(5 minutes)*
➤ Exercise: "Discovering Opportunities" *(45–90 minutes)*
➤ Homework: Success Stories *(5 minutes)*
➤ Wrap-up *(5 minutes)*

Opening Remarks

Welcome participants, especially those who haven't attended previous meetings. Briefly introduce everyone who will help conduct the meeting. Review the agenda. Make necessary announcements. Acknowledge everyone who helped make this meeting possible, especially the volunteers who compiled the information generated in Step 3.

Indicate the availability and location of handouts from previous meetings. Ask if anyone has any thoughts or questions from the previous meeting.

Display an outline of the ER process, briefly review it, recap the points covered in Step 3, and explain where this meeting fits in. Describe the procedure you'll be following, and ask for questions. While you may have covered much of this information at previous meetings, it's a helpful reminder. Say that you'd like the program team to assemble briefly following this session.

Exercise: 'Discovering Opportunities'

With this exercise, your community will find opportunities for economic renewal right in your own backyard. Once it gets under way it's creative and fun, but at first it may seem a bit awkward or confusing, so take time to clearly explain it.

Draw everyone's attention to the flip-chart sheets on the wall. Say: *"The task now is to link the assets with the problems and needs that we identified in the last meeting. In other words, find certain assets that might fulfill needs or solve particular problems. Before we start the exercise, does anyone have any assets, problems, or needs they'd like to add?*

"Now, we need to be clear about the meaning of the items recorded on the wall. They were written in the context of a discussion that some of us didn't hear. Out of that context, their meaning may not be obvious. Therefore, let's take fifteen minutes or so to review the sheets. Notice items that seem unclear so that you can ask for clarification in a moment."

When participants seem to have read all the sheets, ask if they have any questions. When a question is asked about a particular item, don't seek out the person who wrote the item. They might be shy or embarrassed. Instead, ask the whole group so that anyone may offer clarification.

When clarification is complete, say: *"Making connections is a comprehensive, challenging process, but it's also fun. Here's the way it works. Pick, for instance, a problem you're interested in, write it in large letters on a slip of paper, then read through the assets lists to find items that might somehow solve that problem. If you find a connecting asset, tape the problem slip to the wall nearest it. Or use the same procedure starting with a need. Or find an asset and tape it next to a problem it might solve or a need it might fulfill. When you've made a connection, go back and find more. Start with items that interest you, then seek out connecting items.*

"Pinning the tail on the opportunity" is an effective and fun way to find hidden opportunities.

*"Be creative. Don't feel an obligation to explain what your connections mean or know what they might lead to. If it just **feels** like there might be some relationship between two items, go ahead and make the connection."*

Let those instructions sink in, then ask for questions. When they're answered, say: *"You also may find multiple connections—more than one item connecting to another. Connections may not be obvious at first, so we'd like to offer a few examples."* At this point you can demonstrate the procedure using your prepared slips of paper. Following your examples, say: *"Though the primary purpose of this step is not to identify projects, ideas for projects will come up. When they do, let's make sure to capture them. Record them on the flip-charts titled 'Project Ideas.' OK, let's get started."*

As the exercise proceeds, many participants will probably begin talking instead of working on the exercise. If so, ask for everyone's attention, review the procedure, then playfully acknowledge that this a difficult exercise and we've noticed in other communities, when participants do this exercise, they often get into conversations with friends instead of doing the exercise because it's easier to talk than focus on this challenging exercise. (You might add that you know that wouldn't happen here, but you just thought they'd like to know what happened elsewhere.)

(Optional) When the process of making connections begins to slacken or when you're thirty or forty minutes into the exercise, ask participants to put a mark under the three needs or problems they think are most important or challenging. Urge them to just pick the first three good ones that come to mind—this isn't intended to be an exact poll. Write the three problems or needs receiving the most marks onto three slips of paper and tape them to the wall beside one another with plenty of blank space below. Then ask participants to find assets that might deal with these issues and place them below each. Emphasize that this work isn't meant to supersede the earlier

connections work, only to offer another perspective on it. When they select project ideas in Step 7, remind them of this vote.

Call the exercise to a halt, thanking participants for their work and creativity. Explain that this information will be used in the next step to identify project ideas.

If you feel that the exercise didn't produce enough connections, you may want to ask for volunteers to take time outside the meeting to attempt to develop additional connections.

Homework: Learning from Success Stories

In every town there is a tendency to focus on well-worn project ideas. This isn't necessarily bad. Some of these ideas may be excellent. (You'll probably hear them all in the next step.) But one important purpose of Economic Renewal is to open the door to many other opportunities by exploring the successes of other towns. To create a rich basis for thinking about ideas for strengthening the local economy, it's vital that participants read the community success stories that you've compiled.

You might say: *"Before the next meeting, please read the examples of community success stories we've provided. These case studies can do more than just inspire us. More importantly, they can help us get past preconceived notions and open our eyes to the huge range of possibilities available to a town like ours. This information will help us develop realistic projects to revitalize our economy.*

"As you read through the materials, make a note of examples that just might work in our community."

Wrap-up

Thank everyone for their creative analytical work. In making connections, they've moved an important step closer to economic renewal.

Summarize what will happen at the next meeting. Announce the date, time, and place, and ask for a show of hands to see who plans to attend. Say: *"Talk about this meeting to your friends, neighbors, and co-workers; encourage them to attend the next meeting."*

Before everyone leaves, ask for volunteers to collect the flip-chart sheets and attached slips of paper. Be sure to preserve these sheets and slips so that you can post them again during the next meeting.

Before the Next Meeting

Convene the program team and, if you wish, the coordinating committee. Distribute copies of the "Project Idea Evaluation" worksheet (pages 166-7). This worksheet is important because participants will use it to screen project ideas in Step 6 and it is the basis upon which final projects will be selected in Step 7. It must be acceptable to participants and tough enough to help them select the best project ideas.

Ask everyone to carefully review the questions on the worksheet, striking any that they feel are inappropriate and adding any that would be useful. For instance, if there is currently a strong feeling in the community that youth should be involved, then "potential for youth involvement" might be added to your evaluation worksheet. Don't strike a question just because it may generate controversy. Steps 6 and 7 are the points at which respectful arguments may be appropriate. It's far better to risk a little disagreement now than to live with the long-term effects of a bad project that slipped through a loose screen. If you make changes to the worksheet, assign someone to retype it in time for the next meeting.

Separately, you'll need to transcribe the project ideas recorded during this session onto clean flip-chart sheets. Eliminate duplication, group similar ideas, and write clearly. These will be displayed during the next meeting.

Step 5: Generating Project Ideas

In this creative step, participants will generate lots of ideas for renewing the community and the local economy. They'll move beyond conventional top-down approaches and come up with their own project ideas based on the connections they made in the previous step and the experiences of other communities. Finally, they'll form committees to evaluate the ideas during the next step.

"Project idea" is a shorthand way of referring to an idea for any project, action, or program that the community might pursue. At this point projects are still only "ideas"—nothing has yet been decided. Stressing this will reassure new participants that they can still play a part in the decision-making process, and it will also tend to minimize problems associated with pride of ownership.

Be prepared, should circumstances permit it, to combine this step with the previous one or the following one. For instance, if participants generated plenty of project ideas during Step 4, this meeting may not be much more than a recap of those ideas and a quick brainstorming session to come up with a few more. In that case, you could adjourn the meeting early or modify the agenda to begin work on the next step.

The facilitator's role in this session is focused primarily on conducting the brainstorming and being sensitive to the point at which the work of this step (generating project ideas) is complete and the next step (evaluating project ideas) should be begin.

Preparations and Materials

Study this chapter and the "Preparations" section in Chapter 6 before the meeting. Write out the brainstorming guidelines on page 89 on a large flip-chart sheet.

Set up two additional flip-charts for recording project ideas. Have masking tape on hand to attach completed sheets to the wall. Post the lists of project ideas from the previous session nearby. Post the flip-chart sheets listing the community's problems, needs, and assets (along with their "connections") off to one side of the room.

AGENDA

- ➤ Opening *(5–10 minutes)*
- ➤ Exercise: "Generating Project Ideas" *(15–90 minutes)*
- ➤ Create project evaluation committees *(15–40 minutes)*
- ➤ Wrap-up *(3 minutes)*

Recruit a volunteer or two to serve as recorders of project ideas. They must be able to print clearly and large enough to be seen by the group.

Be prepared to offer several of your own project ideas, some based on "making connections," others based on the readings that you assigned in the last meeting. Your suggestions may be needed to break the ice when you ask for project ideas from the group. You might ask a few friends to be prepared to offer their own ideas.

Make copies of the "Project Idea Description" and "Project Idea Evaluation" worksheets, found in the next chapter, for as many participants as you expect to attend. Have on hand copies of handouts from previous meetings for people who missed earlier sessions.

Opening Remarks

Welcome participants. Make introductions and announcements. Review the agenda and indicate how long this meeting is expected to take. Describe the purpose of the meeting.

Explain that the project ideas from the previous session have been transcribed for this meeting. If any interesting ideas or thoughts came up for you while you prepared the project-idea flip-chart, mention them.

Indicate that you'd like the program team to assemble briefly after the meeting.

If you think it's appropriate, discuss the problems of new ideas and risk-taking (see box).

Say: *"In a moment, we'll begin brainstorming to generate more ideas for projects to strengthen the community and the local economy. But first, to encourage creativity, we suggest that you adopt these brainstorming guidelines."* Refer to the guidelines, and ask participants if they agree to abide by them. When they say yes, the guidelines become something imposed on them by themselves, not by someone else.

Exercise: 'Generating Project Ideas'

Say: *"This meeting will be successful when we develop as many diverse project ideas as possible. We're looking for new concepts, as well as ideas that have been discussed before.*

"The ideas we come up with may not be strictly economic development projects. For instance, one project idea may seek to improve community attitude or foster community pride. That's OK. Anything that strengthens the community will contribute to economic renewal."

Point out the flip-chart sheets listing project ideas that participants thought of at the last meeting. Assure participants that they've already made a good start. Remind them of the connections they made between problems, needs, and assets. Suggest they refer back to particular problems and

DANGER: RISKY NEW IDEAS AHEAD

Depending on how people in your community regard innovation, bringing up new ideas may be risky. Therefore, it might be worth saying something about the need to move beyond the same old ideas in order to compete in a changing world.

You may also want to talk about the value of participants offering ideas that may, at first, seem visionary or impractical. Say: *"Most of us avoid the public risk of suggesting new ideas. We may not admit it, but when we think of suggesting a new idea, we also may think, 'How will I look? Will I embarrass myself? Will my friends think less of me?' It's especially risky for anyone to bring up new ideas in a community where everyone knows one another. No one wants to appear foolish. Many of us are apprehensive about what we say publicly, so we tend to limit our suggestions to those that are safe. The problem is that safe is rarely creative. Very little of consequence is achieved without someone taking some risk."*

As a program team or coordinating committee member, one of your responsibilities is to encourage risk-taking. You've already done a lot by helping develop trust among participants during Steps 2, 3 and 4. The more people trust one another, the more comfortable they'll be taking risks with one another. Fortunately, there are other ways to encourage risk-taking. First, ask the group if you can enforce the rules of brainstorming in which no idea is declared inappropriate or preposterous, and no idea is criticized. Second, show that it's OK to take risks, perhaps by offering your own ideas that might seem a little eccentric. Third, call on people who are risk-takers.

needs that they found especially important, then look for additional ideas for addressing them. If necessary, offer your own ideas.

Respectfully encourage participants to state their project ideas as specific actions. For instance, if someone says something very general, like "tourism," ask what they would do about tourism. One way to encourage greater clarity with project ideas is to ask participants to start their ideas with an active verb such as "develop" or "build." But be careful: don't demean their idea or demand perfect clarity. That will only stifle creativity. In many cases, clear definition requires more time. Sometimes a general idea like "tourism" can evolve into the purpose of a committee that decides to take on several related projects.

Economic Renewal adds to the ideas that everyone has for their community.

Record new project ideas on flip-charts.

When people's responses lag, shift their attention from the Step 4 flip-charts to the readings that you assigned at the last meeting. Ask if participants have additional project ideas based on the examples they read. Again, offer one or two of your own ideas if necessary. Record participants' project ideas. If you get little or no response, it could mean that participants didn't read the materials or are too shy to say anything. But it probably means they already offered ideas from the readings.

When the group seems out of ideas, indicate that brainstorming is complete and that the guidelines no longer apply.

Create Project Evaluation Committees and Wrap Up

Say: *"In a moment we'll ask each of you to create committees to evaluate project ideas in the next step, so start thinking about which idea interests you the most. You won't be committing to actually carry out the project, only to describe and evaluate it for the selection process. If you have concerns about a particular project, you may want to work with its evaluation committee to ensure that it's evaluated fairly.*

"Team efforts are usually more effective than individual ones. Therefore it's preferable that more than one person evaluate each project idea. There's no limit to the number of people who can evaluate one project. There will probably be some projects that nobody offers to evaluate, which is fine. If nobody wants to evaluate a project, then it's very unlikely that anyone would volunteer to actually develop it. But those that aren't chosen won't be discarded, they'll be set aside for consideration in the future."

Ask if participants need clarification of any of the items on the project ideas list.

Go down the list of project ideas one at a time, asking for a show of hands of those who would like to evaluate each. When you get just one taker for a project, ask if anyone else would like to help. Keep asking until no one else wants to volunteer for that project. If you're getting only one or two volunteers per project, you may need to cajole the group a little to get more. Three or four is a good minimum number.

When you've run through the list of project ideas, ask if there's anyone who didn't get a project. Ask which project they'd like to evaluate.

Often, several project ideas will be closely related and, therefore, might be pursued together by one group. For instance, participants in an Economic Renewal effort in Colorado's Plateau Valley had a list that included, among many other items, "press local apples for cider," "establish a farmers' market," and "develop alternative crops." A group of participants formed an agriculture committee to evaluate all three projects.

Distribute the "Project Idea Description" and "Project Idea Evaluation" worksheets (see pages 163 and 166-7). Explain that these will be used during the next step. Tell participants that they're welcome to work on their responses to the worksheets between now and the next session.

Thank everyone for their hard work and determination. Say when and where the next meeting will take place.

Step 6: Evaluating Project Ideas

After several sessions of talking about community values, assets, problems, needs, and opportunities, it's now time to start focusing on actual projects. In this step, participants will critically evaluate the project ideas they generated in the previous session to find those that are practical, sustainable, and consistent with community values. This process of narrowing down the list of potential projects began at the end of the last step, when some project ideas weren't chosen for evaluation. It will continue through the next step, when participants will compare project ideas and choose which to develop. The community probably doesn't have the time or resources to pursue them all. But remember, don't discard any ideas just because they haven't yet been chosen. Keep them on file for future consideration.

Procedurally this step resembles Step 3, in that participants will break up into small groups, but this time the groups have already selected themselves—they're the project evaluation committees formed at the end of the last meeting—and you'll let them appoint their own facilitators. Most of the meeting will consist of the committees filling out the two worksheets that you passed out at the last meeting. The "Project Idea Description" worksheet will help them clearly define, and perhaps refine, their chosen project idea. The "Project Idea Evaluation" worksheet will guide them in more fully examining the implications of their project ideas and deciding if they should go ahead.

The committees could conceivably complete their worksheets on their own outside of this group process, but they're less likely to let the work slide if they do it during a general meeting.

AGENDA

➤ Opening remarks *(5 minutes)*
➤ Break into groups *(5 minutes)*
➤ Exercise: "Defining Project Ideas" *(45–60 minutes)*
➤ Review evaluation questions *(15 minutes)*
➤ Exercise: "Evaluating Project Ideas" *(45–60 minutes)*
➤ Wrap-up *(3 minutes)*

Preparations and Materials

Study this chapter and the "Preparations" section in Chapter 6 before the meeting.

The room requirements for this meeting are much the same as for Step 3 (see page 132). You'll need several tables around which groups of two to ten participants can talk and fill in their worksheets.

Make copies of the worksheets contained in this chapter for participants who didn't bring theirs or who missed the previous session. Set out copies of handouts from previous sessions for people who missed them.

Write on a flip-chart sheet:

➤ What is the project?

➤ What are its benefits?

➤ Does it have any problems?

➤ Should it proceed?

➤ Who will do what, when?

Post the flip-chart sheet in a prominent place, along with the one outlining the ER process.

Opening Remarks

Welcome participants, make introductions and announcements, and briefly introduce everyone who will help conduct the meeting. Acknowledge everyone who helped make this meeting possible, especially the volunteers who compiled the information generated in Step 3. Ask if anyone has any thoughts or questions from the previous meeting.

Review the agenda and describe the purpose of this step. Say something along the lines of: *"Given limited time, money, and resources, we can't realistically attempt to implement every project we've considered so far. We'll need to choose a few priority projects. We'll use two worksheets to help us select projects that will make the most of community assets. Right now our purpose is not to design the projects, nor to determine how they can be developed. Rather, we're here to determine what the projects are, what they mean, and if they should be pursued. Based on that information, in the next step we'll narrow the list of projects down to a few hot prospects. Then, in Step 8, we'll carefully think through how to develop those projects."*

Indicate that you'd like the program team to assemble briefly following this session.

Exercise: 'Defining Project Ideas'

Until now you've encouraged participants to freely contribute their ideas. Now many of these same ideas will come under careful scrutiny. Create an atmosphere of friendly discussion that allows participants to speak their minds without offending others. You might say, *"We'll have the best chance of success when we pick the best possible projects. The only way we can find the best ones is by being tough on all of them, by carefully examining each to see what it means and ensure that it will actually benefit us. Therefore, everyone who is evaluating a project idea needs to work very hard at setting aside their pride of ownership and being willing to hear constructively critical comments. That said, those who have something critical to say should do so respectfully. They should comment on things they like about a project before indicating possible problems."*

Ask participants to assemble in the project evaluation committees they signed up for in the previous session. For those who haven't selected a project idea to evaluate, read out the project ideas and indicate where their committees are seated. Pass out extra copies of the "Project Idea Description" and "Project Idea Evaluation" worksheets. Each committee will only fill out one copy of each, but participants will find it useful to have their own copies so they can follow along as you give instructions. Ask each committee to appoint a facilitator (someone to lead the discussion) and a recorder (someone to fill out the worksheets according to the group's instructions).

Direct participants' attention to the "Project Idea Description" worksheet. Explain that the most important item in this worksheet is the first: identifying what the project idea actually is. Until now, discussion of the project may have been general or vague. But now, to evaluate it effectively, everyone needs a clear picture of what it is.

Warn participants not to get bogged down in details when completing this worksheet. It requires only brief answers. Precise responses and extensive research are not needed at this early stage. Suggest, too, that the purpose of the worksheet is not to complete it but to learn from it. The questions are important only to the extent that they help evaluation committees think through their projects.

Start the exercise. Circulate among the committees, sitting in on each for a few minutes to see how discussions are going. If one seems to be falling behind, encourage members to move more quickly. Committees often lose sight of the big picture or digress into related topics that don't contribute to completing the worksheet. If this happens, gently bring them back to the task at hand.

Call a ten-minute warning. When time is up, respectfully close discussion. Bring the meeting to order and thank everyone for their efforts on this worksheet.

Exercise: 'Evaluating Project Ideas'

Having defined their projects, committees can now evaluate them.

Introduce the "Project Idea Evaluation" worksheet. Say: *"At this point in the process, we have more project ideas than resources to implement them. Therefore, we need to whittle the list down to a very few that will be best for*

Worksheet: Project Idea Description

1. What, specifically, is the project? Before answering, consider these other questions: Does it have several component projects or phases? Is it a series or group of projects? If so, does success require that they all proceed? Or should you pick one of the projects, phases, or components to evaluate now, and wait to consider others later?

_____

_____

_____

_____

2. What would the project achieve? (Why do it?)

_____

_____

_____

3. What problems would the project solve, what needs would it fulfill, or what barriers to success would it address?

_____

_____

_____

4. Whom would it benefit? The whole community? One segment of the community? If one segment, which? Would it harm other segments of the community?

_____

_____

_____

5. The project would require: (circle all that apply)

Paid staff   Volunteers   Technical assistance   Equipment   Construction   Financing

Project ideas require careful scrutiny before they proceed.

our community. To do this, we'll first use this worksheet to develop the information everyone needs to know to choose projects. In the next meeting, the information will be summarized on a wall-sized chart for everyone to see and select the best projects."

Emphasize: *"This evaluation is only preliminary. Except for the simplest project ideas, you won't know everything you need to know to make a final determination that, yes, the project deserves the support and energy of this community. Therefore, your answers should be estimates based on what you and your fellow committee members know now."*

"Despite incomplete information, you can make valid choices. In most cases, it doesn't require extensive analysis to see that a project is practical and will improve the community.

"Before we use the worksheet, let's take a quick look at the questions. In effect, you'll be screening your project idea based on these questions. Please skim them and, if necessary, ask for clarification."

Give participants a few minutes to look over the questions. Indicate that they've been thoroughly reviewed (and, if applicable, revised) by the program team. When most participants seem to be finished, ask if they're comfortable using these questions to screen project ideas. Though it's important to get the group's support for the questions, try to avoid an extended discussion of changes that might be made. It could derail your meeting schedule. If someone asks for changes that won't be easily accomplished, ask if they can live with the current questions, despite problems.

Say: *"To come up with these project ideas we were free-wheeling and creative. Now we need to be practical and take a hard look at them. We need to be constructively critical in this step so that we choose projects that stand the best chance of success.*

"Some committees may tend to develop sales pitches for their project ideas that gloss over potential problems and concerns. We urge you, instead, to do your evaluations fairly and impartially. If you find that your project idea has problems, be up-front about them. It's better to face problems now, before significant time and money are spent. The goal here is not to develop a certain project, but to strengthen the community by the best means possible. Those means will be found only through impartial evaluation. Another reason for being tough on your project idea is that you'll be reporting your findings to the whole group in

the next session. If you gloss over problems, the others will notice and let you know about it. They'll grill you.

"Be sure to designate someone, probably your recorder, to make your presentation at the next session. Each committee member should be prepared to answer questions, discuss the project, and compare it to the other projects.

"As you conduct your evaluation, be thinking about the best way to present it to the rest of the group. There won't be enough time at the next meeting to go over your entire evaluation, so you'll have to highlight the information that will be most useful to others who are trying to decide if the project should be pursued. Here are the things the rest of us will most need to know." Point to the flip-chart sheet with the five bulleted items beginning with "What is the project?"

Ask for questions, then have the committees get started. Give them a completion time, and warn them that if they aren't finished by then they'll need to meet independently before the next session. As in the previous exercise, circulate among the committees and encourage them to keep on track.

This process may reveal that certain projects are too ambitious as originally conceived. If so, encourage participants not to give up, but instead to look for realistic, short-term projects that can act as steps toward achieving the larger goal. For instance, if a committee starts realizing that a complete renovation of downtown storefronts and streetscape is too much to tackle, it might propose initially planting a dozen trees along Main Street.

Wrap-up

Thank participants for being willing to stick with the process. Reassure them that there's light at the end of the tunnel: by the end of the next step, projects will be chosen and under way. Announce the location and time of the next meeting.

Meet with the program team to determine how best to select projects in Step 7. Review the next chapter to help you in that decision. You may need to schedule a separate program team meeting to handle this important issue.

Worksheet: Project Idea Evaluation

Use this worksheet to evaluate the relative strengths and weaknesses of your project idea. Though your project may require more information before you decide to definitely go ahead, answer these questions based on what you know today.

Project idea: _____

1. **Problems and needs.** Would the project actually address community problems and needs?

   Yes   No

2. **Preferred future.** In judging the project's compatibility with the community's preferred future, consider these questions: Would it truly better the community? Or would it spoil something the community wants to preserve? Would it disregard important community values? Would it obstruct important community goals? Would it prevent positive change?
   Overall compatibility with the community's preferred future:

   High   Moderate   Low

3. **Environment.** What would the project change about the environment? Would that change be acceptable to the community? What would the indirect, long-term, or cumulative impacts be? What waste would be produced? Where would it wind up? If the project involves hazardous materials, how would they be handled?
   Overall environmental impact:

   Positive   Neutral   Negative

4. **Fairness.** Would the project unfairly burden a particular segment of the community? Who would pay for the project? Who would benefit and who would be harmed? Fairness issues are hard to assess, but asking these questions will help you set aside blatantly unfair projects.
   Fairness rating:

   Good   So-so   Poor

5. **"Social capital."** Would the project increase or decrease trust, neighborliness, and the capacity of people to work together? Would it enhance or damage the community's networks of relationships? Would it increase residents' ability to come together to work, play, or socialize?
   Net contribution to the community's "social capital":

   Positive   Neutral   Negative

6. **Sustainability.** A project isn't sustainable if it depletes community resources or has significant, negative off-site or long-term effects. If it's not sustainable, it won't build the community for the future; it will begin to tear the community down. Like fairness, sustainability is difficult to determine, but well worth considering.
   Sustainability rating:

   Good   So-so   Poor

7. **Controversy.** Would the project be controversial? Are certain residents likely to be upset by it or try to stop it? The fact that someone may oppose a project may not be sufficient reason to reject it, but all things being equal, non-controversial projects are preferable.
   Potential for controversy:

   High   Moderate   Low

8. **Leadership.** Who would be responsible for getting the project going?

Volunteers	Government
Nonprofit group	Church
Business	Individuals
Educational institution	Co-op

9. **Cost.** Low-cost projects can be done with volunteers and donated resources. Medium-cost projects require more sub-stantial sums and possibly even grants or financing, while high-cost projects require major financing that will take many years to pay back.
   Likely cost:

   High   Medium   Low

10. **Difficulty.** Is the project realistic, accept-able, and technically feasible? Are resources available for it? How difficult would it be to pull it off?

    Hard   Medium   Easy

11. **Time frame.** When would tangible results be seen? Short-term is a couple of months or less, medium-term is about a year, and long-term is more than a year.

    Short   Medium   Long

12. **Economic Benefits.** Several meetings ago we discussed four principles of local eco-nomic development. If you need to refresh your memory about the principles, please ask for a handout.
    Economic benefits: (circle all that apply)

    Plug the leaks

    Support existing business

    Create new local enterprise

    Recruit compatible business

Additional considerations:

13. What are the project's weaknesses or problems, if any?

    _____

    _____

14. Could the project be changed to address its weaknesses? If so, how?

    _____

    _____

15. Based on what you know so far, should this project be developed?

    Yes   Maybe   No

16. Would you rate the project as a:

    High priority?   Medium priority?   Low priority?

17. Are there important questions about the project that need further examination? If so, what are they? Could answering these questions be made into a project itself?

    _____

    _____

Step 7: Selecting Projects

This step will energize participants. Finally, after weeks of planning and thinking about development ideas, they'll select specific projects and leave the session with clear, achievable goals. Therefore, make an extra effort to get community leaders and media people to attend. At this meeting, they'll see enthusiasm and the blossoming of creative yet practical projects.

The main purpose of this step is to identify two to five projects—including at least one relatively short-term easy one—that will strengthen the community, secure more support and involvement, and demonstrate that your Economic Renewal effort is at last bearing fruit.

During this session, committees will deliver their project idea evaluations. Following each presentation, the facilitator will record the group's perceptions of how that project stacks up against various criteria. Participants will then compare the projects and, by consensus, select a well-rounded combination to develop. For each chosen project, they'll form a committee to develop an action plan. Lastly, they'll begin the process of creating a permanent local organization to carry on the work of Economic Renewal.

Depending on the number of projects to be presented, this step could easily require two meetings. It's an important step, so don't rush to fit it into one meeting.

Preparations and Materials

The main prop for this session is the "project menu," a big wall-mounted matrix designed to give participants a quick overview of all the projects in relation to one another. You can create it on a series of flip-chart sheets or newspaper end-rolls taped to the wall, or on a schoolroom-sized blackboard, but either way you'll need a writing surface roughly eight feet wide by four feet tall. If more than about nine projects will be reviewed, then

---

AGENDA

- ➤ Opening remarks *(5 minutes)*
- ➤ Report project evaluations *(20–30 minutes per project)*
- ➤ Select projects *(30–90 minutes)*
- ➤ Create project development committees
       (5 minutes per project)
- ➤ Create an ER Council organizing committee *(20 minutes)*
- ➤ Wrap-up *(5 minutes)*

you'll need an even taller surface (or a second menu). The figure on page 170 shows what the menu should look like.

The headings refer to the questions in the "Project Idea Evaluation" worksheet that committees filled out in the previous step. You might choose to add a few headings of your own if you think there are other factors that should be considered in project selection.

Before the session, the program team should decide how project selection will be handled (see page 174).

Use a room that's large enough to seat all participants without tables. You'll be offering a large display on the wall that you'll want all participants to read, so arrange the seating classroom-style or, better still, in semicircles that radiate out from the display.

Reuse the "What is the project?" flip-chart sheet from the previous session.

Make five or six copies of the "Creating the Economic Renewal Council" section at the end of this chapter. Set out copies of handouts from previous sessions for people who missed them.

The Meeting

Opening Remarks

Welcome participants. Make introductions and announcements. Review the agenda and indicate how long this meeting is expected to take. Describe the purpose of this step. Indicate that it marks the end of the planning process, and that the next step will be to develop action plans for the projects selected at this session.

Report Project Evaluations

Say: *"In a moment we'll ask the various project evaluation committee reporters to report their findings."*

Display the flip-chart with five bulleted items beginning with "What is the project?" Say: *"We don't have time to hear everything each committee found. So reporters will just tell us the important points they found. At a minimum, they'll tell us these five things."* If, despite your suggestion, some reporters just read everything on the worksheet, you'll need to remind them to state only the important points of each project.

Before you call on the first committee to report, call the group's attention to the project menu on the wall. Say, *"Following each report, we'll ask for your questions and comments. Then, we'll fill out the various columns on the project menu according to your instructions. For instance, under the heading 'Difficulty,' you'll say to write 'hard,' 'medium,' or 'easy.' This discussion will be an excellent opportunity to ensure that the issues and concerns surrounding each project are clarified.*

Project Menu

Project	Problems / Needs	Preferred Future	Environment	Fairness	Social Capital	Sustainability	Controversy	Leadership	Costs	Difficulty	Time Frame	Economic Benefits

The Project Menu gives a quick overview of all the project ideas, enabling participants to compare their relative strengths and weaknesses.

"But let's try to be constructively critical. We often express our concerns and criticisms as attacks. In turn, responses tend to be defensive. To avoid this pitfall, let's offer constructive, not argumentative, criticisms. An argumentative comment is: 'How can you think of doing that? It'll just make a big mess of traffic.' A constructive question would be: 'Has your committee considered whether the project will affect traffic?'

"We also want to urge evaluation committees to avoid being defensive. It's natural, when someone criticizes or questions your project, to respond by defending it and covering up potential problems. But defensiveness widens the gaps between us and quickly breaks down consensus. More constructive, and conducive to collaboration, is to **include** the concern in the future development of the project idea. For instance, an inclusive response to criticism might be: 'We hadn't thought of that. Could you meet with us later so that we can look for ways of including your concern in the project?' Or, 'Yes, we talked about that issue and concluded such and such. Does that address your concern?'

"None of these suggestions is meant to discourage criticism or controversy. We shouldn't play polite and avoid saying negative things. That would simply put a lid on a problem that could blow up later. Criticism and controversy are important and useful ways to get the best results, but only if they're offered and taken in a civil manner."

One excellent way to set the stage for constructive discussion of project ideas—and to begin to make future community discourse more constructive—is to demonstrate the difference between defensive and inclusive responses through a role-play. You could write a short script of an exchange between an evaluation committee member and someone with a question about the project. The script would include two alternative dialogs, one in which the committee responds defensively, one in which the committee responds inclusively. Ask two aspiring local actors to play out the script.

Keep the Discussion Civil

Ask for a volunteer to make the first project report. To ensure that the group's attention is on the presentation and not you, sit down or stand far aside. Come back to front-and-center only when the report is complete. This method is not only respectful of the speaker, it's also a useful way to deal with a too-long presentation—if the speaker is dragging on, you can slowly move back toward the front of the room. Most speakers will get the hint and wrap up.

When the report is complete, thank the presenter and start a round of applause. Then ask for questions and comments from other participants.

If no one offers a comment or asks a question, you should have one ready. Think about whether the presentation included all that was needed. Was anything unclear? Is anything being glossed over? Are questions not being asked because none are needed, or because the group is being polite?

On the other hand, difficult and even adversarial questions may be asked. This is where your facilitation skills need to be particularly keen. Tough questions are OK, because these are important issues—but you need to ensure that questioners are tough on the *issues*, not the *people*. Your job is to keep the discussion civil and productive. Help make the critical questions constructive, and help committee members respond inclusively. Without trying to avoid valid controversy, you may need to suggest ways to reframe questions, comments, and responses so that they get the point across without the rough edges.

But be careful: don't demean the styles of others in demonstrating a more constructive style. If you're able to set a positive example as the first argument starts to emerge, your style will become the model for the rest of the discussion.

These attempts to maintain constructive dialog don't always work. Sometimes legitimate differences regarding certain projects divide the community. When division occurs, you have three options: let the ensuing battle run its course; intervene in an attempt to find common ground; or ask the group if you can halt the discussion and come back to it at the end of the process. In the latter case, participants may ultimately conclude there are enough projects supported by consensus that the controversial project can be put on the back burner. If it seems politically wise, set a date for reconsidering the project idea.

Fill in the Project Menu

When questions regarding a project idea are complete, write its name in the left-hand column of the project menu, then ask the group how you should fill in the blanks under each heading. Invariably, this exercise is a lot of fun; it's active and hopeful.

Ensure that questioners are tough on the *issues*, not the *people*.

This is not an exacting process. You're not seeking definitive answers to these questions. At this early stage, you're looking for everyone's best guess. Responses will be relative, not absolute. For example, the group might initially rate a project as "hard"; later, in light of the other projects that have been considered, they might revise that rating to "medium."

The project menu is supposed to give participants a quick overview of the projects, so try to be as brief as possible when filling it in—one-word answers are best. Freely use contractions and abbreviations (for example, "biz" for business, "gov" for government). You might use other shorthand symbols to indicate when the group's verbal response is emphatic. For instance, if the environmental effect of a project is especially positive, you might write (++) instead of (+). If the group responds to one of your questions with a resounding "No!" you might want to add the exclamation point.

Select Projects

When the project menu is complete, it's time to discuss the various projects in relation to one another and decide which ones should be developed.

If there are more than three of four projects being considered, say, *"These are great projects, but if we attempt to proceed with all of them, we'll probably spread our limited energy and resources so thinly that all will fail. Experience has shown time and again, whether in business, government, or community affairs: it's far more effective to start small, experience success, and grow comfortably to take on bigger challenges. Therefore, to concentrate our efforts on just a few, let's select the ones that stand the best chance right here, right now. Projects that aren't chosen this time can be revisited at a later date."*

Regardless of how many projects are being considered say, *"As participants in this process, we have no formal authority to approve or reject a particular project. We're here to find and support the most effective development projects, not to take it upon ourselves to control development. If someone wants to go off on their own and start a project that gets little support here, that's their right. On the other hand, those who are considering doing a project on their own may find the wisdom of this group useful in their own decision-making.*

"The strongest economies are those that are most diverse. To be most effective, we should seek diversity in our final choice of projects. To give one example: if we were to choose three projects that all relied on town hall to carry them out, we'd be in danger of putting all our eggs in one basket and overburdening the town; we'd be better off just keeping the best one of the three, and choosing two other projects that rely on other organizations.

"Similarly, our lineup shouldn't consist only of projects that are long-term, difficult, and expensive—it should include at least one that's quick, easy, and cheap. Though long-term projects can be vital, early successes will build confidence and create momentum. We'll be most effective if we choose at least one

project that shows visible signs of success in a short period of time. It could be a small project, or it could be a big one capable of being developed in stages to produce early tangible results."

Using your best consensus-building skills, lead a discussion of the various project ideas and select projects based on your team's choice of the following procedures.

Selection Procedures

Selecting projects as a group is a potentially delicate task. It's important to select projects in a way that's sensitive to people's feelings and to the unique dynamics of your community.

In most situations, your best bet is to have participants stick colored dots next to the names of their favorite projects. Give everyone a certain number of dots—three is a good number, since that's probably how many projects you're aiming to select. (Alternatively, have them put ticks with colored pens next to their preferred projects, or chalk marks if your project menu is on a blackboard.) This is a gentler form of voting than the customary winner-take-all process. Afterwards, lead participants in a consensus-building discussion (see pages 46 and 90) regarding which projects should proceed, based on the number of dots received by each project idea. You might give committees that presented ideas receiving few dots an opportunity to say more. Some committees may graciously withdraw their ideas. If the discussion leads to new information, redefines projects, or regroups projects, you could run a second dot exercise.

If there are only four or five projects to choose from and selection seems obvious, you can probably dispense with the dots and move right into the consensus discussion. With more than five projects, however, this discussion is apt to be very complicated and hard to keep track of. Also, there's always the danger that selecting projects solely by consensus may lead to lukewarm final choices that are the least offensive but also the least useful.

Some sensible-sounding selection methods are generally not appropriate for this process. Voting, for example, is fast and decisive, but it creates winners and losers, not consensus. The losers may not support chosen projects; worse, they might oppose them.

Analyzing the costs and benefits of each project idea would appear to be a logical and dispassionate way to make the cut, but community decision-making can't be so easily reduced to economic equations, nor is money the only variable. Residents may feel more comfortable with less risky projects that result in smaller benefits. One project may generate big monetary benefits but also entail big non-monetary costs (for example, pollution or the loss of a local landmark). Another may cost money and generate no revenues, yet if it builds the community and creates a more supportive atmosphere, it will lead to concrete economic benefits. A project that looks tech-

It's far more effective to start small, experience success, and grow comfortably.

nically correct to an economic-development professional, but has unacceptable impacts on local culture or sensibilities, will probably fail without community support. In contrast, a strongly supported project will succeed even if it doesn't conform to conventional criteria.

Keep in mind that any selection method can create problems in certain circumstances. Picture a situation in which a minority group with a long history of under-representation in community affairs is sponsoring a particular project. If their project seems to be losing, its members may feel they've been rejected again. Voting in any form may cause damage to these folks. They may oppose selected projects or stop participating in community affairs. If you see this happening, you'll need to marshal your best diplomatic skills. Without referring to any group in particular, ask participants if they think the direction that the selection process is going is genuinely fair. If not, ask if a particular project should be given greater consideration in the name of fairness.

Create Project Development Committees

Once projects have been selected, it's time to create committees to develop them. Explain to participants that the committees will meet together in the next step to formulate action plans for their projects.

Read out the name of one of the selected projects, and ask who on the committee that evaluated it would like to serve on the committee that will develop it. Then ask for other volunteers to join the development committee. Seek especially those whose projects weren't selected. It's important to keep them involved and to make them feel included. Do this for each selected project. Though this is a critically important task, it should take no more than about five minutes per project.

Ask all participants to think carefully about who else in the community might help with their projects. Many who weren't willing to participate in the planning process may be enthusiastic about helping develop projects. Ask participants to contact those people and invite them to join their project development committee at the next meeting.

An excellent outcome of this step would be, say, two to five committees each working on a group of related projects. It's important, however, that the committees remain realistic about what they can achieve in the short term. Success is most likely when they proceed with one project at a time, though there may be sufficient enthusiasm that more than one project can proceed simultaneously.

When a good idea becomes identified with one individual (either as an advocate or a beneficiary), it tends to skew other people's perspective on that idea. They tend to think more about the person, and less about how the idea might benefit the community.

For instance, a community that needs a doctor will do almost anything to get one, including building the prospective doctor a house. In contrast, a community that already has a young doctor (who can't afford a house) may resist providing her with a house even if she is compelled to leave due to inadequate housing. Jealousy or resentment about her in particular may overshadow the fact that the community needs a doctor.

It may become clear that some individuals may benefit from a certain project. Resentful participants may think or say that the project should be rejected because it will directly benefit someone.

If you notice resentment stirring, without naming names, you might use the doctor analogy. Also say, *"There's a possibility that a certain project might benefit certain individuals. This is not a reason to reject the project. On the contrary, if one person may benefit directly, he or she will probably be willing to go to great lengths to assure its success.*

"If this project also benefits the community (for instance, saving money or creating new jobs), then it's probably something worth community support, regardless of who benefits most. It's only a problem if someone benefits at the community's expense. Self-interest can easily be mistaken for selfishness. But when exercised in an enlightened way, self-interest can be entirely compatible with community goals."

That said, when participants ask for community support for a project that will benefit them directly, they'll be most effective if they can clearly demonstrate that the community will also benefit. If someone is pushing a personal project without disclosing his interests, it's your job in the meeting to diplomatically ask him the questions that will expose his position.

Initiate a Permanent Organization for Economic Renewal

Before wrapping up, you've got one more big task to set in motion: establishing an organization to ensure that the Economic Renewal effort endures. It's best to initiate this project now. If for any reason this isn't possible, make absolutely certain to do it at the *beginning* of the next step, before participants get completely engrossed in developing their projects.

Say, *"We've accomplished important work, but we have one final item on our agenda that's brief but crucial. If the community's effort to develop sustainably is not to wither and die when these projects are complete, we need a permanent organization—maybe a new one, maybe one that's already here—but one that will coordinate and carry this effort into the future. For the time being, we'll call it the 'Economic Renewal Council.'*

"To make this happen, we need at least three volunteers to form an organizing committee that will start this effort off in the right direction. They'll help determine the functions of the council, the type of organization required, and whether an existing group can fill the role or whether a new one will have to be created. We have materials to guide the volunteers in this effort. They'll start creating the council during the next session, while the rest of us are developing action plans for our projects."

Recruit at least three people—seven would be better. Since this organizational work will parallel the development of project action plans, these people should not be members of project committees, unless they think they have time to do both. Give each one a copy of the "Creating an Economic Renewal Council" section (below), and thank them for their commitment. Ask them to attend the next session to work alongside the project development committees.

Wrap-up

Offer an uplifting send-off. Congratulate the group for having selected some excellent projects and being prepared to begin the process of developing them. Give a brief preview of Step 8—the last step in the Economic Renewal process, but the first step in project implementation. Emphasize that their ER effort is already on the road to success.

Creating an Economic Renewal Council

In a 1994 study, the National Governors' Association analyzed the importance of various factors in determining the success of community development efforts. To the researchers' surprise, none of the expected factors—proximity to an interstate or a city, the amount of federal aid received, skills of the population—correlated strongly with success. The single most important ingredient of community economic development, they found, was long-term commitment by the community.

Notes former NGA senior economist DeWitt John: "Fundamentally, what we found out is that the key ingredient appears to be organized, persistent, long-term economic development at the local level. It's just as clear as a bell."

For your community to maintain an "organized, persistent, long-term" development effort, it must create (or revitalize) an organization to coordinate and promote it. That organization is referred to here as the Economic Renewal Council, but you can call it whatever you think is appropriate for your community.

Without an ER Council, your community's development efforts probably won't continue over time. People will tend to drift away. Participants in one project may run into difficulty, find no one to help, and give up. Participants in another project may get sidetracked by other activities and fail to find people to replace them. Without coordination, it will be more difficult for your project development committees to share information and resources.

Your council may already exist in some form. It may have emerged as a natural outgrowth of Economic Renewal. If not, consider turning ER Council responsibilities over to an existing group. But do so only if you can find one:

> Whose goals and objectives are consistent with your ER efforts.
> Whose resources (skills, staff capacity, time, money, services, credibility, and political strength) are sufficient to fulfill the functions that you determine are needed (see list below).
> That isn't seen as being on one side of local controversies.
> That's enthusiastic about doing so.

The remainder of this section is written as if you've decided to create a new organization, though parts of it will be helpful if you decide to work with an existing group. Whatever you do, you'll need to be at least as diplomatic and collaborative as you were when you started the ER process. Community leaders will definitely take notice. If they're not involved, or at least fully informed, they may stop the council before it starts. Therefore, begin by reviewing Chapter 3, "Collaborative Community Decision-Making."

Without coordination, your community's efforts probably won't continue over time.

Membership

For your ER Council to be regarded as a serious and important organization, it must include several respected community members. These could include decision-makers from local government, civic organizations, the chamber of commerce, ethnic organizations, local businesses, unions, churches, schools, industries, financial institutions, or utility companies. The process of identifying and recruiting members for your council will be similar to the one you used to mobilize the community in Step 1 (see Chapter 7). In many cases, you'll be contacting the same people. The council should also include a representative from each project development committee and other citizens with relevant interests and skills.

It's useful to also create an executive committee of council members to provide leadership, notify members of meetings, make necessary arrangements, set agendas, and coordinate with project committees. An executive committee can offer suggestions as to the structure, function, goals and policies of the council, but final determinations should be by vote of the entire council.

The council should meet roughly twice a year, while its executive committee should meet about once a month. All meetings should be well publicized to encourage full participation by all interested citizens.

Functions

An Economic Renewal Council can fulfill a number of beneficial functions in your community, although some may already be handled by other groups. Discuss each of the functions listed below and determine which should be the responsibility of your council. They're listed in order of priority for most communities, but your priorities may be different. In its early stages, the council should perform at least the first three functions.

➤ **Advocacy.** Support and promote initial ER projects, as well as future economic development efforts, within the community and among local government and funding agencies.

➤ **Assistance.** Follow the project development committees' work closely, and help in whatever ways possible.

➤ **Leadership.** Bring participants in the community's economic development effort back together, at regular intervals or for special meetings, to celebrate successes, review progress, select new projects, and rekindle enthusiasm.

➤ **Leadership development.** Seek out, support, and find training for people who demonstrate interest in and commitment to the community's development. Choose skill-oriented, not strictly issue-oriented, training.

➤ **Recruitment.** Bring new people into the effort. Help them understand it, listen to their ideas, and give them responsibilities with an eye toward preparing them for leadership.

➤ **Resource allocation.** Receive resources (including money) from foundations, corporations, and local, state, and federal governments, and distribute them to appropriate project development committees and entrepreneurs.

➤ **Communication.** Act as liaison between ER participants and other groups. Bring speakers to the community.

➤ **Record-keeping.** Maintain a history of the community's Economic Renewal effort, archiving the information for use in an ER plan (see page 66) or other funding proposal.

➤ **Inclusion.** Ensure that all relevant community groups, interests, and individuals are involved and are being treated fairly.

➤ **Project management.** The council may choose to take on the responsibility of developing and implementing projects, but if not, then make it clear that these tasks aren't part of its mission. Otherwise, if the going gets tough, project committees may tend to dump their implementation work on the council.

Activating the Council

Much the same way you got ER started, begin with a core group and expand it as you secure the support of community leaders. When roughly a dozen leaders have agreed to participate, meet to determine which of the functions listed above will be part of your council's mission. Develop a mission statement based on those functions plus your community's preferred future or vision statement.

Choose a name. It might refer to a historic event that community residents can be proud of, a nearby landmark or natural feature, a community achievement, or the character of the community.

If you don't already have it, seek support from all key organizations in the community. At a minimum, the strong support of local governments and business and development groups should be secured. One very clear way that these organizations can express their support is by granting money to the committee. Even if it's only a small amount, a grant, donation, or contract invests these organizations in the committee's work. They become partners.

Explore possible methods for hiring a paid director to coordinate volunteers, assure that tasks are completed, handle paperwork, and develop relationships with the various outside organizations that will be helpful in your efforts. These tasks can of course be carried out by volunteers, but it'll be hard to maintain the same level of reliability and professionalism. If you hired someone to coordinate the ER process, this person would be an obvious choice for the director position.

The director's salary might be paid by local government or business organizations; local nonprofit groups and educational institutions might also help. If leaders from these sectors are involved in your ER effort, they'll better understand the need. If a director is too expensive, explore the possibility of applying to the state or a foundation for grants, or seeking the loan of staff from a local corporation, utility, or local government. But be careful: you could end up spending more time and energy trying to find a director than strengthening the local economy. If you aren't able to hire a director right away, concentrate on developing a "track record" of one or more visible successes. With proof of success, potential funders will become confident that their money will be well spent.

Choosing Another Form of Organization

In time, your council may see advantages to evolving into, creating, or turning its responsibilities over to one of several types of specially consti-

> **Explore possible methods for hiring a paid director.**

tuted organizations. After your council has gotten its feet on the ground, review the kinds of organizations described here and decide if one would be appropriate in your circumstances.

> **Economic development commission (EDC).** An EDC is created through the governing body of a city, town, or county by the adoption of a resolution or ordinance. Its members are appointed by the governing body. It has the duty to investigate, study, and survey the need for additional job opportunities and economic diversification, and to recommend action. Specifically, an EDC has the power to acquire land; issue bonds; sell facilities; exercise the power of eminent domain; make direct loans to users or developers for the cost of construction of facilities; and purchase, lease, construct, remodel, rebuild, enlarge, or substantially improve facilities, including machinery and equipment.

> **Nonprofit corporation.** A nonprofit corporation's board of directors should represent a broad range of community interests—not unlike the ER Council. Because it provides a vehicle through which major improvements can be funded and through which parcels of land can be assembled for development or redevelopment, a nonprofit corporation is best suited to a community with ambitious plans. It can also serve to attract new businesses by buying and renovating commercial property. It offers the advantage of raising capital within the community through tax-deductible contributions (under section 501[c]3 of the tax code). It can involve a large number of local citizens, institutions, and businesses (all of them investors or contributors) in decision-making. An attorney can assist in the incorporation process, which is relatively simple and requires only filing out an application with the state and paying a nominal filing charge.

> **Local development corporation (LDC).** An LDC can be a for-profit or nonprofit organization. Under many states' laws, LDCs are authorized to promote and assist the growth and development of small businesses. Formed by a minimum of 25 stockholders or members, an LDC is a very flexible organization offering many possible functions. For example, it can lease and improve real property, acquire property, make equity investments in new and young small businesses, sell notes and debentures to finance projects, borrow and re-lend money to assist businesses, receive grants from federal, state, and local agencies, develop industrial parks, provide state income-tax credits to program contributors for eligible activities, establish and operate a small-business resource center, and undertake historic preservation activities.

> **Regional development organization.** Some communities are seeking new patterns of cooperation with their neighbors. It's not easy to

form links between places that used to think of themselves as rivals, but this new idea has some powerful potential benefits. When communities work together they can provide goods and services more efficiently to larger markets. They have a better chance of attracting new business and industry because they represent a larger trade area and work force. They can take full advantage of all area tourist attractions to fully develop that resource. And they have more political muscle to attract governmental grants and loans and to seek needed changes at the county and state level.

Regional development organizations can be formal or informal. Most states provide legal authority for intergovernmental cooperation. Under this authority, neighboring communities can cooperate to provide services they now provide separately. The nonprofit-corporation organizational structure can also provide a mechanism for cooperation.

Step 8: Developing Project Action Plans

This is the last step in the Economic Renewal process, but it's only the first step in developing the projects you've chosen. The public meetings and consensus-building have served their purpose. Now comes a less visible—but equally challenging—phase. One last group meeting will be necessary to get the project development committees started on the right track. After that, the program team will probably disband and pass the baton to the Economic Renewal Council (see page 177). The project committees will continue their work separately at their own pace, each according to the special requirements of its project, and be coordinated through the ER Council.

Every project is unique. This chapter can't tell you how to implement a particular project, but what it can do is suggest a generic process for deciding how to do so. The basic outcome of this process will be a project action plan. To create their action plans, committees will refine their project descriptions, analyze alternative ways to achieve the same goals, identify barriers to implementation, outline tasks, develop budgets, and seek support (financial and otherwise).

They'll start on these tasks during a group meeting—the last one of the Economic Renewal process. The ER Council organizing committee will begin its work at the same meeting. There are good reasons for gathering these committees together one last time before cutting them loose to work independently. First, the effort will be more exciting, reassuring, and important if all the committees start their work together. Second, some committees may have questions that other committees can answer. And third, the meeting ensures that the committees will actually start their work instead of putting it off. This meeting should create enough momentum to carry them through to completion.

Preparations and Materials

List and invite all key community leaders and members of the media, even those who didn't attend previous ER meetings. Make an extra effort to get commitments from leaders who may be in a position to support projects, as well as those who just might scuttle one or more projects. If they seem reluctant, ask them to attend at least the first half-hour: non-participating leaders need to see the amount of work that went into this effort and the strength of support for chosen projects.

Choose your most upbeat program team member to lead the meeting. Although it will involve serious work, the meeting should begin and end with a strong feeling of celebration of the good work that's been accom-

Opening remarks *(20 minutes)*

Project committees
    Get organized *(25 minutes)*
    Refine project description *(30 minutes)*
    Consider alternatives *(20 minutes)*

ER Council organizing committee
    List potential council members *(20 minutes)*
    Determine responsibilities *(20 minutes)*
    Develop a mission statement *(20 minutes)*
    Brainstorm names *(15 minutes)*

Wrap-up *(10 minutes)*

plished through the ER process. Think of opening and closing remarks to give everyone an inspirational send-off. You might ask one or two respected leaders to make a few comments, but if you do, pick these people very carefully. Their comments must be upbeat and brief—no boring speeches.

Make copies of pages 186-200 and 205-7 to distribute to each project development committee member during the meeting. Give a copy to at least one member of each committee several days before the meeting. Urge them to study it and ask questions. This preparation will expedite the work of the committees during the meeting. Also offer a copy of Chapter 6 to committee chairpersons.

Room requirements are similar to those for Step 3 (see page 132). You'll need a large space—possibly a high-school cafeteria—with one table for each committee. Large committees may need multiple tables joined together. Set up another table or two for attendees who aren't committee members. Space the tables so the committees don't disturb each other. Place signs on the tables indicating committee names; signs on the non-committee tables might read, "New Participants."

The Meeting

At the end of the last meeting, participants formed separate project committees and a committee to organize the ER Council. As they arrive for this meeting, ask them to seat themselves in their committees. Those who haven't chosen a project may join one of the existing committees or sit at one of the "new participant" tables.

Opening Remarks

Take plenty of time to thank everyone who's made your Economic Renewal effort such a success. Briefly review the process so far, and offer an enthusiastic assessment of your community's ER work. You might say something like: *"We've come a long way. We've accomplished something that very few communities have. We've brought together people from all walks of life, overcome previous antagonisms, worked together side by side, and decided on these hopeful projects to strengthen our community and its economy.*

"Tonight is the last step of this public-meeting process, but it's the first step in actually developing the projects we've chosen. Each project committee will begin developing an action plan for its project. Also joining us is the committee that will help organize our Economic Renewal Council. After tonight, you'll all carry on meeting separately, probably several more times. Be sure to make arrangements for your next meeting before you leave here tonight."

Ask someone from each project committee to describe their project very briefly. After they're done, announce: *"If anyone hasn't yet chosen a project, talk with us after these opening comments. We'll describe each project in more detail so you can decide which committee to join. If you choose not to join a committee, feel free to listen in on the work of any of the groups."*

Review the agenda and introduce the concept of action plans (see next page). Pass out the copies of pages from this chapter. Ask for questions. Indicate that one member of each committee has studied the chapter before the meeting and will be helpful keeping the committee on track. Ask them to begin.

If implementing a project is like building a house, the project action plan is the blueprint.

CHAPTER 14

The Action Plan

First of all, why develop an action plan? Why not just do the project? There are several reasons:

➤ **It attracts support.**
Your plan will be especially helpful in generating community support and financial assistance. A realistic and properly prepared plan demonstrates the project's potential for success and fully informs people who might consider investing their time or money.

➤ **It's a grant proposal.**
Your plan will contain most of the ingredients of a grant proposal, should you need to do one. It will answer most questions you might be asked in making presentations to a local government, chamber of commerce, or other source of support. Elements of it can simply be reorganized to meet various potential funders' requirements. The plan will demonstrate that you confronted and solved problems instead of avoiding them, and that you were sensitive to the issues that often concern potential supporters (for example, community involvement).

➤ **It's a business plan.**
Your action plan will also include much of the information you'd find in a business plan. Most projects, even if they're nonprofit or volunteer efforts, require some form of budget to show that they're viable. And like a business plan, your action plan will help reveal whether your proposal has big holes in it, and if so, it will force you to fix them.

➤ **It builds teamwork.**
Creating an action plan will encourage project committee members to work closely on the practical issues and constraints that come with any project development effort. In the process, they'll get to know one another well enough to work through the difficulties that nearly always arise.

The process outlined in this chapter is designed to help committees examine their projects systematically and critically to produce solid, well-thought-out action plans. The outline below highlights the main elements that an action plan should probably contain, but each project will have its own considerations. The length and complexity of your plan will depend on your project: for a simple project, the plan need only be a few pages long and could probably be developed in two or three committee meetings; a complex one will require a more extensive plan, including detailed financial information, and more meetings with participation from an increasing number of people, especially those with resources and expertise to contribute. You may need to coordinate this effort with other project committees through the newly formed Economic Renewal Council.

The process of developing your action plan will be as important as the written document itself. Before you ever show the finished plan to prospective supporters, you'll be seeking their input on it. The relationships you form in this way—with community leaders, with staff members of agencies and organizations, with potential critics—may be the greatest contributing factor to your project's success. In addition, developing your action plan will help you to re-examine assumptions, be flexible, and find creative solutions, and in the process it will almost certainly improve your project.

Take occasional breaks from your committee's problem-solving to reflect on what you've done so far. Celebrate progress and even the smallest successes. Ask yourselves what has worked and what hasn't. What have you learned? What will you avoid next time? Keeping in mind ways in which the project or community conditions may have changed, is your project still likely to achieve your stated goals? Remember that the project itself isn't the goal—it's only a way to achieve the goal. If barriers become too difficult, if the project changes too much over time, there may be better ways to achieve the original goal.

Action Plan Outline

When you've completed the process in this chapter, your action plan will probably contain:

➤ **Project description.**
   A detailed description of the project, including its goals, the community needs it will address, and its intended effects.

➤ **Alternatives.**
   Brief descriptions of any alternatives that were considered, and why they were rejected.

➤ **Sources of support.**
   A list of organizations and notable individuals who support or are willing to support the project, whether by providing endorsements, advice, technical assistance, money, or in-kind contributions.

➤ **Technical needs.**
   An assessment of technical assistance that will be needed, and who will provide it.

➤ **A budget.**
   This may range from a simple list of projected expenses to multiple spreadsheets detailing cashflow and balance sheets.

➤ **Tasks.**
   A list of tasks required for implementation of the project, noting who will carry them out and when.

➤ **Personnel.**
   A list of project committee members (and, if appropriate, their qualifications).

Project Committee Tasks

Some project committees will accomplish more than others during this meeting, but they all should try to get through the following preliminary tasks. Those that finish early can start on the further tasks on page 191.

Get Organized

Select someone to serve as chairperson. He or she should review Chapter 6 ("Conducting Effective Meetings") prior to the next session. Besides facilitating the meetings, the chair is responsible for assigning tasks and making sure people clearly understand what they've volunteered to do. Pick someone else to serve as liaison to the ER Council, a role that entails attending council meetings and keeping the council and the project committee informed of each other's activities. Select a recorder to keep track of decisions made, tasks assigned, and deadlines set. (Tip: To enliven descriptions of tasks, begin each with active verbs such as "write," "contact," "make," "list," or "develop.")

Circulate a contact list for each person to write his or her name, address, and phone number. Ask for a volunteer to copy and distribute the list to everyone.

Choose at least three dates for future project committee meetings to complete work on your action plan. Because there will be some homework to do for each session, schedule them approximately two weeks apart.

Inventory members' skills and contacts. For instance, one person may have experience writing grants, another may be good at gaining community consensus or preparing budgets. Think about whether there are any risks for the people involved in your project. If so, discuss those risks as a group. What might be done to minimize them? Are there ways your committee can support individual members who are taking a risk?

Think about who isn't on your project committee and should be. Who can help with various aspects of the action plan? Who would be interested in this kind of project? Start a list of people to contact between now and the next time your committee meets. You'll probably find that your committee grows as you make contact with more and more people in the course of developing your action plan.

When seeking volunteer help, remember that your project will have to compete with many other activities for volunteers' discretionary time. No matter how important you think your project is, the people you contact will be weighing it against going to the Rotary meeting, high-school baseball game, 4H picnic, etc. Give careful thought to how your project can compete. Can you sell it as a short-term commitment? An opportunity for high-profile public service?

Keep the entire committee and its supporters involved and informed at every stage of the development of the action plan and the implementation of the project.

Refine the Project Description

You began this task when you completed the "Project Idea Description" worksheet (see page 163), but that work was preliminary. Your project and your thinking may have changed since then. Take more time to consider it now.

What if you were asked by someone in your community, such as the newspaper editor or the mayor, to explain what the project will achieve? Would your answer be clear? To attract supporters, you'll need a concise answer to this question. A short (less than two pages) project description will form the basis for measuring the project's success and for reporting its benefits to the community.

Review the "Project Idea Description" worksheet, then discuss:

➤ **Project or program?** Is yours a one-time project or an ongoing program? Projects have a beginning, middle, and an end: a consultant might be able to help in attracting grants and creating visible signs of success. Programs can be more difficult: they have a beginning but no end; they require ongoing commitment, political maintenance, and often cash support. If it's a program, is there any way to divide it up into separate projects?

➤ **Goals.** How will the project contribute to your community's goals or preferred future? Identify several objective and subjective indicators of success for the project. For example, objective measures might be the percentage increase in sales tax revenue or the number of jobs created. Subjective measures might be greater optimism among business people or positive stories in newspapers. Also think about what would constitute your personal measure of success— what needs to happen for you to feel your time has been well spent?

➤ **Needs.** What community problems or needs will the project address? The answer to this question may come right out of the "Project Idea Description" worksheet, or it may have undergone considerable rethinking and refining since then.

➤ **Effects.** What positive effects do you intend the project to have? What are its possible negative effects? What are its possible unintended consequences? What will be different in your community when the project is complete?

Have someone write a first draft of your project description based on these criteria.

Consider Alternatives

A big part of the process of developing a project action plan is making sure you haven't overlooked better ways of doing it. You'll analyze your alternatives more fully at a later meeting, but if there's time now, spend a

What if you were asked to explain what the project will achieve?

Though your action plan is necessary, writing it will not by itself cause your project to be implemented. Success isn't a fill-in-the-blanks exercise. You won't submit your plan to someone who will award you with a completed project.

The primary factor that will make your project a success is the relationships that you develop in the process of creating your action plan and developing your project. These important relationships may form:

➤ among committee members;

➤ with key local leaders;

➤ with staff members of agencies or organizations that are in a position to help; and

➤ with people who may be uneasy about your project.

Your project will succeed when these people feel good about you and believe in your cause. That success doesn't need a hot salesperson, but it requires your commitment, patience, and clarity of purpose.

few minutes thinking about alternative locations, phasing, and other criteria described on page 194. Creating a preliminary list of alternatives now will make the analysis easier later.

ER Council Organizing Committee Tasks

While the project committees are working on their action plans, members of the ER Council organizing committee can be getting on with the tasks described in the "Creating an Economic Renewal Council" section that you gave them at the last meeting (see page 177). They may need some help getting started. Be sure to impress on them that, whatever sort of council they choose to create, it must be prepared to accept the leadership of your community's Economic Renewal process from now on. Encourage them also to brainstorm names for the council, and tell them you'll give them a few minutes toward the end of the meeting to try their ideas out on the other participants.

Wrap-up

Save the last ten minutes of the meeting for your final Economic Renewal wrap-up. Quietly circulate among the committees to give them five minutes' warning.

This final portion of the meeting should be just as celebratory as the opening, though briefer. Thank everyone for their work on their action plans. Remind committees to be absolutely certain to schedule the time and location of their next meeting before they leave, and to use their liaisons to keep in touch with the ER Council. End with brief comments from a respected leader or members of the program team. Thank everyone for coming and wish them good luck with their projects.

Further Project Committee Tasks

Seek Support

Though this section is placed here, you'll need it to seek an expanding circle of support at each subsequent stage in developing your action plan and your project.

You're looking for three distinct kinds of support:

Endorsement

Endorsement is where a person or group is willing to say publicly that your project is a good idea and they're behind it. Don't regard this as mere token aid. As your project progresses through the planning stages, those who endorsed it early on may later decide to provide additional support. When you have several important endorsements, you'll increase your chances of getting someone to assist or even adopt the project.

Think carefully about whether there are any individuals whose endorsement will be necessary for the project to proceed, or whose opposition could hamper the project. If so, involve them early. Let them know what you're doing and why. Ask for their suggestions and support.

Unless your project is a genuine blockbuster, support will come slowly at first. Be patient: the first person or group to stand behind your project may be taking a bit of a risk. But as endorsements mount up, your project becomes a legitimate and important effort that others will want to be associated with. One way to break the ice is to ask for a provisional endorsement. For instance, you might say, "I understand that you're privately behind our project. If I can get the backing of three other people (or some particular person), can I then say that you endorse it?"

Assistance

Assistance is an offer of substantial help to the project—advice, equipment, staff time, or money. Inventory your needs to determine who to approach for assistance. The section starting on page 205 will help you think about the kinds of organizations that might be approached.

Money is an important need, but save that worry for later. Your main short-term priority is to find people who can assist the project *as part of their regular job*. They might be a government, nonprofit, or industry employee whose organization has decided to support your project. Seek their assistance because they've got the resources or skills to help make your project fly. Give serious thought to who might make your project part of their job description. It will be a short but crucial list. Think about how these people might benefit from your project. Will it look good on their resumé? Will it improve their professional status? Will it please the people they answer to? If you plan to approach Ms. Smith about making your project part of her job, first get a clear understanding of who she works for. Make a special effort to make sure her boss(es) fully understand your project. Maybe ask the boss to join your committee or serve as an advisor to it.

If it appears that your project will require technical assistance, seek it first from local institutions and individuals: town or county government, a community college, a state university, local business people, or retirees. Ask each about ways they might provide important help, and inquire about any other skills and resources that might be found within and outside the community. Research what other communities have done regarding this kind of project.

If you exhaust local resources, expand your search outside of the community. Consider a regional development or government organization, large industries and businesses, the U.S. Small Business Administration, state universities, state government agencies, local and regional foundations, or a small-business development center.

Of course, most problems don't require experts. Therefore, before seeking professional solutions, thoroughly exhaust the potential of your committee to solve problems internally. Identify who on your committee is good at confronting and solving problems; not everyone is.

Adoption

The most encompassing form of support is when some group or agency—for example, the chamber of commerce, local government, or a regional development agency—adopts your project as part of its work plan. As your project progresses, a group that offered its endorsement or assistance early on may later agree to take full responsibility for it.

Your committee's work may be relatively easy if you can turn the project over to another organization. For example, if your project is a rest area and information kiosk on the highway, at some point you may turn it over to the highway department, although even an organization as large and well-funded as the highway department is likely to require your continued participation.

But understand that if you give your project up for adoption, it's no longer yours. Unless you strike some agreement to the contrary, the adopting organization will assume full control.

How to Solicit Support

The most effective way to get support is to set the stage for someone to volunteer their help. Get them involved offering advice. Seek it in informal

Seek technical assistance first from local institutions and individuals.

settings, over coffee, one on one. Keep them involved. Then, as project needs emerge, they may offer to assist or even take full responsibility for the project.

Be confident but respectful. Don't hard-sell anyone on your project—just describe it, indicate its purposes, say why you're excited about it, and maybe ask how it might serve their needs and interests. Your attitude can be something like, "We know this is a terrific idea and it has the support of the community, but we need help in refining it, making it practical." Ask for their suggestions. Take time to get to know them, to get frank responses, and to get them feeling comfortable with your committee. Keep them posted on the project's progress. When the time feels right, ask what additional information they need to offer their support for the project.

If you're planning that kiosk on the highway, for example, you might offer your preliminary ideas to a gathering of highway department engineers, landscape architects (or students of landscape architecture), local government officials, and the chamber director. Ask them how to do it better. Make the session as informal as possible—maybe after work with beer and pretzels (or cookies and milk). As these advisors become involved in the project and develop rapport with your committee, they may begin to feel ownership in the project. This "buy-in" could lead to more substantial support by these people or their agencies.

Create a list of organizations and individuals that might support your project, noting which committee member will contact each potential supporter and when. Later, when you write your project action plan, include lists of all those who have indicated they're willing to endorse, assist, or adopt your project. Remember that those who assist or adopt your project must be acknowledged publicly (unless they ask to remain anonymous).

Analyze Alternatives

Are there better ways to do your project, or other projects that could achieve your goals better? It might seem strange to ask such questions now, after you've already put so much thought into your project, but it's wise to consider all the alternatives before committing to a single course of action. Alternatives analysis may suggest ways to improve the project; it will certainly give the project greater resilience, by generating a menu of fallback options that could be considered should the original idea run into difficulties.

This is potentially a very creative process. Most of the alternatives you come up with will only tweak the original idea in subtle ways, but some of them may alter it dramatically. In the case of the highway rest area/information kiosk project, you might consider shifting its location to the main road into town, or changing it from a kiosk to a billboard, or broadening the scope of its information from local to regional. But an even more fundamental alternative might be to create an Internet Web site to distribute the information electronically, instead of physically.

Discuss alternative project scenarios based on the following criteria. Two or three will probably emerge as the most practical and appropriate. Write them out and include them in your action plan. Later, you'll develop budgets for each to see how they compare financially.

➤ **Location.** Where else might the project take place?

➤ **Phasing.** Should the project be implemented in phases? Can one or more of these phases be regarded as a projects in themselves? For instance, a downtown revitalization project may require a series of smaller projects (installing street lights, making facade improvements, etc.). Can the early phases stand on their own and be used to demonstrate progress to the community?

➤ **Existing or new?** Should you expand existing services and structures, or create new ones?

➤ **Staff.** Most projects require one or two people who devote a significant amount of their time and energy. These may be volunteers, donated personnel (see page 191), or paid staff. Which of these staffing alternatives are worth considering?

➤ **Assistance.** Are there additional experts who might be willing to advise you on your project? If expert advice isn't available or is too expensive for your project in its current form, are there other ways to achieve the same goals for which technical advice isn't needed or can be obtained more cheaply? If expert advice indicates significant technical problems with your project, are there alternatives that appear more promising?

➤ **Adoption.** Are there additional organizations that might be willing to adopt your project? Can your project be modified to become more attractive to potential adopters?

➤ **Partnership.** Is yours a single-group effort, or should two or more organizations (e.g., nonprofit groups, municipalities) work together to make it happen? Which ones? Such a partnership facilitates the sharing of skills, resources, and even political influence, and can also demonstrate broader support for your project.

➤ **Regional cooperation.** Should the project be attempted locally only, or should several areas (e.g., towns, counties, valleys) work together to make it happen?

➤ **Funding.** Of the funding sources you now know of, which ones may be interested in this project?

➤ **Revenue.** In what ways might the project might generate revenue? Some possible revenue sources: fees or charges for services, membership dues, individual contributions, ticket sales, assessments, new taxes, retail sales, fund-raising events, a share of United Way or a local equivalent, grants, corporate donations, advertising, space rental, commissions.

Discussion of these factors will probably generate at least as many questions as answers. If questions come up that require additional information or professional advice, assign committee members to find the answers and report back.

Identify Barriers to Implementation

Barriers to implementing your project will almost certainly emerge. If, from the beginning, you assume that barriers will arise, you'll be less likely to be disappointed, and more able to deal with them constructively. Instead of avoiding barriers, seek them out and overcome them. Here are some common ones:

➤ **Legal or financial requirements.** Are there legal constraints or financial difficulties? Does the project require any local, state, or

---

FERRETING OUT ASSUMPTIONS

Most of us approach a new project with certain assumptions and expectations. We may be disappointed, frustrated, or angry if they aren't fulfilled. An incorrect assumption can lead your committee down the wrong path. Perhaps, for instance, the highway department will provide the paving and guttering for your highway information kiosk—but if that assumption turns out to be false, your committee will be in for some serious backtracking.

While analyzing alternatives, be on the lookout for unexamined assumptions that need to be addressed in the project action plan. Do project committee members appear to be making contradictory or mutually exclusive assumptions? If so, question each party about the goals, reasons, or objectives that underlie or drive their assumptions. Ask them to temporarily set aside those conflicting assumptions and focus on the underlying goals. Look for common goals and alternative ways to achieve them. Include those options in your alternatives analysis.

Some assumptions are difficult to detect. They may be so deeply ingrained that they seldom come to the surface. One way to ferret them out is to visualize yourself involved in the project six weeks, then six months, from today. Think about what it will look like, who will be involved, when it will be completed, who will benefit, how much time you'll spend on it, what will need to happen to fulfill your personal goals, how often you'll meet, and who will support the project with their resources.

federal approvals? For example, does it require a license or permit, a change to a municipal ordinance, or perhaps a resolution from city council?

➤ **Opposition.** Is there anything about this project, or the way you're proposing to carry it out, that will be so different from the usual ways of doing things that it will cause general concern or opposition in the community? If so, can you change your plans so that they'll accomplish your goals without causing problems? (See page 201.)

➤ **Fear of failure.** Some committee members may be thinking, "We're just a bunch of people. Who are we to do something like this? We have no power." The perception that you lack the permission and know-how to get it done—that you'll fail and look foolish—is a subtle but real barrier to success. There's no easy way to overcome it except to realize that you do *too* have power, as much power as you care to take—the kind of power that gets things done. You have no more or less permission to do your project than anyone had when they had a great idea. And as for know-how, you'll pick that up as you need it or find others to provide it. Yes, you could fail, but very few worthwhile endeavors require no risk-taking. So go for it!

If you come across a barrier that appears particularly challenging, ask yourselves: Should we try to overcome the barrier? Should we change the project to avoid the barrier? Or should we set the project aside and help with others that stand a better chance?

Include in your action plan a list of potential barriers and proposals for overcoming each.

Develop Budgets

Developing budgets may be easy or quite involved, depending on the scale and complexity of your project alternatives. It will take at least one meeting, perhaps more. To streamline the process, have a couple of committee members do some preliminary number-gathering first.

Ask this "budget subcommittee" to estimate likely expenses (the box on page 198 lists many common ones) for each of your project alternatives, and to report their findings at the next meeting of the full committee. They'll get most of their information from local experts. In the case of the highway information kiosk, for example, they might contact local contractors, a building inspector, and highway or road department folks. These advisors should be invited to the project committee's next meeting. The budget subcommittee should also look for comparable projects developed in other communities and (if possible) obtain copies of their budgets.

The full project committee should set aside an entire meeting to refine the budget subcommittee's preliminary figures, assess the relative costs and feasibility of the various alternatives, and look for ways to cut costs. In the

---

Fear of failure is a subtle but real barrier to success.

case of community-development projects, the best way to cut costs is to get people and businesses to contribute their services for free. As you discuss each projected expense, think about who might provide it as an in-kind contribution; assign a committee member to approach each of these people in a low-key, inclusive way. List in-kind contributions in your action plan. Potential funders will regard them as substantial demonstrations of support, as well as a way to gain greater "leverage" with their own contribution. In-kind contributions are often regarded just as favorably as cash contributions.

As the budget discussion takes place, additional questions may arise. If so, ask for volunteers to find the answers and report back at a follow-up session.

Creating realistic, professional budgets is a specialized skill. The local experts that provided you with cost estimates may also be able to help you format them into appropriate budget spreadsheets. If not, seek the help of a local accountant, or consult a book on writing business plans (check your library).

Go/No-Go

Many tough questions have been answered. Many potential advisors and supporters have been contacted and have begun to help you with your project. Finally, having scrutinized various alternatives and with your budgets before you, it's time to decide which alternative (if any) will actually be implemented.

If you decide that no project should go ahead, then someone will need to write a letter to the ER Council indicating why the project won't proceed. If the decision is to go ahead with a project, then the committee will need to determine next steps: writing grant proposals or loan applications, obtaining necessary approvals, hiring staff, etc. Such determinations are beyond the scope of this book—you're on your own now!

If your project will be completed in phases, celebrate the completion of each phase with a community event and local media attention. Try to schedule sub-projects so that you achieve at least one early success, so that activities are occurring throughout the project, and so that you're constantly gaining momentum. These celebrations will generate continuing community support for your efforts.

Keep expanding your circle of supporters. Think of groups whose goals might be served by your project, identify specific points of common interest, and determine who in your group would best contact each group. Determine who to approach for letters of support and resolutions, and what information and meetings are required to secure each commitment.

Keep all key organizations and the community at large fully informed about your progress. Be prepared to make the case for your project whenever it's mentioned. Designate a spokesperson and use the media techniques outlined in Chapter 5.

EXPENSES

Start-up Expenses	Ongoing Expenses
Site purchase	Utilities
Site preparation	Maintenance
Utility extensions	Materials
Road access	Supplies
Parking	Insurance
Labor	Auditing
Materials	Bookkeeping
Design and engineering	Legal services
Sketches	Accounting
Permits, fees, tests	Cash-flow analysis
Furnishings, signs, equipment	Postage
Renovation, cleaning, replacement	Telephone
Deposits, account start-up	Fax
	Copier
	Computers
	Advertising
	Security
	Salaries, benefits
	Travel
	Dues, memberships, licenses
	Trash pickup
	Reporting, monitoring
	Rental fees
	Repair, replacement
	Fees
	Printing, design, layout
	Storage
	Vehicles
	Taxes
	Signs, banners

Secure Financial Assistance

Success in fund-raising depends largely on your relationships with potential lenders or grant-makers, and relationships take time. There's no guarantee that putting time into these relationships will result in money, but it may pay off in other ways—an organization that turns you down for financial assistance may still provide technical help, referrals to other funders, or suggestions for improving your proposal.

Identifying potential funders is a great networking adventure. The more people you talk to, the more likely you are to discover an unusual source of funding. This brief section is only intended to get you started. Books and organizations listed in the appendix can give more detailed information, but ultimately you'll just have to follow your nose.

Some projects attract grants, while others are more appropriately financed through loans; a few may qualify for both. Needless to say, a grant will tend to have fewer strings attached to it than a loan, but a for-profit venture (or even a not-for-profit one that's intended to generate revenue) will usually have to receive its funding from lenders or investors.

Grant-Based Projects

When seeking a grant, start with local sources—a retiree devoted to the community, a community foundation, maybe local government—then expand your network of contacts outward to regional and national foundations and state and federal agencies.

There are literally thousands of grant-making foundations in the United States alone. Search the foundation directory in your library for institutions that give money to projects like yours. Corporations and local governments also may make grants to locally significant projects. See the section starting on page 205 for more information on foundations', corporations', and local governments' funding capabilities.

Most states offer a number of financial assistance programs that promote community economic development and business creation/expansion. Some federal agencies also provide financial assistance, although more typically they deal in loans and loan guarantees. Get agency phone numbers from the appendix, the government section of the phone book, and your local government. If you have computer networking capabilities, an Internet search may turn up further opportunities (see page 219 for addresses). A business consultant may be able to steer you toward the most applicable programs.

Grant-writing is a skill in itself, and it's well worth trying to get an experienced grant-writer to volunteer his or her time to help you with it. Your project action plan will provide the raw material for the application, but each institution has its own specific requirements.

The best government agencies and foundations design their grant and assistance activities to support projects generated through community collaboration. When they ask for evidence of that collaboration, you'll be way ahead of most applicants. All you have to do is describe what you did in the Economic Renewal process to choose projects. If you've created an ER plan (see page 66), it will fulfill this requirement handily; if not, the records you've been collecting all along will make it easy to write something up.

Be prepared to give a cogent two- to five-minute summary of your request. Make sure you mention the name of the person who referred you. If the organization indicates an interest in your project, ask what they'd like to see to take it to the next step. Getting them involved on their terms is more important than prematurely sending them too much information.

Ask if they have any literature on their funding criteria and projects they've funded that may be similar to yours.

Grant-makers don't like to say no, but they want to spend their money wisely. They need to take part of the credit for success. They need a win just as much as you do (maybe even more, since their job depends on the wise use of funds). So don't feel offended if they're tough on you, make you jump through lots of hoops, and ask you to prove that your project is strongly supported by the community.

Loan-Based Projects

For loan-based projects, start by finding a trusted advisor. Look for someone who's done a project similar to yours, perhaps a successful local business person. It's best to find someone you know well. You might even ask the advisor to take you under his or her wing and serve as your mentor, a source of ongoing support and advice.

It may also be useful to enlist the services of a financial intermediary— an investment banker, loan broker, CPA, or business consultant—to connect you with likely sources of financing. Try to get a direct referral to an intermediary from someone you trust (looking in the Yellow Pages is a last resort). A competent intermediary will probably save you money and help you obtain financing on more favorable terms than you could on your own, not to mention sparing you the frustration of cold-calling lenders.

Most traditional lenders—banks, insurance and equipment-leasing companies, commercial finance companies, credit unions, community development corporations, etc.—are risk-adverse, have strict credit standards, and prefer not work with new businesses (unless the financing can be made extremely safe). Also, they'll expect you to commit a significant portion of your own assets to the venture. Fortunately, your community-oriented project will probably qualify for more lenient forms of non-traditional financing. The section starting on page 205 highlights several avenues to pursue. Try also local "angels"—private investors who take the same risks as venture capitalists but generally on less demanding terms.

Some community development projects require more than one type of financing. Lenders can take different levels of risk and accept different levels of return in the same transaction. Combining funding sources—hybrid financing—is often the key to getting a large project financed.

Any prospective lender or investor will want to see a business plan. Writing a compelling business plan takes a lot of work, knowledge of the market, and persuasive abilities. Many books have been written on the subject—check your library. Your project action plan is a good start, but your business plan will probably also have to include a detailed market analysis, spreadsheet financial projections, and other elements that demonstrate the venture's potential to pay back its lender or shareholders.

Dealing With Resistance to Your Efforts

You've just completed an extraordinary effort to build consensus for a project based on your community's own goals and values. But, as mentioned in Chapter 3, consensus-building is far from foolproof. It's not some warm fuzzy vision of everyone holding hands and walking off into the sunset, nor does it mean you should give up or give in every time someone objects. On the contrary, it's a means to seek mutually satisfactory solutions that maximize community interest and minimize discord. But sometimes interests are so divergent that consensus simply isn't possible.

Resistance may come from people who heard a rumor about your project, whose information is incomplete or erroneous, who didn't participate in the ER process, or who feel that they must sacrifice too much for too little benefit. Resistance might also come from people who fully understand your project but just think it's a bad idea. In any case, your project will be more successful if you're able to satisfactorily respond to all, or at least a portion of, these people's concerns.

When in doubt, use the simple negotiation process described here. It requires patience and time, but in most cases it will take less time in the long run than dealing with the conflicts that would otherwise occur. It will reduce anger and resentment on all sides, and will make the business of implementing your project much less stressful for you and your committee. It may well result in a better project.

This process requires clear intentions. If you go into it trying to convince the concerned parties that your project is best or that they're wrong, you'll probably fail. In contrast, if your intention is to find a solution that will benefit both you and your opponents, then your potential for success will be higher. The ideal solution is one in which everyone wins. A realistic solution is one that everyone can live with.

This method is neither foolproof nor unique, but it has been found to work in many circumstances. You can do it without professional assistance, although in difficult cases a trained mediator will increase the likelihood of success. If you feel you need help, ask around to find out who in your area is a mediator, and check their references.

Meet with Your Project Committee

If you hear of residents who are troubled about your project, your first step should be to meet with your project committee and carefully review your own position. Are you being unreasonable? What are your project goals? What interests and desired outcomes drive those goals? Have you sought an alternative that would achieve your goals while alleviating the concerns of others? Is your project genuinely in the long-term interest of the community? You might ask a neutral party to help you answer these

Dealing with resistance saves time in the long run.

questions. This shouldn't be a discussion about how right you are and how wrong they are. Rather, it should be an honest attempt to clearly identify your committee's intentions.

Once you've carefully thought through your own position, it's essential that you communicate with the concerned parties as quickly as possible. The success of your project may depend on it.

Meet with 'Mr. Warry'

Break the ice by meeting one-on-one with a key representative of the concerned group—let's call him Mr. Warry. Your purpose will simply be to get to know one another and talk about how your respective groups might meet. It won't be easy. Don't be surprised if you find an excellent reason to miss it—your daughter's basketball game, something at work, you're not feeling well, whatever. But resist the temptation to call it off; make it a high priority. Once it's under way and the two of you begin to understand and respect each other, the feeling of relief will make it all worthwhile. Then you can focus your attention on the tasks at hand.

If it goes well with Mr. Warry, convene a more formal meeting with, say, three people from each side where you can begin to negotiate the issues. (Inviting the same number of participants from each side will reduce the risk that one side feels threatened.) Arrange the meeting in a comfortable setting in a neutral location; that is, the meeting shouldn't be held at the home or office of one of the parties. Church meeting rooms often work well.

Take your time—don't try to get all the issues ironed out in one meeting. In fact, don't go more than two hours in one sitting (90 minutes would be better). Feel free to call a third or fourth meeting if necessary.

Listen Actively

After all the thought and work you've put into your project, it would be understandable if you started the meeting by reacting to Mr. Warry's objections with indignation and anger, or with aloof coolness. Though these reactions may be justified, if acted on, they'll probably only cause Mr. Warry to become more determined to stop your efforts. Similarly, it would be natural for you to try to convince Mr. Warry that he's wrong to oppose your project. But doing that will only force him to defend his position. He won't hear the points you're making because, while you're talking, he'll be thinking about how to show you that you're wrong.

The most effective approach is to ask Mr. Warry what his concerns are—after all, he may have a point. Therefore, the first objective of the meeting must be to carefully and sincerely listen to what Mr. Warry has to say. This will be difficult, but he won't begin to listen to you until he feels you've heard his points. And he won't feel that you've heard him if you merely lis-

Trying to convince Mr. Warry he's wrong will only force him to defend his position.

ten passively—you must listen *actively*, using the techniques described on page 88.

When Mr. Warry makes a point that you like, *acknowledge* it—that is, interject to say that you liked what he said. He'll begin to feel that you may not be so bad after all. If he seems angry, upset, or frustrated, or if he exhibits some other strong emotion, *empathize* with him—that is, sincerely indicate that you notice that he's angry, frustrated, or whatever. If you don't understand something he says, ask him to *clarify* it. He'll sense that you're sincerely interested in his ideas. When he's finished, or during the course of the discussion, you can further clarify by summarizing what you think he said, then ask if you got it right. He'll then feel satisfied that you've heard him and he'll become more comfortable with the conversation.

Don't interrupt, and don't defend yourself. If you interrupt, Mr. Warry will think you aren't listening, and he'll be right. You cannot listen thoroughly to someone when you start talking before they're finished. If you attempt to defend yourself in response to each point he makes, the discussion will get lost in the details and never get to the real issues.

If your active listening is insincere, Mr. Warry will sense it and you'll get nowhere. He'll keep repeating his points and he won't listen to you. But if you use these three techniques—acknowledging, clarifying, and empathizing—or even just one of them—he'll probably be ready to hear your ideas. If he was angry, most of his anger will be gone. If he was fearful, his fear will subside. The two of you will have begun to communicate.

Early in the discussion, ask Mr. Warry if he minds if you take notes. Explain that you want to be sure that you remember everything correctly. Keep a record of Mr. Warry's goals, interests, and desired outcomes. Later, you'll be able to compare them to your own to find common interests.

Explain Goals

Your foremost intention should be to achieve your goals, not to implement a particular project. If you focus first on your goals, you may find that there are other ways to achieve them that also accommodate Mr. Warry's concerns. You may find that a different or changed project will achieve both your goals and his.

Therefore, the second objective of your meeting with Mr. Warry should be to give him a clear understanding of the goals of your project. Don't try to "sell" your project. Rather, ask him how he feels about each of your goals and interests. If he's comfortable with one, move on to the next. If he's not, ask him if there are related goals that he would support. They may be consistent with your goals. He may say the same thing in different words. Don't quibble over details; look at the big picture.

Describe the Project

Don't assume that Mr. Warry understands your project. Your third objective should be to carefully explain the project and the community process by which it was chosen. Refer gently to the extent of community support for the project, but don't use that support as a weapon to better him.

Having described the project, listen to his concerns. Summarize the points of agreement and apparent disagreement. Check with Mr. Warry to see if he agrees with your summary. If there are any disagreements you think you can resolve or accommodate on the spot, do so. (Note: don't make any actual promises to change something about your project until you've had a chance to talk it over with your group.) Then, to assure Mr. Warry that you understand the points that remain as problems, recap them. Ask if he has any additional suggestions as to how to reconcile his concerns with the goals and purposes of your project.

End the meeting by telling Mr. Warry you appreciate his having taken the time to meet with you so that you could understand his concerns and describe your project. Indicate that you'll get back to him after you take his concerns back to your group to see how they might be accommodated.

After the Meeting

Reconvene your group. Review Mr. Warry's goals, interests, and desired outcomes. Discuss ways in which they're similar to your own. Talk about whether they might be the basis for negotiations with Mr. Warry's group. Could your project be changed to accommodate Mr. Warry while supporting your original goals?

Discuss ways in which Mr. Warry's goals, interests, and desired outcomes are at odds with your own. Are you so far apart that you'll have to remain adversaries?

Try to anticipate what Mr. Warry's next steps will be if you change your project to accommodate him, and if you don't.

Get back to Mr. Warry. If you made changes to the project, let him know how he has helped improve it. If you didn't, let him know in detail how you carefully considered his concerns but couldn't find a way to accommodate them. Since he now knows you better and understands your goals and interests, he may be satisfied that you sincerely tried.

If you feel that Mr. Warry has a constructively critical attitude, you may want to ask him to join your effort. It wouldn't be the first time that someone started as an opponent and became an ally.

The following types of organizations, as well as those described on page 181, may be useful in your quest for project funding. Though some will clearly be more applicable to your project than others, the type of organization is less important than the people who run it and the kind of relationships you develop with them. Further details on specific agencies, programs, and information clearinghouses can be found on pages 214-20.

When thinking about who might provide assistance, bear in mind that many nonprofit organizations, government agencies, and public institutions tend to take the public perspective, undertaking projects that serve overall community interests. They're accustomed to public scrutiny, and they're usually more willing to devote the additional time needed to deal gingerly with the community's diverse interests, which frequently collide. In contrast, private-sector organizations are better able to undertake projects that require quick, independent decision-making. They often stress the need for measurable results from their efforts.

➤ **Government agencies.** The Small Business Administration (SBA) is a great place to start looking for money, or at least information. Other key federal agencies include the Economic Development Administration (EDA), Rural Economic and Community Development (RECD), and Department of Housing and Urban Development (HUD). These agencies collectively run hundreds of programs. Among the most popular are loan-guarantee programs, which take out most of the risk for lenders, and hence stimulate lending to companies that wouldn't normally be able to access capital (or at least not on such favorable terms). Some of these agencies also administer micro-enterprise loan funds, which make very small, short-term loans to individuals to start up or expand small businesses. These funds often serve only very low-income people, and loans are coupled with strong hands-on technical assistance. For information on state-sponsored loan programs, contact your state's office of economic development. Some states have agencies that provide assistance specifically to business start-ups.

➤ **Local governments.** Cities, towns, and counties may provide money, staff, or technical assistance to community economic development, depending on the inclination of elected officials. They can also help develop infrastructure, acquire land, promote the community to attract new investment, and offer economic incentives to lure new business. Some local governments own facilities that support the local economy. For instance, the Packers football team will never be taken from Green Bay, Wisconsin, because the city owns it.

➤ **Foundations.** These can be important partners in community economic development, providing both direction and financial assistance. Because they can accept tax-exempt contributions, they offer an attractive means for companies to make contributions to community development efforts. Many make direct grants and, increasingly, loans (called "program-related investments" in foundation lingo) to business enterprises or programs. Community-based projects are in an excellent position to create joint public/private initiatives with foundations and local governments or corporations.

➤ **Corporations.** For-profit or other corporate entities, such as utilities, sometimes have programs to loan personnel or facilities, sponsor community activities, underwrite certain project costs (e.g., publishing materials), or provide education and training.

➤ **Educational institutions.** Colleges and universities can often provide education and training in business and economic development. They may help with such efforts as leadership training, improvement and expansion of workplace skills, and evaluation of development alternatives. Small-business development centers (see page 218), with their own staff and technical assistance programs, are often found in community colleges. Many state universities have extension services that offer technical assistance to communities interested in economic development.

➤ **Religious investors.** Religious pension funds and other religious institutions are increasingly lending to impoverished urban and rural communities. Through alternative investments, they play a major role in supporting community efforts to meet essential human needs, such as affordable housing, health care, elder care, business formation, etc. These investors provide loans directly to both for-profit and nonprofit entities, often channeling their funds through intermediaries such as community development loan funds and minority-owned banks.

➤ **Venture capital funds.** Contrary to popular belief, most venture capital investments are *not* made in business start-ups. However, a small but growing number of "community development" venture capital funds make small-scale equity investments to stimulate community development and to support regional businesses that foster sustainable business practices.

➤ **Community development corporations.** CDCs are often subsidiaries of commercial banks or multi-bank corporations, formed to serve the unmet capital needs of a community. Many have been created as part of an effort of their parent banks to adhere to the

Community Reinvestment Act, which requires financial institutions to demonstrate that they serve the credit needs of the communities in which they're chartered. Unlike regular banks, CDCs can function as real-estate developers and make equity (stock) investments in local businesses and community development organizations, as well as make loans.

➤ **Revolving loan funds.** These specialized funds are created by towns, cities, or regions to provide alternative financing to small businesses and non-profit organizations. Often these funds are administered by a CDC or specially created nonprofit organization. Each fund operates for a specific purpose, such as to support job creation/retention, affordable housing, business start-ups, business expansion, etc. Because of their focus on community economic development, revolving loan funds generally lend money on terms that are more flexible and at lower rates than conventional lenders.

➤ **Community development loan funds.** Backed by foundations, private donors, or religious organizations, these funds lend money to small businesses and community projects that have typically been denied access to traditional capital sources. They work with organizations that are community-centered and community-controlled. Typical borrowers include worker-owned businesses, consumer cooperatives, housing cooperatives, minority- and women-owned businesses, and nonprofit housing developers.

➤ **Local development corporations.** The economic backbone of many small communities, LDCs are certified Small Business Administration lenders that specialize in lending to small and medium-sized businesses for job creation or retention.

➤ **Downtown development authorities.** These nonprofit entities are often created by local government to support downtown businesses in their efforts to improve marketing, create events, finance improvments, and upgrade public facilities (e.g. streets, vegetation, and streetlights). The National Trust for Historic Preservation helps downtown associations create historic districts, preserve historic buildings, encourage compatible new construction, and find new economic options for historic downtowns.

➤ **Special-purpose districts.** Another nonprofit category, these taxing districts provide such public infrastructure and services as sewer, water, streets, recreation facilities, and weed control. They can help with Economic Renewal projects—for example, a recreation district might build rest rooms that tourists could use in a park near downtown.

Explaining Economic Renewal to Others

You'll probably be called upon to talk about Economic Renewal often in the early stages of your effort, even though you haven't actually had direct experience with the process yourself.

Here are two ready-made presentations you can give, or at least draw from. The first is a brief verbal description of ER you can use when your audience has very little time. Spoken the way it's written, it should take roughly three minutes. If you have even less time than that, the first two paragraphs will suffice as a quick summary. The second presentation will take about ten minutes. If you want to add detail, cite different examples, or make up your own presentation from scratch, use material from Chapters 1, 2, and 3 (especially Chapter 2).

Open your presentations by thanking the sponsors of the meeting, introducing yourself, and explaining why you're presenting the information in this place at this time. Have copies of Chapters 1, 2, and 3 available for distribution to your audience.

Also included below is a sample letter you can use when first contacting community leaders to become involved in ER.

Three-Minute Presentation

Economic Renewal is a different way of looking at economic development. Based on the experience of real people in real towns, it shows us that economic development is not just about business, it's about many ways to make our economy and our community stronger without doing any damage to the environment. In fact, it shows us that the economy, the community, and the environment are really one thing in the long run. It's when we separate them that we get into trouble.

Economic Renewal is also a different way of going about economic development. Instead of letting a few people make decisions that generate lots of nasty controversy, it involves people from all walks of life in a collaborative decision-making process that's creative, practical, and fun.

The Economic Renewal process is a series of carefully thought-out town meetings. In the first, we'll envision our "preferred future"—how we want the community to be. In the next, we'll figure out what we have to work with—our community's problems, needs, and assets. In later meetings, we'll look for ways to use our assets to solve problems or fulfill needs; we'll study successes from other towns and talk about ideas for projects to strengthen our community and its economy; and we'll carefully evaluate our ideas and choose the projects that make the most sense for our particular circumstances.

Not only will these sessions result in practical projects that we can implement to make this a better place to live, they'll help us find common ground and learn to work better with one another—even with people we disagree with. It won't be quick or easy. It'll take eight to ten meetings to do it right. But it'll be creative and fun, and it'll definitely set us off in a better direction.

Instead of just figuring out who to blame or searching high and low for someone outside the community to come save us, we'll focus first on how we can do better with what we have. For instance, we could find ways to save money by using resources more efficiently. We might create jobs by figuring out ways to produce locally some of the things we buy from the outside. Or we could focus on keeping the jobs we've got. Also, we'll probably look for ways to keep local businesses strong.

Economic Renewal will help us identify what we want, find creative new ideas, put those ideas to work, and access resources. But it doesn't guarantee results. Results depend on our ability to work together, despite our differences. The Economic Renewal process will help us do that, too, so we can get genuinely creative results.

And, by the way, if you want to learn more about these ideas, we have materials you can read on your own. We've got one paper on sustainable development (Chapter 1), one on this particular approach to development (Chapter 2), and one on how communities can work together more effectively (Chapter 3).

Ten-Minute Presentation

I'd like to talk briefly about some ingenious things that other communities have done, and what we can do to develop a more prosperous and sustainable local economy here in our community.

There are many theories about what's happening to the economy—at least as many theories as there are economists. But we can't afford to base our actions on theory. Instead, we must be prepared for an ever-changing world economy. We must become more resilient, so that we can withstand economic changes that are outside our control. And, equally important, we must base our actions on what we know is working in the real world.

For instance, we could do something as straightforward as what they did in Tropic, Utah. The timber mill had shut and ranching was part-time for most. But high school students in a business class noticed that tourists were buying a lot of water. They started producing and selling Bryce Canyon Mist, locally sourced spring water bottled with an attractive label depicting the nearby national park. Bryce Canyon Mist hasn't single-handedly saved the town, but it has taught residents an important lesson: you can improve the local economy by replacing imports with local products. That's one way to *plug the leaks*, which is the first principle of Economic Renewal.

Even when a commodity can't be produced locally, it can often be used more efficiently to achieve the same result—which is probably the most reliable development strategy of all. For instance, most towns spend more than 20 percent of their gross income on energy—and 80 percent of those dollars immediately leave the local area. Plugging this leak through efficiency is much easier (and cheaper, as it turns out) than trying to produce more energy.

Thanks to locally initiated weatherization and energy-efficiency efforts, residents of Osage, Iowa enjoy electric rates 50 below the state average. That may not sound like much until you add up the overall effects. All told, the town of 3,800 people has plowed more than $7.8 million back into its local economy since 1974.

Leak-plugging opportunities abound. When folks in the Williamsburg, Kentucky, Firestone plant read the Economic Renewal materials, they decided to stop buying their uniforms out of state and order them locally instead, helping out a nearby business.

It's simple stuff, it just requires that our community get together and think carefully about where we're headed and what we might do differently. But I'll talk about how to do that in a moment.

The second principle of Economic Renewal is *support existing businesses*. It sounds obvious, but many towns throw open their front doors for new industry—providing tax breaks and giving away land and buildings—while existing businesses are quietly falling out the back door.

There are plenty of ways to help existing business. For example, "community-supported agriculture" supports one of our most vital businesses—farms—by providing them with up-front capital and securing markets for their products. Farmers sell "shares" of their crops in the fall and winter, when farm income is typically lowest. For their investment, customers are assured a supply of fresh fruits and vegetables. Everyone benefits: the farmers get winter cash, consumers get summer discounts, and the community strengthens its local food supply and agricultural economy.

Local retailers are often intimidated when "big-box" retailers come to town. But Economic Renewal inspired local retailers in Alamosa, Colorado to fix up their downtown despite the big-box store on the outskirts. Now, restaurants, a coffee shop, a record store, a natural foods co-op, a clothing store, art galleries, and artists' studios thrive where boarded-up storefronts used to collect trash.

And back in Osage, they found that leak-plugging also supported local businesses and jobs. A major employer, Fox River Mills, was able to cut its production costs by 29 percent thanks to lower electric rates and more efficient electric motors, making possible a plant expansion that nearly tripled jobs.

The third principle of Economic Renewal is *encourage new local business*—look for business opportunities by fully using underused local assets, skills, and resources. Farmers in Alamosa used to grow only such traditional crops as potatoes, but now they're fully using local know-how and soil by growing and selling organic quinoa [pronounced *keen-wa*], canola, garlic, and various veggies. They've even used local hot springs to make year-round fish-farming a reality.

A group of farmers in Saskatchewan, inspired by Economic Renewal, built a facility to process their organic grain products instead of shipping them unprocessed. They showed that "adding value" is a powerful strategy for creating more jobs without harvesting or extracting more of limited natural resources and without increasing environmental impact.

But local start-ups are often so small or risky that banks won't touch them. So "micro-enterprise" loan funds are beginning to fill the gap. One, pioneered by a foundation in Arkansas, loans money to very small businesses often started by low-income people who want to work for themselves.

The fourth principle is to *recruit compatible new business* to the community. When a town has bootstrapped itself using the first three principles, it's more attractive to outside companies. And it's in a stronger position to ensure that the new business fits with community conditions and values, therefore ensuring that the community will receive a net gain.

Business recruitment may be fine in our situation, but we just can't rely on it. First, we need to build on our strengths and do better with what we already have. Old, worn-out industrial recruitment schemes require decisions made outside the community by people with no regard for it. That's very different from plugging leaks and supporting existing business. They depend on decisions made inside the community by people with a personal stake in it.

The stories I've mentioned are examples of what is now called "sustainable development"—development that makes sense in the long run as well as the short term, that creates jobs in the present without jeopardizing future livelihood; development that uses resources—such as soil, water, and trees—no faster than they can be renewed.

These stories demonstrate two important ideas. First, we can make our economy stronger ourselves. We need not always look for someone to come in and save us. Second, we need not give up our community's qualities and values in order become stronger economically.

We can develop success stories right here. The Economic Renewal process is a democratic way to make community decisions about economic development. It's based on the principle that community decisions are most effective when developed collaboratively—that is, when people from all walks of life are involved from the very beginning.

APPENDIX

ROCKY MOUNTAIN INSTITUTE

THE ECONOMIC RENEWAL GUIDE 211

Economic Renewal is a eight-step process that begins when we *mobilize the entire community* to be involved. When all different kinds of people collaborate, you get more and better ideas. Also, the resulting proposals are far less likely to run into opposition because potential opponents were involved from the beginning. They had a hand in it. Their concerns were addressed.

The second step is to *envision the community's "preferred future"*—identify what everyone wants the town to be, say, twenty years from now. Our preferred future is, in effect, the reason why we're doing economic development. I'm betting that we'll find a surprising level of agreement on this big picture, which will make it easier for us all to work together, despite things that may have happened in the past.

The third step is to *identify what the community has to work with*—its assets, needs, and problems. We'll divide into small groups that will use written materials to examine various aspects of the local economy such as infrastructure, quality of life, access to capital, and human resources.

Fourth, we'll begin *finding opportunities*, many of which may never been considered. We'll do this by looking for ways in which we might use our assets to solve problems or fulfill needs.

Fifth, we'll apply what we've learned to *generate project ideas* to strengthen the community and the economy. Economic Renewal materials will offer additional ideas for local opportunities.

Then, in the sixth step, we'll *evaluate project ideas* based on many criteria, including their compatibility with our preferred future.

That information will be used in the seventh step when we *select projects*—the ones that are best and most practical for our particular circumstances. Hopefully, at least one will be completed quickly for a short-term success that everyone can see and get excited about.

Last, we'll *create action plans* for the chosen projects so that we can be sure that they'll actually get going.

But while those projects are getting under way, something else will have happened. We'll feel more in control of our future, less dependent on experts, less inclined to find someone to blame. We'll know that we can strengthen our own economy. We'll be far more creative. Like the residents of Colorado's Plateau Valley. Spread over hundreds of square miles, they had no effective way to communicate as a community. Their only newspaper came from a city forty miles away that virtually ignored them. So their first Economic Renewal priority was to create a local newspaper. It was their way to build their own capacity to strengthen their community and economy.

They understood that Economic Renewal isn't a quick fix. It's not a long pass to win the football game. Rather, it's like a "ground game," won a few yards at a time. That's a game this community knows how to play.

Yes, it will take time and work. But when the stakes are this high, it's well worth it.

And, by the way, if you want to learn more about these ideas, we have materials you can read on your own. We've got one paper on sustainable development (Chapter 1), one on this particular approach to development (Chapter 2), and one on how communities can work together more effectively (Chapter 3).

A Draft Letter to Community Leaders

Your initial contact with local leaders might be in the form of a letter. If so, you might use some of the following sample letter. Adapt it to your needs, and have several team members sign it. But keep in mind that, though a letter is a one way to make a first contact, to be effective, it must be followed by a phone call or a visit.

Include with the letter background materials on Economic Renewal—a photocopy of Chapter 2 should do the trick.

Dear (Name):

The purpose of this letter is to introduce you to a new economic development program that is available to our community, and to request your support for it. The program, called Economic Renewal, will be conducted by local people. Because you are a key leader in our community, your participation is important to the success of this effort. We will call you in the next few weeks to arrange a meeting to talk further about this idea.

Economic Renewal is a series of carefully designed community meetings and workshops supported by easy-to-use written materials. It enables us to develop practical projects to revitalize our local economy. We have learned how to conduct this program in our community, but we can't do it alone. We need the support of people like you. The enclosed material will give you a complete description of the program.

The Economic Renewal program was developed by Rocky Mountain Institute, an independent, non-profit research organization in rural Colorado. Our community's Economic Renewal effort is supported by (sponsors' or funders' names).

We would like to hear your ideas about the community and its development. We will be very pleased to answer any questions that you may have regarding the enclosed material. Also, because you are a trusted member of the community, we will ask if you would be willing to endorse and actively support our Economic Renewal effort. We feel that your support will encourage a significant portion of the community to participate in it.

Thanks for your time. You'll be hearing from us soon.

Resources

ROCKY MOUNTAIN INSTITUTE

Rocky Mountain Institute (RMI) is a nonprofit organization that conducts research, publishes reports, and consults on a wide variety of topics. Though this work cuts across many disciplines, it focuses primarily on: energy, water, community economic development, land and building development, and transportation. RMI's mission is to foster the efficient and sustainable use of resources as a path to global security. RMI believes an informed market can often solve environmental problems faster and more surely than bureaucratic coercion. The Institute employs a non-confrontational approach, working with corporations and environmental groups alike, and emphasizes positive action over doomsaying.

Three RMI programs provide assistance on issues relevant to community economic development:

Economic Renewal Program

RMI's Economic Renewal program offers:

- ➤ **Oral presentations.** These introduce the ideas of sustainable development and community collaboration to conferences and community gatherings.
- ➤ **Seminars.** Economic Renewal seminars teach the ER process to community leaders, active citizens, and professionals. Participants hear how other communities have successfully strengthened their economies using sustainable development. Through discussion and practice, they learn how to conduct each step in the ER process with the support of this workbook. Seminars may be arranged by community groups, nonprofit organizations, corporations, governments, professional groups, and foundations who hire RMI to conduct them in locations of their choice.
- ➤ **Consultation and follow-up.** RMI helps find ways to introduce Economic Renewal ideas while remaining sensitive to local politics. Its field staff work with key local people to assess the community's readiness for ER. They also conduct ER town meetings and trouble-shoot problems that may arise.
- ➤ **Publications.** Written for community volunteers, leaders, and development professionals, RMI publications provide communities with innovative ideas and practical steps for achieving sustainable and collaborative economic development. See listings below for *The Community Energy Workbook*, *The Business Opportunities Casebook*, and *Financing Economic Renewal Projects*.

Green Development Services

RMI's Green Development Services program fosters energy-efficient, environmentally responsive, and community-sensitive land and building development. The team's consultants work mainly with architects, planners, developers, and corporations on ways to integrate cost-effective "green" design into specific projects. RMI also publishes papers and books on green development.

RMI Water Associates

Another consulting unit of RMI, Water Associates helps water utilities and communities plan and evaluate efficiency programs as a least-cost alternative to expensive and environmentally damaging supply increases.

Rocky Mountain Institute
1739 Snowmass Creek Road
Snowmass, Colorado 81654-9199
(970) 927-3851
http://www.rmi.org
Periodical: *RMI Newsletter*

RURAL DEVELOPMENT CENTERS

The following regional centers offer extensive publications and technical assistance for rural development.

North Central Regional Center for Rural Development
317D East Hall
Iowa State University
Ames, IA 50011-1070
(515) 294-8321
jstewart@iastate.edu
http://www.ag.iastate.edu/centers/rdev/RuralDev.html

North East Regional Center for Rural Development
7 Armsby
Pennsylvania State University
University Park, PA 16802
(814) 863-4656

Southern Rural Development Center
PO Box 9656
Mississippi State University
Mississippi State, MS 39762
(601) 325-3207
bonniet@mces.msstate.edu
http://www.ces.msstate.edu/~srdc

Western Rural Development Center

307 Ballard Extension Hall
Oregon State University
Corvallis, OR 97331-3607
(541) 737-0123
WRDC@ccmail.orst.edu
http://www.orst.edu/dept/WRDC

OTHER NONPROFIT ORGANIZATIONS

American Planning Association

1776 Massachusetts Ave. NW
Washington, DC 20036
(202) 872-0641
scochran@planning.org
http://www.planning.org./
Periodical: *Environment and Development*

Offers conferences and extensive publications to citizen and professional planners. APA's Community Planning Teams of experienced and committed professionals work with communities on a cost-only basis. On-site work is organized around four- to five-day sessions in the communities, which may be repeated over a two- to three-year period.

Association for Enterprise Opportunity

320 N. Michigan Ave., Suite 804
Chicago, IL 60601
(312) 357-0177
Periodical: *AEO Exchange*

A volunteer-based national trade association of more than 500 micro-enterprise development organizations serving economically disadvantaged entrepreneurs across the country. AEO provides its members with a forum, information, and a voice to promote enterprise opportunity for people and communities with limited access to economic resources.

Center for Community Change

1000 Wisconsin Ave. NW
Washington, DC 20007
(202) 342-0519
Periodical: *Community Change*

A national nonprofit organization that supports low-income and minority neighborhoods in establishing small businesses and replacing tenements with safe housing. The most important objective of CCC is to see these communities mobilize themselves through grassroots action. CCC is active in providing long-term, on-site assistance to urban and rural grassroots groups that address a daunting range of poverty-related issues.

Center for Living Democracy

RR1, Black Fox Rd.
Brattleboro, VT 05301
(802) 254-1234
ans@ans.sover.net.com
Periodical: *Doing Democracy*

Working to make democracy a way of life, CLD demonstrates that it's possible to change essential elements of society from the bottom up. The center focuses on three areas: changing public perceptions of what's possible; linking different democracy trailblazers through the "living democracy learning center"; and offering training programs in how to become an effective citizen problem-solver.

Center for Neighborhood Technology

2125 W. North Ave.
Chicago, IL 60647
(312) 278-4800
http://www.cnt.org/Welcome.html
Periodical: *The Neighborhood Works* (tnwedit@cnt.org)

Seeking a healthier urban environment, a sustainable economy, and viable neighborhoods, CNT offers practical tools for neighborhood organizations, especially in the areas of energy, jobs, housing, food, and materials use.

Center for Rural Affairs

PO Box 406
Walthill, NE 68067
(402) 846-5428
HN1721@handsnet.org
http://www.forages.css.orst.edu/
Organizations/Agriculture/CRA.html
Periodical: monthly newsletter

An advocate for progressive action on social, economic, and environmental issues affecting rural America, especially the Midwest and Plains regions. Among its activities are creating self-employment opportunities in farm and non-farm businesses, developing a loan fund, reforming the way public schools are financed, and working for fairer prices for livestock producers.

Center for the Study of Community

4018 Old Santa Fe Trail
Santa Fe, NM 87505
(505) 982-2752

Offers training that develops and enhances the leadership skills of individuals to effectively address community needs and support the common good.

Clearinghouse on Alternative Investments

475 Riverside Dr., Room 566
New York, NY 10115
(212) 870-2293

Provides information on religious loan funds (see page 206).

Community Economic and Ecological Development Institute

1807 Second St., Studio #2
Santa Fe, NM 87501
(505) 986-1401

Operates the Right Livelihood Revolving Loan Fund, which focuses primarily on ecologically sustainable community development and the financing of environmentally sound businesses.

Community Information Exchange
1120 G St. NW, Suite 900
Washington, DC 20005
(202) 628-2981
cie@comminfoexch.org
Periodicals: *Exchange News!, Strategy Alert*

A national, nonprofit information service providing community-based organizations with customized information for community revitalization—especially on affordable housing and economic and community development. It also offers technical assistance and publications on business and development finance.

Corporation for Enterprise Development
1725 K St. NW, Suite 1401
Washington, DC 20006
(202) 408-9788

Provides technical assistance, training, and information to public, private, nonprofit, and community organizations. It expands the pool of entrepreneurs through improved policy, practice, and support systems for individuals and small businesses.

The Foundation Center
79 Fifth Ave.
New York, NY 10003-3076
(212) 620-4230
http://fdncenter.org/2aboutfc/2whatis.html

Fosters public understanding of the foundation field by collecting, organizing, analyzing, and disseminating information on foundations, corporate giving, and related subjects. It's used by grant seekers, grant makers, researchers, policy makers, the media, and the general public.

Heartland Center for Leadership Development
941 'O' St., Suite 920
Lincoln, NE 68508
(402) 474-7667

An independent, nonprofit organization developing local leadership that responds to the challenges of the future. A major focus of its activities is practical resources and public policies for rural community survival. It offers workshops and technical assistance.

Highlander Research and Education Center
1959 Highlander Way
New Market, TN 37820
(423) 933-3443
hrec@igc.apc.org
Periodical: *Highlander Reports*

An independent, nonprofit training center involved in a variety of social change issues in the South, including economic development and education. The center develops its research and publications by drawing together people most affected by particular issues and recording their experiences and ideas on how to approach solutions.

Institute for Community Economics
57 School St.
Springfield, MA 01105-1331
(413) 746-8660
Periodical: *Community Economics*

Developed the community land trust and community loan fund models to help lower-income communities secure access to land, housing, and capital.

International City/County Manager's Association
777 N. Capital NE, Suite 500
Washington, DC 20002
(202) 289-4262
http://www.icma.org
Periodicals: *Public Management Magazine, ICMA Newsletter*

Provides technical and management assistance, training, and publications to help local government administrators improve their skills and increase their knowledge. Also serves as a clearinghouse for the collection, analysis, and dissemination of information and data about local government.

Lincoln Institute of Land Policy
113 Brattle St.
Cambridge, MA 02138-3400
(800) 526-3873
lincolninfo@lincolninst.edu
http://www.igc.apc.org/lincoln/
edu@lilp.html

A school for land-use policy, including land economics and land taxation. It offers courses, conferences, and publications.

MDC, Inc.
1717 Legion Rd.
PO Box 2226
Chapel Hill, NC 27514
(919) 968-4531
hn4406@handsnet.org

A private, nonprofit organization providing research and technical assistance to identify and develop responses to the economic development, employment, and education challenges facing the South. MDC works closely with state and local organizations in the public, private, and nonprofit sectors to establish and institutionalize model economic development and job training programs.

National Association of Community Development Loan Funds
PO Box 40085
Philadelphia, PA 19106-5085
(215) 923-4754
nacdls@aol.com or
71231,2211@compuserve.com
Periodical: *Capital for Economic, Social, and Political Justice*

A clearinghouse, mentor, and resource to help communities create and manage community development loan funds (see page 207). Also, it advocates reform of the financial system to increase the flow of capital to distressed and disinvested communities.

National Association of Counties

440 First St. NW
Washington, DC 20001
(202) 393-6226
cnnewsnaco@aol.com
Periodical: *County News*

NACo's primary objective is to create a bridge between various levels of government and act as a national flag-bearer for county government. It studies issues, evaluates current policies, and reviews proposals submitted by its membership.

National Association of Towns and Townships

1522 K St. NW, Suite 703
Washington, DC 20005
(202) 737-5200, (202) 624-3550
Periodical: NATAC Townscape Supplements (distributed on disk to members)

Offers educational conferences, training workshops, and specialized periodicals that help local officials cope with and manage change in small towns.

National Civic League

1445 Market St., Suite 300
Denver, CO 80202-1728
(303) 571-4343
ncl@csn.net
http://www.ncl.org/ncl
Periodical: *National Civic Review*

Helps citizens and public and private officials develop a community culture that is aware of and responsive to its divergent needs. Its Civic Index assists communities in developing their problem-solving capacities. Its Healthy Communities Initiative helps communities identify their collective needs, priorities, and resources to address a broad range of social as well as health problems.

National Cooperative Bank Development Corporation

1401 Eye St. NW, Suite 700
Washington, DC 20005
(202) 336-7700
http://www.ncb.com

Provides advice and technical assistance to groups considering forming a cooperative or expanding their services. It assess options, reviews business plans, identifies resources, and provides financial analysis. Also, it assists in the creation of employee-owned businesses.

National Development Council

51 East 42nd St., #300
New York, NY 10017
(606) 291-0220

Offers technical assistance, training, and financial services to local governments and nonprofit groups for economic and housing development finance in distressed communities.

National Economic Development and Law Center

2201 Broadway
Oakland, CA 94012
(510) 251-2600

Provides legal services, planning, training, program assistance, and publications on economic and community development to community-based organizations.

National Main Street Center

National Trust for Historic Preservation
1785 Massachusetts Ave. NW
Washington, DC 20036
(202) 588-6219
http://www.nthp.org
Newsletter: *Main Street News*

Conducts training courses and provides technical assistance to conserve historic commercial buildings. Emphasizing public-private partnerships, it helps downtown groups create historic districts, preserve historic buildings, encourage compatible new construction, and find new economic options for downtowns.

Sonoran Institute

6842 E. Tanque Verde Rd., Suite D
Tucson, AZ 85715
(602) 290-0969

Promotes community-based conservation strategies that preserve the ecological integrity of protected lands, and at the same time meet the economic aspirations of adjoining landowners and communities. Underlying the institute's mission is the conviction that community-driven and inclusive approaches to conservation produce the most effective results.

Southwest Research and Information Center

Box 4524
Albuquerque, NM 87106
(505) 262-1862
Periodical: *The Workbook*

Offers information on clean energy, convenient transportation, safe streets, economic justice, clean air and water, and other issues.

Small Towns Institute

PO Box 517
Ellensburg, WA 98926
(509) 925-1830
Periodical: *Small Town*

Collects and disseminates information on new ideas concerning the issues facing small towns.

SMALL BUSINESS ADMINISTRATION PROGRAMS

The SBA works with the private sector to benefit small businesses through financial investments, loan guarantees, and technical assistance. Of particular interest to community economic development efforts, its "Low Doc" program streamlines the loan-guarantee process and allows for a two- to three-day response with minimal front-end documentation requirements for loans of $100,000 or less. Businesses apply for the loans through their local bank.

Small Business Administration

U.S. Department of Commerce
409 3rd St. SW
Washington, DC 20416
(800) 827-5722
www@www.sbaonline.sba.gov

OTHER SBA PROGRAMS INCLUDE:

Small Business Development Centers

http://www@www.sbaonline.sba.gov/SBDC

SBDCs are funded by the SBA along with various private-sector partners, and administered by various colleges and universities. They provide counseling, training, and technical assistance in all aspects of small-business management. Topics include accounting, organization, finance, management, engineering, and marketing. Special SBDC programs and economic development activities include international trade assistance, procurement assistance, venture capital formation, and rural development. Contact your nearest SBDC by visiting the website or calling SBA's 800 number (above) or the SBA office in your state capital.

Service Corps of Retired Executives (SCORE)

(800) 634-0245
http://www@www.sbaonline.sba.gov/SCORE

Through free, in-depth counseling and training, SCORE volunteers—primarily retired business people—help business owners solve problems, improve management skills, evaluate expansion, modify products, and meet other business challenges. SCORE also offers inexpensive workshops to present and prospective small business entrepreneurs.

Small Business Innovation Research

(202) 653-7875
http://www.darpa.mil/sbir/sbir/sbir.html#sbir

Encourages participation of small businesses in developing innovative research ideas for marketing, using federal (especially defense) R&D money.

OTHER GOVERNMENT AGENCIES

Office of Community Planning and Development

U.S. Department of Housing and Urban Development
451 Seventh St. SW
Washington, DC 20410
(202) 708-0270
http://www.hud.gov/prgcednp.html

Its mission is to help people create communities of opportunity. The Community Development Grants program provides annual grants on a formula basis to be used for a wide range of activities directed toward neighborhood revitalization, economic development, and improved community facilities and services. Under the Community Development Block Grant Program, local governments can receive grants, the proceeds from which can be lent to local businesses at low interest rates. Loan applicants must demonstrate that the loan will retain or create new jobs for low- and moderate-income workers.

Cooperative State Research, Education and Extension Service

U.S. Department of Agriculture
Room 3328-S
14th & Independence SW
Washington, DC 20250-900
(202) 720-3029
csrees@reeusda.gov
http://www.usda.gov

Works to improve economic, environmental, and social conditions in the United States and globally. Focuses include improved agricultural and other economic enterprises; safer, cleaner water, food, and air; enhanced stewardship and management of natural resources; healthier, more responsible and more productive individuals, families and communities; and a stable, secure, diverse, and affordable national food supply.

Natural Resources Conservation Service

U.S. Department of Agriculture
PO Box 2890
Washington, DC 20013
(202) 720-4525
http://www.ncg.nrcs.usda.gov/who.html

Works with private landowners to conserve natural resources. Through financial assistance, advisory services, and counseling, it assists local people in initiating and carrying out long-range programs of resource conservation and development. Call the number above to find the contact for your RC&D (Resource Conservation and Development) district.

Regional Economic Information System

Bureau of Economic Analysis
U.S. Department of Commerce
Washington, DC 20230
(202) 606-4500
webmaster@bea.doc.gov
http://www.lib.virginia.edu/socsci/reis/reis.html

Provides local-area economic data for states, counties, and metropolitan areas. Statistics in the data base include: personal income by source, per-capita personal income, earnings by two-digit Standard Industrial Code, full- and part-time employment by industry, and regional economic profiles.

Rural Community Assistance

U.S. Forest Service
U.S. Department of Agriculture
PO Box 96090
Washington, DC 20090-6090
(202) 205-1394
http://www.rurdev.usda.gov/
programs.html

Helps communities that are faced with acute economic problems associated with federal or private-sector land-management decisions and policies, or that are located in or near a national forest and are economically dependent upon forest resources. Provides project grants, direct loans, and use of property, facilities, and equipment to affected communities to help them diversify their economic bases and to improve the economic, social, and environmental well-being of rural areas.

Rural Development (formerly Farmers Home Administration)

U.S. Department of Agriculture
3003 N. Central, #900
Phoenix, AZ 85012
(602) 280-8700

Its Community Facility Loan Program provides loans and technical assistance to local governments, non-profit organizations, and Native American tribes in towns of not more than 25,000 to develop and improve public facilities.

Rural Information Center

U.S. Department of Agriculture
National Agricultural Library, #304
Beltsville, MD 20705-23551
(800) 633-7701
ric@nal.usda.gov
http://www.nal.usda.gov/ric

Provides information and referrals to people working to maintain the vitality of rural areas. It combines the technical expertise of the Cooperative Extension Service's nationwide educational network with the resources of the largest agricultural library in the world. For instance, its website includes "The Planning Commissioner's Journal," which offers information for volunteer members of local planning commissions, and "The Applied Rural Telecom Resource Guide," a directory of economic development resources related to telecommunications.

INTERNET RESOURCES

All communities—especially small or remote ones—should secure access to the Internet. It contains a wealth of information, much of which could otherwise only be found after weeks of calls and an extended visit to the nearest university library. At least a couple of people involved in your community's development effort should become proficient in the use of the Internet. Discussion groups are useful for trading ideas and seeking answers to specific questions. The World Wide Web, the most user-friendly portion of the Internet, can easily be searched for generic information on desired topics (try keywords like "community," "economic," "development," and "finance"). Many of the organizations listed above have their own websites and can be contacted by e-mail.

The following resources were also available as of late 1996. However, everything on the Internet changes quickly, so some listings may be out of date by the time your begin your search.

Community Economic Development Discussion Forum

An unmoderated discussion group for anyone interested in trends and opportunities in community economic development. Users help each other access information, programs, markets, and funds. Topics include: what makes communities most likely to succeed or fail; technology and local development; computer net-working; local financial capacity; entrepreneurship; and sustainability.

To subscribe, send mail to <Majordomo@sfu.ca>. In the message body, type "subscribe ced-net" followed by your email-address.

On-line Resources for Rural Community Economic Development

For a copy of this "pamphlet" by e-mail send a message to <goodstuff@lists.aspeninst.org>, typing the words "send guide" in the subject field and your name in the body of the message. The paper will be sent to you automatically as straight text. Alternatively, download it from the Web at <http:// www.aspeninst. org/rural>.

Rural Update

An electronic newsletter of events and innovations in rural community economic development, including leadership development and environmental stewardship. It also covers sustainable agriculture, lending, telecommunications and networks, human services, and business development. Its primary focus is the USA, but it often includes resources from Canada, Europe, and other countries. It's delivered via e-mail twice a month.

To subscribe, send mail to <ruralupdate@lists.aspeninst.org>. On the subject line type "subscribe", and in the message body type your name, organization, mail address, phone, and fax.

Sustainable Community Indicators Website

http://www.subjectmatters.com/
indicators

Sustainable indicators are measures of how well a community is meeting the needs and expectations of present and future residents. Designed for volunteers and community residents working toward sustainability, this website explains how indicators relate to sustainability, how to identify effective indicators, what data sources are available, and how indicators can be used to measure progress toward building a sustainable community. It lists hundreds of indicators currently being used by communities in North America.

Sustainability Project
sustain@web.apc.org
http://www.ccn.cs.dal.ca/
Environment/SCN/CommLink/
sustain.html
Offers documents and carries on network discussion regarding sustainable development.

Sustainable Development Discussion Forum
An unmoderated discussion for anyone interested in sustainable development. To subscribe, send a message to <majordomo@civic.net> (not to the list itself). The message should contain the command "subscribe sustainable-development".

PUBLICATIONS

Many of the following books are out of print, and most of them aren't available in bookstores. When in doubt, try your library. Rocky Mountain Institute publications can be ordered by mail using the form at the back of this book.

SYSTEMS THINKING AND RESOURCE ECONOMICS

Beyond the Limits
Donella H. Meadows (Chelsea Green, 1992).

Earth in the Balance
Al Gore (Houghton Mifflin, 1992).

The Ecology of Commerce
Paul Hawken (HarperCollins, 1993).

The Economic Pursuit of Quality
Thomas Michael Powers (M.E. Sharpe, 1988).

The Fifth Discipline Fieldbook: Strategies and Tools for Building a Learning Organization
Peter Senge et al. (Bantam Doubleday Dell, 1994).

For the Common Good: Redirecting the Economy Toward Community, the Environment, and a Sustainable Future
Herman E. Daly and John B. Cobb, Jr. (Beacon Press, 1989).

The Gaia Atlas of Green Economics
Paul Ekins, Mayer Hillman, and Robert Hutchison (Doubleday, 1992).

If the GDP Is Up, Why Is America Down?
Clifford Cobb, Ted Halstead, and Jonathan Rowe (article in *The Atlantic Monthly,* October 1995).

Lost Landscapes and Failed Economies: The Search for a Value of Place
Thomas Michael Powers (Island Press, 1996).

When Corporations Rule the World
David Korten (Kumarian Press, 1995).

COMMUNITY POLITICS

Beyond Polarization: Emerging Strategies for Reconciling Community and the Environment
Kirk Johnson (Northwest Policy Center/University of Washington, 1993).

Making Democracy Work
Robert Putnam (Princeton University Press, 1994).

The Quickening of America: Rebuilding Our Nation, Remaking Our Lives
Frances Moore Lappé and Paul DuBois (Jossey-Bass, 1994).

FACILITATION AND MEDIATION

Getting to Yes
Roger Fisher and William Ury (Penguin/Harvard Negotiation Project, 1985).

How to Make Meetings Work
Michael Doyle and David Straus (Berkeley Publishing Group, 1985).

Joining Together
David W. Johnson and Frank P. Johnson (Prentice-Hall, 1987).

The Skilled Facilitator: Practical Wisdom for Developing Effective Groups
Roger Schwarz (Jossey-Bass, 1994).

SUSTAINABLE COMMUNITY ECONOMIC DEVELOPMENT

Building Sustainable Communities: An Environmental Guide for Local Government
(Center for Study of Law and Politics, 1990).

The Business Opportunities Casebook
Barbara Cole (Rocky Mountain Institute, 1988).

The Community Energy Workbook
Alice Hubbard and Clay Fong (Rocky Mountain Institute, 1995).

Creating Successful Communities
Michael A. Mantell, Stephen F. Harper, and Luther Propst (Island Press, 1990).

The Environmental Industry: Open for Business. A Review of Emerging Trends and Economic Opportunities
Skip Laitner (Economic Research Associates, 1992).

Helping Ourselves: Local Solutions to Global Problems
Bruce Stokes (W.W. Norton & Co., 1981).

Monitoring Sustainability in Your Community
Benedict Hren, Nick Bartolumeo, and Michael Signer (Izaak Walton League, 1995).

Sustainable Cities: Concepts and Strategies for Eco-City Development
Bob Walter, Lois Arkin, and Richard Crenshaw (Eco-Home Media, 1992).

Toward Sustainable Communities: A Resource Book for Municipal and Local Governments
Mark Roseland (National Round Tables, 1992).

ECONOMIC DEVELOPMENT

Broadening the Base of Economic Development: New Approaches for Rural Areas
(MDC, Inc., 1986).

Building Communities from the Inside Out: A Path Toward Finding and Mobilizing a Community's Assets
John P. Kretzmann (Center for Urban Affairs/Northwest University, 1996).

Communities in the Lead
Harold L. Fossum (Northwest Policy Center/University of Washington, 1993).

Community Economic Development Strategies
Glen C. Pulver (University of Wisconsin, 1986).

Community Economic Development Strategies: Creating Successful Businesses
Linda M. Gardner (National Economic Development and Law Center, 1983).

Designing Development Strategies in Small Towns
Glen Pulver and David Dodson (Aspen Institute, 1992).

Economic Development: What Works at the Local Level
Matt Kane and Peggy Sand (National League of Cities, 1988).

From the Grassroots: Profiles of 103 Rural Self-Development Projects
Jan L. Flora et al. (U.S. Department of Agriculture, 1991).

From the Roots Up
David P. Ross and Peter J. Usher (Bootstrap Press, 1986).

Harvesting Hometown Jobs
Nancy T. Stark (National Association of Towns and Townships, 1986).

How Superstore Sprawl Can Harm Communities
Constance Beaumont (National Trust for Historic Preservation, 1994).

Managing Change: Coping with the Uncertainties of Unpredictable Growth
Barbara Cole and Philip Herr

(National Trust for Historic Preservation, 1994).

Organizing a Small Town Development Corporation
Robert O. Coppedge (New Mexico State University, 1989).

Profiles in Rural Economic Development: A Guidebook of Selected Successful Rural Area Initiatives
Margaret G. Thomas (Midwest Research Institute/U.S. Department of Commerce, 1988).

Rural Economic Development: A Resource File of Selected Technical Assistance Providers
Margaret G. Thomas (Midwest Research Institute, 1987).

Rural Economic Development Source Book
Margaret J. Thomas (Midwest Research Institute, 1989).

The Rural Futures Program: A Guide for Trainers
Julie Thomason and David Dodson (MDC, Inc., 1991).

The Small Town Survival Guide
Jack McCall (William Morrow & Co., 1993).

Take Charge: Economic Development in Small Communities
Janet Ayers et al. (North Central Regional Center for Rural Development, 1990).

Taking Charge: How Communities Are Planning Their Futures
Ronald L. Thomas, Mary C. Means, and Margaret A. Grieve (ICMA, 1988).

ECONOMIC DEVELOPMENT
FINANCE

Financing Economic Renewal Projects

Barbara Cole and Meredith Miller (Rocky Mountain Institute, 1988).

Funding Sources for Community and Economic Development: A Guide to Current Sources for Local Programs and Projects

(Oryx Press, annual).

Innovative Grassroots Financing: a Small Town Guide to Raising Funds and Cutting Costs

Nancy T. Stark et al. (National Association of Towns and Townships, 1990).

National Guide to Funding for Community Development

(The Foundation Center, 1996).

STATISTICAL MANUALS

Besides the manuals listed below, several U.S. Census Bureau publications can help you get useful data on local business conditions, income, and employment: *County and City Data Book* (published every five years), *State and Metro Book* (every five years), *Statistical Abstract* (annually), and *Survey of Current Business* (monthly). If they're not in your library, order them through the U.S. Government Printing Office at (202) 782-3238.

Community Economic Analysis: A How-to Manual

Ron Hustedde, Ron Shaffer, and Glen Pulver (North Central Regional Center for Rural Development, 1984).

A Community Researcher's Guide to Rural Data

Priscilla Salant (Island Press, 1990).

Identifies a wealth of current data sources, illustrates how they can be used to analyze social and economic change, and provides ordering information. Individual chapters in the book describe data on local population and community resources, economics, and government.

How to Conduct Your Own Survey

Priscilla Salant and Don Dillman (John Wiley & Sons, 1994).

How to Research Your Local Economy: A People's Guide to Economic Development

Tom Schlesinger (Southern Exposure, 1986).

Measuring Change in Rural America: A Workbook for Determining Demographic, Economic and Fiscal Trends

Ray Rasker, Vicky York, and Jerry Johnson (The Wilderness Society, 1995). A manual designed to enable any community to gather and use the information it needs as the basis for its development effort.

Index

Talk to us!

We want to learn from you. Please give us your comments on this book and any thoughts you have on how to improve it. If you tried to use any part of this book in your community, please let us know what worked, what didn't, and what kind of results you achieved.

Are you a(n):
- ❐ interested citizen?
- ❐ local government staff person?
- ❐ elected official?
- ❐ state or federal government staff person?
- ❐ other?

How would you rate this book?
- ❐ very useful
- ❐ moderately useful
- ❐ not useful

Please tell us how it could be improved:_____

_____

What effect did this book have in your community? _____

_____

Name_____

Address _____

Phone _____

Please send your comments to:
Rocky Mountain Institute
Attn: Economic Renewal Staff
1739 Snowmass Creek Road
Snowmass, CO 81654-9199
(970) 927-3851 or (970) 927-4510

Order Form

Rocky Mountain Institute
1739 Snowmass Creek Road
Snowmass, CO 81654-9199
Tel: (970) 927-3851 / Fax: (970) 927-3420
Email: orders@rmi.org
Web site: http://www.rmi.org

Please send me the following RMI publications:

ER97-2	*The Economic Renewal Guide*	_____	$17.95
ER91-7	*The Food and Agriculture Workbook*	_____	$15.00
ER95-4	*The Community Energy Workbook*	_____	$16.95
ER88-39	*The Business Opportunities Casebook*	_____	$10.00
E95-3	*The Energy Directory Kit* (please call for details)	_____	$99.00
ER88-25	*Financing Economic Renewal Programs*	_____	$15.00
ER95-5	"Paying for Growth, Prospering from Development"	_____	$5.00
	RMI Catalog	_____	Free

Shipping & Handling Charges		
Order Amount	*U.S.*	*Canada*
$0.00–12.00	$2.50	$3.00
12.01–20.00	3.50	4.50
20.01–35.00	4.50	5.50
35.01–50.00	6.00	7.50
50.01–100.00	7.00	9.00

For orders over $100, express delivery, or shipments outside the United States and Canada, please call.

SUBTOTAL: _____

SHIPPING/HANDLING: see box at left _____

SALES TAX: Colorado residents add 3% _____

DONATION: Donors of $10 or more receive RMI's Newsletter (3 issues/1 year) _____

TOTAL ENCLOSED: _____

® My check or money order is enclosed (U.S. funds only)
® Please charge my: ® Visa   ® Mastercard

Card #: _____   Exp. date: _____

Signature: _____

Please send the publications to: (PLEASE PRINT OR TYPE)   ® Check here if this is a new address

Name: _____

Organization: _____

Address: _____

Town/City: _____

State: _____ ZIP/Postal code: _____ Country: _____

Daytime Telephone: _____
(in case we have questions about your order.)

ALL PRICES SUBJECT TO CHANGE.